WORLD WAR I

WORLD WAR I

Neil M. Heyman

Greenwood Press Guides to
Historic Events of the Twentieth Century
Randall M. Miller, Series Editor

Greenwood Press
Westport, Connecticut • London

Library of Congress Cataloging-in-Publication Data

Heyman, Neil M.
    World War I / Neil M. Heyman.
       p. cm.—(Greenwood Press guides to historic events of the
  twentieth century, ISSN 1092–177X)
    Includes bibliographical references and index.
    ISBN 0–313–29880–7 (alk. paper)
    1. World War, 1914–1918. I. Title. II. Title: World War One.
  III. Title: World War 1. IV. Series.
  D521.H428 1997
  940.3—DC21   97–1686

British Library Cataloguing in Publication Data is available.

Library of Congress Catalog Card Number: 97–1686
ISBN: 0–313–29880–7
ISSN: 1092–177X

First published in 1997

Greenwood Press, 88 Post Road West, Westport, CT 06881
An imprint of Greenwood Publishing Group, Inc.

Printed in the United States of America

∞

The paper used in this book complies with the
Permanent Paper Standard issued by the National
Information Standards Organization (Z39.48–1984).

10 9 8 7 6 5 4 3 2 1

Front cover photo: German soldiers in trenches, March 1918. By
permission of Corbis-Bettman.

For Mark and David

Contents

A photo essay follows page 80

Series Foreword

As the twenty-first century approaches, it is time to take stock of the political, social, economic, intellectual, and cultural forces and factors that have made the twentieth century the most dramatic period of change in history. To that end, the Greenwood Press Guides to Historic Events of the Twentieth Century presents interpretive histories of the most significant events of the century. Each book in the series combines narrative history and analysis with primary documents and biographical sketches, with an eye to providing both a reference guide to the principal persons, ideas, and experiences defining each historic event, and a reliable, readable overview of that event. Each book further provides analyses and discussions, grounded in both primary and secondary sources, of the causes and consequences, in thought and action, that give meaning to the historic event under review. By assuming a historical perspective, drawing on the latest and best writing on each subject, and offering fresh insights, each book promises to explain how and why a particular event defined the twentieth century. No consensus about the meaning of the twentieth century emerges from the series, but, collectively, the books identify the most salient concerns of the century. In so doing, the series reminds us of the many ways those historic events continue to affect our lives.

Each book follows a similar format designed to encourage readers to consult it both as a reference and a history in its own right. Each volume opens with a chronology of the historic event, followed by a narrative overview, which also serves to introduce and examine briefly the main themes and issues related to that event. The next set of chapters is composed of topical essays, each analyzing closely an issue or problem of interpretation introduced in the opening chapter. A concluding chapter suggesting the long-term implications and meanings of the historic event brings the strands of the preceding chapters together while placing the event in the larger historical context. Each book also includes a section of short biographies of the principal persons related to the event, followed by a section introducing and reprinting key historical documents illustrative of and pertinent to the event. A glossary of selected terms adds to the utility of each book. An annotated bibliography—of significant books, films, and CD-ROMs—and an index conclude each volume.

The editors made no attempt to impose any theoretical model or historical perspective on the individual authors. Rather, in developing the series, an advisory board of noted historians and informed high school history teachers and public and school librarians identified the topics needful of exploration and the scholars eminently qualified to examine those events with intelligence and sensitivity. The common commitment throughout the series is to provide accurate, informative, and readable books, free of jargon and up to date in evidence and analysis.

Each book stands as a complete historical analysis and reference guide to a particular historic event. Each book also has many uses, from understanding contemporary perspectives on critical historical issues, to providing biographical treatments of key figures related to each event, to offering excerpts and complete texts of essential documents about the event, to suggesting and describing books and media materials for further study and presentation of the event, and more. The combination of historical narrative and individual topical chapters addressing significant issues and problems encourages students and teachers to approach each historic event from multiple perspectives and with a critical eye. The arrangement and content of each book thus invite students and teachers, through classroom discussions and position papers, to debate the character and significance of great historic events and to discover for themselves how and why history matters.

The series emphasizes the main currents that have shaped the modern world. Much of that focus necessarily looks at the West, especially Europe and the United States. The political, commercial, and cultural expansion of the West wrought largely, though not wholly, the most fundamental changes of the century. Taken together, however, books in the series reveal the interactions between Western and non-Western peoples and society, and also the tensions between modern and traditional cultures. They also point to the ways in which non-Western peoples have adapted Western ideas and technology and, in turn, influenced Western life and thought. Several books examine such increasingly powerful global forces as the rise of Islamic fundamental-ism, the emergence of modern Japan, the Communist revolution in China, and the collapse of communism in eastern Europe and the former Soviet Union. American interests and experiences receive special attention in the series, not only in deference to the primary readership of the books but also in recognition that the United States emerged as the dominant political, economic, social, and cultural force during the twentieth century. By looking at the century through the lens of American events and experiences, it is possible to see why the age has come to be known as "The American Century."

Assessing the history of the twentieth century is a formidable prospect. It has been a period of remarkable transformation. The world broadened and narrowed at the same time. Frontiers shifted from the interiors of Africa and Latin America to the moon and beyond; communication spread from mass circulation newspapers and magazines to radio, television, and now the Internet; skyscrapers reached upward and suburbs stretched outward; energy switched from steam, to electric, to atomic power. Many changes did not lead to a complete abandonment of established patterns and practices so much as a synthesis of old and new, as, for example, the increased use of (even reliance on) the telephone in the age of the computer. The automo-bile and the truck, the airplane, and telecommunications closed distances, and people in unprecedented numbers migrated from rural to urban, indus-trial, and ever more ethnically diverse areas. Tractors and chemical fertiliz-ers made it possible for fewer people to grow more, but the environmental and demographic costs of an exploding global population threatened to outstrip natural resources and human innovation. Disparities in wealth increased, with developed nations prospering and underdeveloped nations starving. Amid the crumbling of former European colonial empires, Western technology, goods, and culture increasingly enveloped the globe, seeping into, and undermining, non-Western cultures—a process that contributed to a surge of religious fundamentalism and ethno-nationalism in the Middle East, Asia, and Africa. As people became more alike, they also became more aware of their differences. Ethnic and religious rivalries grew in intensity everywhere as the century closed.

The political changes during the twentieth century have been no less profound than the social, economic, and cultural ones. Many of the books in the series focus on political events, broadly defined, but no books are confined to politics alone. Political ideas and events have social effects, just as they spring from a complex interplay of non-political forces in culture, society, and economy. Thus, for example, the modern civil rights and woman's rights movements were at once social and political events in cause and consequence.

Likewise, the Cold War created the geopolitical framework for dealing with competing ideologies and nations abroad and served as the touchstone for political and cultural identities at home. The books treating political events do so within their social, cultural, and economic contexts.

Several books in the series examine particular wars in depth. Wars are defining moments for people and eras. During the twentieth century war became more widespread and terrible than ever before, encouraging new efforts to end war through strategies and organizations of international cooperation and disarmament while also fueling new ideologies and instruments of mass persuasion that fostered distrust and festered old national rivalries. Two world wars during the century redrew the political map, slaughtered or uprooted two generations of people, and introduced and hastened the development of new technologies and weapons of mass destruction. The First World War spelled the end of the old European order and spurred communist revolution in Russia and fascism in Italy, Germany, and elsewhere. The Second World War killed fascism and inspired the final push for freedom from European colonial rule in Asia and Africa. It also led to the Cold War that suffocated much of the world for almost half a century. Large wars begat small ones, and brutal totalitarian regimes cropped up across the globe. After (and in some ways because of) the fall of communism in eastern Europe and the former Soviet Union, wars of competing cultures, national interests, and political systems persisted in the struggle to make a new world order. Continuing, too, has been the belief that military technology can achieve political ends, whether in the superior American firepower that failed to "win" in Vietnam or in the American "smart bombs" and other military wizardry that "won" in the Persian Gulf.

Another theme evident in the series is that throughout the century nationalism has continued to drive events. Whether in the Balkans in 1914 triggering World War I or in the Balkans in the 1990s threatening the post–Cold War peace—or in many other places—nationalist ambitions and forces would not die. The persistence of nationalism is yet another reminder of the many ways that the past becomes prologue.

We thus offer the series as a modern guide to and interpretation of the historic events of the twentieth century and as an invitation to consider how and why those events have defined not only the past and present but also charted the political, social, intellectual, cultural, and economic routes into the next century.

Randall M. Miller
Saint Joseph's University, Philadelphia

Introduction

Although remote in time, World War I continues to exercise a powerful attraction on the popular imagination. A continuing flow of academic and popular writing on the conflict, accompanied by a number of strikingly effective documentary films, attests to a wide interest in the struggle—tragic and fascinating—that dominated the world eight decades ago.

This volume is intended to offer an introduction to the subject to the general reader and students at the secondary school and college level. It seeks to be interesting as well as informative, and to present the results of recent historical study while giving an accurate view of the war's major features. I have placed my emphasis upon the war as conducted and experienced by the major countries of Europe as well as the United States. Events in Africa, the Middle East, and the Pacific attest to the fact that this was, indeed, a "world war," but the focal points of developments from 1914 to 1919 were on the continents of Europe and North America, as well as on or under adjacent bodies of water. With only a few exceptions, such as the Battle of Coronel and the Battle of the Falklands, those are the events we will explore.

The book begins with a chronology of events of World War I, followed by an overview of the war, examining the roots of the conflict, then proceeding to an examination of the major military events and their most important political and diplomatic consequences. Next come five more specialized chapters, examining important aspects of this titanic struggle of nations and peoples. Chapter 2, "Anatomy of Catastrophe," takes up the war's most familiar and depressing image: the seemingly fruitless and costly Allied offensives on the western front. The Battle of the Somme (1916) and the Battle of the Chemin des Dames (1917) serve to illustrate the technical conditions within which the war was fought on the western front and the strategic and mental limitations of generals and politicians. Chapter 3, "Anatomy of Success," reminds us that bloody failure was not the result of all military efforts in World War I; the fight against the submarine, when it reached its decisive point, was conducted with skill, intelligence, and rapid success.

Chapter 4 examines the role of the United States in the wartime years. Geographically remote and politically neutral, the great republic of North America was, nonetheless, an influence on the conflict from its early stages. Thereafter, when it was drawn officially into the war in the spring of 1917, the United States played a military and political role of escalating importance. Like other major countries, it discovered that the war had a transforming effect on the individual lives of the people at home and the society they inhabited. Chapter 5 considers the overlapping issue of life on the home front in three major belligerent countries in Europe: Great Britain, France, and their antagonist, imperial Germany. Immersed for four years in a war vast beyond pre-1914 imagining, these societies found themselves facing such major issues as food shortages, new roles for women, and bereavement on an unknown scale.

Chapter 6 considers how two countries, one from the Central Powers, one from the Allied side, collapsed under the strain of the war. Austria-Hungary and Russia demonstrate how structural weaknesses evident before 1914 combined with the strain and turmoil of the war to bring down the old order. Chapter 7 looks at the war from the perspective of the present. It considers, in particular, the cliché that World War I has shaped and dominated the twentieth century. No dispute over that view may be reasonably advanced, but the chapter argues that it now seems evident that, in many respects, the impact of the war is fading. From the perspective of the late 1990s, it seems that the war's most notable political consequences have become attenuated, while larger historical trends, antedating the war, are asserting themselves once again.

The next section of the book presents biographical profiles of the major political and military figures involved in the war. Each biographical essay begins by summarizing the individual's role in the conflict. There follows an account of the individual's life designed to indicate his background and circumstances prior to 1914, but stressing his role in the wartime (and sometimes the peacemaking) period. A brief glossary presents a guide to the war's most essential terminology.

A set of documents drawn from memoirs, autobiographies, newspaper editorials, and government papers shows the war from a different perspective than that of historians or biographers, who examine the war from afar and in compressed fashion. By contrast, the war's everyday immediacy and pain for the average European can be found in the memoirs of Stefan Zweig and Vera Brittain, while the fascinated sense of being an observer at an epochal event—the Russian Revolution—is vividly expressed in the recollection of Louis de Robien. The memos of General von Falkenhayn and Matthias Erzberger reveal leaders in moments of dreadful isolation, deciding on a momentous policy and preparing to convince others to follow them. Editorials from the *New York Times* illustrate a significant organ of public opinion responding to a stream of shocking news. The letters of André Cornet-Auquier show how a civilian European responded to combat.

The available literature on the war is beyond the ability of any individual to fully command, and the recommended readings are necessarily the result of a process of selection. The annotated bibliography has been compiled with the hope of providing a range of readable resources for investigating the major facets of the war. The books, many of which are recent and break new ground, have received general acceptance from scholars in the field. Works considered too lengthy, too specialized, or too unreadable for the intended audience have been omitted.

I wish to thank Barbara Rader, executive editor at Greenwood Press, for her help in directing this project. Professor Randall Miller of Saint Joseph's University, the editor of this series, has been—all at once—understanding, sympathetic, stimulating, and demanding as I proceeded in my research and writing. It has been a rare pleasure to work with him. I would also like to recognize the help provided by my research assistant, Tom Materla.

I have been a student of World War I since I was an undergraduate, and my enthusiasm for the subject has grown with time. While I was always certain to be an intrigued reader on the subject, I wish to express my thanks to two splendid historians who helped and encouraged me to move beyond that point. William Richard Emerson, Jr., my teacher when I was an undergraduate at Yale, stimulated and shaped my interest in numerous aspects of military history including World War I. Gordon Alexander Craig, my teacher at Stanford Graduate School, helped me to become a professional historian while providing the model for what a professional historian can be.

Finally, as always, my deepest thanks to Mark, David, and, especially, Brenda.

Chronology of Events

1914

June 28	Assassination of Archduke Franz Ferdinand
July 23	Austro-Hungarian ultimatum to Serbia
July 28	Austria-Hungary declares war on Serbia
August 1	Germany declares war on Russia
August 3	Germany declares war on France
August 4	Germany invades Belgium; Britain declares war on Germany
August 8	British Parliament passes DORA
August 23	Battle of Mons
August 26–29	Battle of Tannenberg
September 6–11	Battle of the Marne
September 1	Falkenhayn replaces Moltke as German commander-in-chief
September 15	Germans complete retreat to the Aisne
September 22	German U-boat sinks three British cruisers off Dutch coast
October 20– November 22	First Battle of Ypres

October 27	German U-boat sinks battleship *Audacious* off Irish coast
November 1	Battle of Coronel; Turkey enters the war
December 8	Battle of the Falklands
December 16	German cruisers raid Yorkshire coast

1915

March 10–14	Battle of Neuve Chapelle
March 18	British naval attack fails at Dardanelles
March 22	Besieged Austro-Hungarian army at Przemysl surrenders to Russians
April 22	Second Battle of Ypres begins with German gas attack
May 2	Central Powers attack Russians at Gorlice-Tarnow
May 7	German submarine sinks *Lusitania* off coast of Ireland
May 9	French launch attack in Artois
May 23	Italy enters the war
May 25	Coalition government takes office in Britain
June 8	William Jennings Bryan resigns as U.S. secretary of state
June 29	First Battle of the Isonzo begins
September 22	French begin offensive in Champagne
September 24	Tsar Nicholas II takes command of Russian armies
September 25–26	Battle of Loos
October 6	Central Powers attack Serbia
October 11	Bulgaria enters the war with attack on Serbia
December 15	Douglas Haig named commander-in-chief of BEF

1916

February 21	Battle of Verdun begins
April 2	Easter Rebellion in Ireland
May 10	Austrian offensive against Italy begins
May 17	British government adopts conscription
May 31–June 1	Battle of Jutland
June 4	Brusilov offensive begins

July 1	Battle of the Somme begins
August 3	Central Powers set up unified command on eastern front
August 27	Rumania enters the war
August 29	Hindenburg and Ludendorff take over the German high command
September 6	Germany and Austria-Hungary set up unified command in all theaters
October 21	Prime Minister Stürgkh assassinated in Vienna
November 7	Woodrow Wilson reelected as president of the United States
November 21	Death of Emperor Franz Joseph
November 23	Venizelos government in Greece enters war
November 25	Jellicoe named First Sea Lord
December 7	Lloyd George becomes prime minister of Great Britain; Germans capture Bucharest
December 1	Nivelle takes over as French army commander-in-chief

1917

February 1	Germany renews submarine warfare
March 1	United States government releases the Zimmermann telegram to public
March 8	Russian Revolution starts
March 15	Tsar Nicholas II abdicates; Germans begin retreat to Hindenburg line
April 6	United States enters the war
April 16	Nivelle (Chemin des Dames) offensive begins; Lenin returns to Petrograd and denounces Provisional Government
May 4	First American destroyers reach British waters
May 10	First successful British merchant convoy leaves Gibraltar for home waters
May 17	Pétain replaces Nivelle as commander-in chief of French army
May 19	French armies begin to mutiny
May 26	Pershing named commander of AEF

June 5	United States Congress passes Espionage Act
July 1	Kerensky offensive begins
July 21	Kerensky becomes Russian prime minister
July 31	Third Battle of Ypres (Passchendaele) begins
October 23	Restored French army begins series of limited offensives
October 24	Central Powers defeat Italians at Caporetto
October 26	Orlando becomes Italian prime minister
November 7	Bolshevik Revolution in Russia
November 9	Diaz replaces Cadorna as commander of Italian army
November 16	Clemenceau becomes premier of France
November 20–29	Battle of Cambrai
December 22	Peace negotiations start at Brest-Litovsk

1918

January 1	United States government takes control of railroad system
January 8	Wilson presents Fourteen Points
February 1	Mutiny in Austro-Hungarian navy
February 6	British women receive the vote
March 3	Peace treaty signed at Brest-Litovsk; Russia leaves the war
March 4	Bernard Baruch takes over War Industries Board
March 21	Ludendorff offensive begins
March 26	Foch named Allied supreme commander
April 23–24	British attack submarine bases at Zeebrugge and Ostend
May 7	Rumania leaves the war
May 31	Americans go into combat at Château-Thierry
June 6	Americans attack at Belleau Wood
July 16–17	Tsar Nicholas II and his family are murdered by Communist officials
July 18	Second Battle of the Marne begins
August 9	Britain recognizes Czech National Council
September 3	United States recognizes Czech National Council

September 12	American offensive at St. Mihiel
September 15	General Franchet d'Esperey begins Allied offensive at Salonika
September 26	General Allied offensive begins on western front; American offensive begins in Meuse-Argonne
September 29	Bulgaria leaves the war
October 3	Max von Baden named German prime minister
October 16	Emperor Charles announces federation in Austria
October 26	Ludendorff resigns as leader of German high command
October 29	Austria leaves the war
October 30	Turkey leaves the war
October 31	Mutiny in German navy at Kiel; start of revolution in Germany
November 9	Germany becomes a republic; Rumania reenters the war
November 11	Germans sign Armistice
December 4	Woodrow Wilson arrives in Europe to lead American peace delegation

1919

January 18	Paris Peace Conference convenes
June 21	German fleet scuttled at Scapa Flow
June 28	Treaty of Versailles signed
September 26	Woodrow Wilson taken ill while touring the United States
October 2	Wilson suffers a stroke
November 19	U.S. Senate rejects peace treaty

1921

August 25	United States signs separate peace with Germany (Treaty of Berlin)

World War I Explained

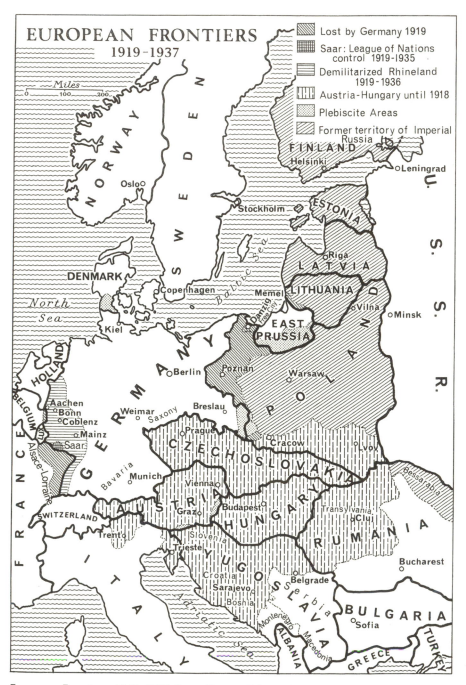

European Frontiers 1919–1937. From Martin Gilbert, *Atlas of Recent History*. Used by permission of Routledge.

I

Overview of the War

In later years, men and women on both sides of the Atlantic remembered the early summer of 1914 as a moment marked by a particular brightness. For both the leaders and those they tried to lead, it was a time of beautiful weather for all and of leisure for many. The season's first day, June 21, found Kaiser Wilhelm II touring northern Germany. His appearances at agricultural fairs and military maneuvers were scheduled to bring him shortly to the annual Elbe Regatta he so much enjoyed. Archduke Franz Ferdinand, heir to the throne of Austria-Hungary, and his wife, Countess Sophie, were visiting their favorite Bohemian castle at Chlumetz. Across the Atlantic the budding young American intellectual Walter Lippmann stayed at a cabin in the Maine woods, writing an analysis of labor problems for ex-president Theodore Roosevelt. In Paris, the Spanish artist Pablo Picasso, who had recently shifted his endeavors from painting to sculpture, was planning a vacation trip to southern France. In Vienna, Dr. Sigmund Freud was preparing for his July vacation at the Bohemian spa city of Carlsbad, and General Helmuth von Moltke, the chief of staff of the German army, expected to be there as well. In Munich, a young fugitive from conscription, Adolf Hitler, who had fled only a year before from his Austrian homeland, was scratching out a living by painting advertising posters. Since May, the Russian revolutionary Vladimir I. Lenin had been on vacation at Poronin, a village in the Tatra Mountains of Austrian Poland located near the Russian border. A little more than a year earlier, he had dismissed the possibility of a major war: "A war between Austria and Russia would be a very useful thing for the revolution in all of Eastern Europe, but it is not likely that Franz Joseph [the emperor of Austria-Hungary] and Nikolashka ["Nicky," the tsar of Russia] will give us that pleasure."[1] Meanwhile, in the Bosnian capital of Sarajevo, a Serb teenager named Gavrilo Princip, along with a coterie of fellow conspirators, counted the days until they could make a risky and inauspicious attempt to murder Franz Ferdinand.

On June 28, when the summer was only a week old, Franz Ferdinand and Sophie lay dead in Sarajevo, while Princip, their assassin, was in police custody. The crisis of 1914, whose results would darken the next four years and haunt the decades following, had begun.

THE WAR'S ORIGINS

War broke out in the summer of 1914 because several of the nations of Europe had differences that could not be settled by peaceful means. The diplomats continued to do their work up to the moment that the first soldiers passed into the territory of the enemy. Their efforts were unavailing.

There were deep and painful conflicts among the countries of Europe that led to the unprecedented calamity of a war that lasted four and a half years, that killed more Europeans than any event since the Black Death of the fourteenth century, and that altered the shape of European life and the geopolitical map. Princip's rash act, two shots fired without aiming by a lad of nineteen who had just learned to use a revolver, set the crisis in motion.

Tensions in Eastern Europe

The Europe of the early twentieth century was marked by instability and unresolved conflicts. In the Balkans, the southeastern portion of the continent, three facts defined the overall situation. The Ottoman Empire's grip over this region, stretching back for five hundred years and slipping for the past century, now disappeared. The peoples of the region had won increased freedom from Turkish rule in the nineteenth century. The Balkan Wars of 1912–1913 virtually eliminated the Turkish presence in Europe. Thus, the old order, long tottering, suddenly vanished.

The second element was the historical tendency of Russia and Austria-Hungary (the Habsburg or Dual Empire) to compete for power and influence in the Balkans as Ottoman weakness presented the opportunity to do so. As Turkish power faded, Russian and Austrian ambitions collided over who would control, influence, or win over the newly independent or newly expanded nations of the Balkans: Serbia, Bulgaria, Greece, and Rumania.

A third element was the ethnic tensions of the region, which reached over international borders in the relationship between the small nation of Serbia and its giant neighbor to the north. Austria-Hungary at the start of the century included a collection of Slavic peoples, increasingly restless under the control of Germans in Vienna and Hungarians in Budapest. The existence of large numbers of ethnic Serbs within the borders of the Austro-Hungarian Empire and the ambitions of the Serbian government to bring these ethnic brothers "home" to the Serbian nation threatened to create an ethnic landslide. Viewing the prospect that the Dual Empire faced total destruction, Austrian leaders like Field Marshal Conrad von Hötzendorf, chief of the general staff, saw Serbia as a deadly enemy that somehow had to be erased from the map.

Tensions in Central and Western Europe

In central and western Europe, the great question of the era was the future role of Germany. United only since 1871, imperial Germany had rapidly emerged as the dominant industrial and military power on the continent. By the close of the century, leaders in Berlin were committed to play an equally great role in European naval affairs and in the world of empire outside Europe. This created a potentially explosive situation.

As recently as 1870, France had considered itself—and had been considered by others—the leading military power of Europe. Its defeat by Germany in 1871 in the Franco-Prussian War meant a lasting antagonism, although one that would ebb and flow over the following decades. French acceptance of the new reality of power was unlikely. This was especially so since Germany's military superiority took geographic form in the seizure of the entire French province of Alsace and part of a second province, Lorraine.

For Great Britain, concern over Germany came later. Germany's insistence on intervening in colonial issues, ranging from Samoa to South Africa to Latin America, challenged a pattern existing for more than a century in which Britain had the main voice in such matters. More immediate was the related German threat to Britain's control of the seas: by the start of the twentieth century, Germany was creating a first-class navy.

The fleet was the most obvious and dramatic illustration of Germany's surging power in many spheres. Since 1870, the new country's industry had grown so rapidly that this part of Europe, which had supplied immigrants to the Western Hemisphere for more than a century, now imported labor from Poland. From higher education and scientific research to the development of a system of social insurance for its working class, Germany could pride itself on being a world leader.

Industrialists anxious to protect their maritime links to a world market and ambitious military leaders like Admiral Alfred von Tirpitz, dreaming of a successful naval war against Great Britain, looked to German power on the sea. They found a crucial ally in Kaiser Wilhelm II. The embodiment and often the director of his nation's restless energies, Wilhelm saw the fleet serving several important functions. "The young German Reich needs institutions in which the unitary idea of a Reich is embodied. The navy is such an institution," he declared to Prime Minister Arthur Balfour of Britain in 1902.[2] But he saw it as a tool of external power as well. Against countries like Britain, Germany's army could make no impression. As Wilhelm's leading biographer has put it, "Only with a fleet could Germany be able to elicit from the British the esteem Wilhelm II believed to be his due."[3]

Tirpitz aimed not at British esteem but at British subordination to a dominant Germany. The German fleet taking shape at Wilhelmshaven and Cuxhaven on the North Sea coast put its emphasis on battleships. These were the most powerful individual weapons of the time, and they were clearly designed to meet the British navy within the confines of the North Sea. Thus, the German navy intended to challenge Britain's control over the oceans, the lifeline of the island nation's existence.

Germany and Russia

A final major element of instability on the international scene was the relationship between Germany and Russia. In the eyes of key German leaders such as Chancellor Theobald von Bethmann Hollweg, the ramshackle Russian Empire, recently defeated in war by Japan and going through the trauma of early industrialization, was nonetheless a growing threat. Humiliation in the Far East turned Russian foreign policy planners toward gains in the Balkans. Russia's new Duma (parliament), established after the Revolution of 1905, brought public opinion into play over foreign affairs. Foreign policy makers like Foreign Minister Sergei Sazonov aimed at containing Austria-Hungary's expansion in the Balkans. The Austrian annexation of Bosnia-Herzegovina in 1908 raised alarm among government circles and in public opinion. Nationalist newspapers like *Novoe Vremya* as well as Duma deputies such as Count Vladimir Bobrinsky of the Nationalist party soon pointed with alarm to German ambitions in the Balkans. The rhetoric of Pan-Slavism, which called for ethnic solidarity between Russia and its Slavic brethren in southeastern Europe, also inflamed the atmosphere.[4]

Reforms in the Russian army, the very size of Russia's population and natural resources—all these elements made it likely that Germany's vast power would be increasingly overshadowed by a resurgent Russia. With Russia allied to France, Germany's permanent foe since 1870, the authorities in Berlin were doubly afraid of the Russian threat. A study by the German general staff in the spring of 1914 predicted that Germany and Austria-Hungary would have to face a Russian army, when it had fully mobilized, of frightening dimensions: ninety-four infantry divisions, twelve rifle brigades, and thirty-five cavalry divisions.[5] German prime minister Bethmann Hollweg himself had returned from a trip to Russia in 1912 "deeply disturbed at his first-hand impressions of that empire's human and material resources.[6]

International Alliances

International tensions led to alliances that, in turn, made tensions more dangerous. Quarrels between two countries could easily expand to involve all of the Great Powers. The Franco-Russian alliance and the link between Germany and Austria-Hungary were both products of the late nineteenth century; the twentieth century brought Britain out of isolation into a web of agreements. British leaders had been shocked by the country's lack of friends during the Boer War, when most of its naval power had been tied up with the conflict in South Africa. Two crises over Venezuela—one in 1895 and a second in 1902—had reminded British leaders of the dangers of a conflict with the United States, and there followed a rapprochement between the two English-speaking Atlantic powers that eased the concerns of the authorities in London. In 1908 American president Theodore Roosevelt expressed the sentiment of friendship and mutual interest to an English friend: "Do you know, I think I have become almost as anxious as you are to have the British fleet kept up to the highest point of efficiency."[7] The warmed relationship with the United States was to pay huge dividends after the outbreak of World War I. But earlier still, Britain found it possible to close out other old quarrels and to make new friends. Between 1904 and 1907, Britain's new ties, first with France, then with Russia, let the island nation concentrate its attentions on the burgeoning power of Germany.

In the formation (and dissolution) of alliances, the wishes of civilian officials—prime ministers, foreign ministers—were paramount. Prime Minister Otto von Bismarck had been the architect of Germany's long-standing tie with Austria-Hungary at the close of the 1870s. Foreign Minister Théophile Delcassé of France had been the dominant voice in his

country in favor of a rapprochement with Great Britain. But the actions of
military leaders strengthened and sometimes reshaped alliances. Messages
from the leader of the German general staff, Helmuth von Moltke, to his
Austrian counterpart, Conrad von Hötzendorf, during the Balkan crisis of
1908–1909 promoted the idea that Vienna could count on German help
against Russia even if armed conflict came at Austria-Hungary's instiga-
tion.[8] And the arrangements for cooperation between the armies and navies
of Great Britain and France bolstered the commitment the men in frock
coats had made.

Civilian and Military Leadership: The July Crisis

In the end civilian leaders and, where present, their monarchs, made the
breathtaking decision to make war or to keep the peace. But the military
men had a strong voice. Possessing enough prestige and authority, as
generals did in Vienna, Berlin, and St. Petersburg in late July 1914, to
demand the mobilization of the country's armed forces made the men in
uniform a force to be reckoned with. No civilian leader could ignore a
high-ranking general claiming that a delay in mobilization would put the
country's future in peril. But the mobilization of huge armies was a process
that, once begun, could be stopped only with the greatest difficulty. In the
eyes of European leaders, mobilization meant war.

Historians View the Origins of the War

For some historians the international tensions throughout the continent
provide a sufficient explanation for the outbreak and spread of war in the
summer of 1914. The assassination of Archduke Franz Ferdinand, the heir
to the Austro-Hungarian throne, by Serb nationalists enticed Austrian
leaders to crush the Serb threat once and for all. Russia's link to Serbia
turned out to be a central element in the road to war as the tsar's empire
supported its small Balkan ally. Germany stood anxious, not only to
preserve Austria-Hungary, its lone ally, but also to humiliate Russia, Serbia's international friend. Therefore, Berlin urged Vienna onward. France
sprang to Russia's defense and, due to the German war plan, faced German
attack. Britain, after some hesitation, moved to aid France, and, in the larger
sense, to contain an overly powerful Germany. Thus, a Balkan crisis in late
June began a vast European war by the start of August.

Arno Mayer has found a crucial cause of the war in the troubled domestic
scene in the major countries of Europe. In his view, leaders drawn from

traditional elites with a weakening grip on power entered the war to subvert the process of internal change. Thus, the growing electoral power of the SPD, Germany's Socialist party, which had won an impressive victory in the national elections of 1912 to become the largest party in the Reichstag, or the possibility of civil war in Great Britain over the issues of Irish Home Rule, loomed large. If such pressures did not dictate entry into war, according to Mayer, they inclined leaders to take risks more willingly than they would have otherwise.[9]

In the end, Mayer is less than persuasive. As Theodore Hamerow has put it, there is no hint of such intentions: "No grand design, no fixed plan can be discerned in what the political leaders were doing during those feverish weeks and days before the outbreak of hostilities." One looks in vain for a revelation by one of the directors of Europe's politics "in some secret diary, in some private conversation with an aide, a colleague, a friend, a wife." Indeed, Bethmann Hollweg and other leaders were more afraid war would promote domestic upheaval.[10]

A further issue that has drawn intense concern is whether or not Germany holds a disproportionate degree of responsibility for the outbreak of war. It is now clear that German recklessness and ambition, mixed with fear that delay in fighting a war against a reviving Russia would prove fatal, inflamed an already dangerous situation and pointed Europe toward war. All of the participant countries in the great summer crisis contributed—by their diplomatic ineptness and their antagonisms—to the grim outcome. None-theless, it was Germany's encouragement of gross aggressiveness in Vienna that counted most in moving the crisis from the conference table to the battlefield.[11]

THE CRISIS LEADS TO WAR

A month after the assassination of Archduke Franz Ferdinand, the crisis developed with lightning speed. On July 23 Austria-Hungary presented Serbia with an ultimatum designed to be rejected. The ultimatum required the government of Serbia to take such humiliating steps as dismissing military and civilian officials to be named by Austria-Hungary. At the same time, officials of the Austro-Hungarian government were to be allowed to participate in Serbia's investigation of the plot to murder the archduke. The inevitable rejection was Austria's excuse to attack Serbia five days later. Russia's support for the Serbs took the form of a military mobilization along its entire western frontier. In short order, Germany responded with a declaration of war against Russia on August 1, then against France, Russia's ally, two days later. When Germany implemented its long-standing war plan and invaded France through Belgium on August 4, Britain immediately joined France and Russia.

When this momentous crisis arrived, a mixture of European crowned heads, civilian leaders, and military commanders moved to meet it. In Germany, Kaiser Wilhelm played an active role in the decision to support Austria's ultimatum to Serbia. Thereafter Prime Minister Bethmann Hollweg and General Helmuth von Moltke took the lead, and the kaiser merely ratified the decision to go to war. In the other great monarchies of the time—Austria-Hungary, Russia, and Great Britain—monarchs had a lesser role. In Austria-Hungary, Foreign Minister Count Leopold von Berchthold took command and decided on war. In Russia, Foreign Minister Sergei Sazonov set the country's policy and persuaded a hesitant Tsar Nicholas II to follow. In Vienna and St. Petersburg (renamed Petrograd in late August 1914), as in Berlin, the generals commanding their countries' armies—Conrad von Hötzendorf, Nikolai Yanushkevich, and von Moltke—pressed for national mobilization and, in so doing, brought each country measurably closer to a declaration of hostilities. By contrast, in Britain, with military leaders far from the inner circle of power, the civilians in the cabinet, Prime Minister H. H. Asquith and his colleagues, decided the issue. King George V ratified their decision. In the hostilities now beginning, monarchs would fade even further into the background, and, in most of the belligerent states, generals and statesmen would wrestle for control of the war effort.

CIVILIAN AND MILITARY LEADERSHIP: WARTIME

The Central Powers—Germany, Austria-Hungary, the Ottoman Empire, and Bulgaria—put their armies under a unified command in September 1916. The countries of the Entente—Great Britain, France, and Italy—and the United States did the same only in the spring of 1918. Thus, the first campaigns were fought by military leaders in clumsy, often strained cooperation with one another. German and Austrian generals, along with their British and French counterparts, fought together as best they could.

From the start, much of the military sphere was walled off from civilian influence. Bethmann Hollweg had as little to say about the conduct of the German offensive into France as French prime minister René Viviani did about the counterstrategy of General Joseph Joffre. In all countries, civilian leaders were discouraged from visiting the front, not only in 1914 but for years thereafter. Only in 1917, when the record of failure and blood had become too obvious to ignore, did leaders like Britain's David Lloyd George and France's Georges Clemenceau try to apply the principle often attributed to Clemenceau that "war is too serious to be left to the generals." And even then, they had only mixed success.

THE WAR PLANS

The campaigning season of 1914 was the shortest of any year of the war, but it built the framework for much that followed. Starting in the first days of August, armies mobilized according to prewar plans: reservists were called up; field armies were moved to national borders. War plans ceased to be documents on paper, previewed in peacetime maneuvers: they now became the guidelines for military operations.

Each of the major warring nations had a war plan, although some were both more elaborate and more ambitious than others. During the first weeks—and perhaps the first months—of the war, while the conflict offered a host of surprises, much of the fighting took place along the lines of prewar expectations. Germany invaded France through Belgium; the British Expeditionary Force (BEF), the bulk of the British army, crossed the Channel to serve alongside the French army; Russian forces invaded both eastern Germany and the northern parts of the Austrian empire; Austrian forces marched into Serbia.

The generals of the time operated on the basis of principles derived from the wars of Napoleon. They directed their efforts toward a quick and decisive defeat of the enemy's main forces. Their tool was the powerful and determined offensive. As one authority on warfare had put it in 1905, "The essence of successful leadership in the future will be . . . a rapid and sustained advance which will overrun all opposition by its very momentum."[12] The vast changes in the size and composition of armies, the equally great alterations in the technology of weapons, in means of transportation, and in tools of communication had not altered such thinking—at least not at the top of the military ladder. In the American Civil War (1861–1865), the Boer War (1899–1902), and the Russo-Japanese War (1904–1905), bold and bloody offensives had not lived up to expectations derived from the time of Napoleon. But Europe's military leaders had not chosen to alter their plans. Instead, they used recent European experience, such as the decisive success of Prussian arms in the Franco-Prussian War (1870–1871), as the norm. As Jay Luvaas has pointed out in regard to the events in North America, "Most of those who studied the Civil War after 1870 were in reality seeking to confirm accepted principles rather than to discover new information that might lead to a change in doctrine."[13] Plans based on the old doctrine of the bold and decisive offensive now had their time of testing.

THE FAILURE OF THE SCHLIEFFEN PLAN

During this first phase of the fighting in 1914, the war was a mobile one, much as prewar planners had anticipated. Field armies confronted one another, either seeking to break through to victory, or, more frequently, to slide around the enemy's flank to gain a decisive advantage. The German army, invading France via Belgium, marched and fought over a distance of 300 miles. Russian troops thrust as much as 75 miles into the German province of East Prussia, while other Russian armies cut deeply into Austrian Galicia. But none of these great sweeps, impressive on the map and conducted in accordance with prewar hopes, brought decisive victory.

The German war plan—known in honor of its creator as the Schlieffen plan—offered the clearest set of goals. In its key feature, it called for German forces to drive through Belgium (a neutral country), thus avoiding the massive French fortifications facing the German border. Moving southward and southwestward, they would push, crowd, and then annihilate the French army against its own eastern border, crushing France's ability to continue fighting in one great offensive campaign. Victory in the west would come in less than two months. German forces then were to move eastward for a longer but no less decisive offensive against the Russians. The failure of the Schlieffen plan built the foundation for the prolonged war that followed in western Europe. The fighting there has offered the most vivid, horrible images of what World War I was like.

The German offensive seemed at first to meet with striking success. The Belgian army and Belgian fortifications offered more resistance than German planners had foreseen, but the march went generally according to the timetable. France's commanders were caught off guard, since they never anticipated such a massive German concentration in the north. And they were off to conduct their own offensive—with objectives far less clear and less ambitious than those of the Schlieffen plan—against the German border regions further south. As German forces advanced westward into Belgium and swung southward toward the undefended Franco-Belgian border, the five divisions of the British Expeditionary Force took their place along the left (western) flank of the French. They too were soon pushed along in the overall Allied retreat.

But the Schlieffen plan did not work. The French and British both conducted a fighting retreat, impeding the German advance while keeping their own forces intact. German efforts to sweep around to the western flank of the enemy never succeeded. Their field armies—advancing each day over vast territories, encountering spirited enemy resistance, and uncoordinated by higher authority—tended to pull away from one another during the advance; this opened dangerous gaps into which the French or possibly the British could counterattack. In a momentous but almost inevitable decision, the generals in the field modified their orders. They would shorten their line of advance, pursuing the French forces while remaining east of the French capital—and powerful fortress—of Paris.

Meanwhile, German troops were exhausted by weeks of marching and fighting. Of course, the British and French had to cover the same ground, but the Germans were pulling perilously far from their supply bases. As German generals, in particular the overall commander von Moltke, grew first uncertain, then pessimistic, and finally panicky, the key figure on the Allied side, France's General Joseph Joffre, remained unruffled and even confident.

In early September the tide turned. The French and British counterattacked northward against the overextended Germans along the Marne River. Meanwhile, a newly created French army based in Paris struck the Germans from the west. By September 9, the Germans were compelled to pull back. The Schlieffen plan had failed, and any hopes of a quick German victory in the west evaporated. But they pulled back only to strong defensive positions, such as those along the Aisne River, that soon expanded to become a steady line of trenches stretching from the Swiss border to the English Channel. If the Germans had failed to win a decisive victory, they ended up occupying most of Belgium and large areas of northeastern France. The war on the western front was to center on efforts to push them from the consolation prize they had taken in the late summer of 1914.

1914: THE WAR IN EASTERN EUROPE

In eastern Europe, the war plans also went into general operation. Two Russian armies drove into East Prussia—one from the south pushing up from Russian Poland, one from the east through the Masurian Lakes region—occupying German territory and threatening further advances. Energetic German commanders, notably General Paul von Hindenburg, his vigorous assistant General Eric Ludendorff, and the key military planner Colonel Max Hoffmann, managed to isolate and annihilate the southern army under General Alexander Samsonov. They then turned and repelled General Paul Rennenkampf's force, which was advancing westward. It seemed a more decisive victory than anything that was occurring on the western front: Samsonov's force of 300,000 was destroyed or captured. But it too left both sides basically intact to fight again.

Russian forces had much greater success penetrating and occupying Galicia, the northern part of the Austro-Hungarian Empire. Their attack met advancing Austrian troops under Conrad von Hötzendorf; the collision between the two ended in Conrad's withdrawal. To add to Austria's embarrassment in the first episodes of the war, several Austrian offensives against minuscule Serbia—seen as Austria's archenemy and the cause of the war—ended in failure. An encouraging event for the Central Powers came in early November, however, when Ottoman Turkey entered the war on their side.

CASUALTIES AND THE DETERMINATION TO CONTINUE

Perhaps the most striking feature of the first months of the war was the bloody nature of the fighting, far beyond what nineteenth-century European models had led prewar planners to expect. Heavy artillery, rapid-fire rifles, and machine guns combined with defensive tools such as barbed wire and trench fortifications to make combat unimaginably costly.

The generals of course knew the casualty figures. But the public could only sense the size of the losses. Newspaper reports offered little accurate information. British war correspondents, for example, in Phillip Knightley's vivid description, "protected the high command from criticism, wrote jauntily about life in the trenches, kept an inspired silence about the slaughter, and allowed themselves to be absorbed by the propaganda machine."[14] This pattern continued in all countries throughout the war. But in the minds of the public and military leaders alike, the determination to go on with the war—and even fight it with larger, better equipped forces—was unchallenged.

1915: THE ELUSIVE VICTORY

The full year of fighting in 1915 produced a record of frustration and disappointment for the Allied powers. In contrast, the Central Powers fended off one threat after another and drove forward in several directions. New countries entered the conflict. Nonetheless, the year ended without having moved the war closer to resolution.

Allied Failures in 1915: The Western Front, Gallipoli, and the Invasion of Serbia

While France failed in its attacks on the western front, the British, losing there as well, were humiliated at Gallipoli. The western front remained

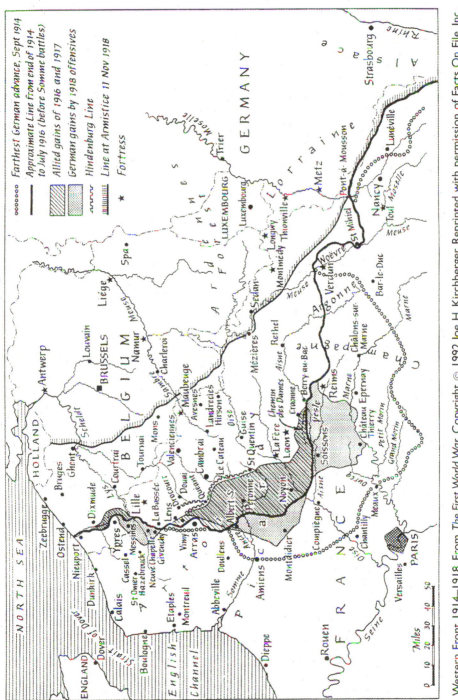

Western Front 1914–1918. From *The First World War.* Copyright © 1992 Joe H. Kirchberger. Reprinted with permission of Facts On File, Inc., New York.

primarily a French responsibility as Britain busied itself building up a large army. General Joffre hurled the vast French forces against the German lines in a series of offensives from March until September. The result was a deadlock marked by long, discouraging casualty lists. Whether striking along the northern portion of the front in Artois or further southward in Champagne, the French could do little more than dent the German line. What ground they took in the face of potent German defenses often fell back into enemy hands following violent German counterattacks.

The experience for the British on the western front was the same, although on a smaller scale. From the spring to the fall of 1915, General Sir John French's divisions conducted a series of offensives. No combination of artillery or gas (the latter was introduced by both the Germans and the British on the western front this year) opened the way for the infantry to take—and to keep—much ground. The final major assault, at Loos in September, was a particularly bloody affair due to the ineptitude of the British high command as well as to the success of the German counteroffensives. In the aftermath, French was forced to relinquish his command to General Sir Douglas Haig.

Britain's humiliation at Loos was compounded by its failure to seize the Turkish Straits and capture the Turkish capital, Constantinople. Some of the more imaginative members of the government, like Winston Churchill, the navy minister, advocated using Britain's sea power to gain a decisive victory away from the western front. But the effort was marked by muddled planning and poor execution. Starting as a failed naval attack on the forts defending the entrance to the Straits in March 1915, it evolved into an amphibious operation in which British, Australian, and New Zealand troops landed on the Gallipoli peninsula to seize Turkish defenses by land attack.

The highly vaunted British navy, undefeated for more than a century, failed in its attack. And, in another reversal of the trends of the nineteenth century, Britain's land forces could not overcome the army of a non-Western power, Ottoman Turkey. By the close of the year, the forces at Gallipoli had to be evacuated.

In the Balkans, Serbia was nearly driven out of the war in the fall. Attacked from the north by German and Austrian forces, and from the east by Bulgaria, which joined the war in October in order to help overwhelm the Serbs, the kingdom of Serbia was overrun. Only by a dramatic march westward through Albania to the Adriatic Sea and the assistance of the French navy did a remnant of the Serbian army survive. Like the story at Gallipoli, the Serbian campaign was a disaster limited only by a skilled naval evacuation of the defeated forces.

Italy Enters the War

In the Mediterranean, Italy joined the Allies in May. The Italians had been courted by both sides. Led by Foreign Minister Sidney Sonnino, the Italian government got a pledge of extensive territorial gains to be won at the expense of Austria-Hungary. These included the South Tirol and vast regions along the eastern coast of the Adriatic. Sonnino expected to wage a limited war in conjunction with Italy's new allies, fighting only against Austria-Hungary and confining military operations to the areas where Italy sought its territorial rewards.

The mountainous border between the two antagonists offered few possibilities for an effective offensive. General Luigi Cadorna, like his counterparts elsewhere a fervent believer in the decisive offensive, hurled his forces against Austrian territory at two points: northward into the Trentino and eastward through the region of the Isonzo River toward Gorizia and Trieste. In June, the poorly equipped and badly led Italians experienced the first of numerous bloodbaths assaulting Austria's mountain defenses along the Isonzo. As in France, the war here bogged down in costly stalemate.

Germany Defeats Russia

Seen from Berlin, Germany's leaders could point to the success of halting enemy offensives everywhere. But there was the even greater satisfaction of massive advances. The conquest of Serbia was one example that paled, however, compared to the German push into the Russian Empire. Germany's spectacular success against Russia came largely out of necessity. In the winter of 1914–1915, Russian forces seemed poised to cut through the last line of mountain defenses and to plunge into the heartland of the Austro-Hungarian Empire. To maintain the security of Germany's most crucial ally, General Erich von Falkenhayn, Moltke's successor, sanctioned a major offensive on the eastern front.

Striking northward through the Carpathian Mountains, a combined German and Austrian force under General August von Mackensen punched through Russian defenses at Gorlice-Tarnow and thrust into the enemy's rear. The desperate Russians were blown aside by one overwhelming artillery barrage after another. Mackensen's artillery at Gorlice outnumbered the Russians in light artillery, 1,272 pieces to 675. And the Russians had no weapons to match the Germans' 334 pieces of heavy artillery. In the face of unlimited supplies of shells on the German side, Russian soldiers had permission to fire only two howitzer shells per day.[15] Starting in early

July, Hindenburg and Ludendorff drove southward from their bastion in East Prussia to add to the Russians' calamity.

Facing certain annihilation, desperate Russian commanders withdrew from vast areas that had constituted the western bastion of the Russian Empire. By the time the German offensives merged in late August, Russia had lost all of its Polish territories and German armies were penetrating the Russian-speaking core of the tsar's possessions. Russian losses, unlike those of the British and the French on the western front, included vast numbers of troops taken prisoner. But the most important result of the 1915 disaster was a Russian military system shaken to its core.

Following this triumph, soon augmented by the advance into Serbia, which the tireless Mackensen also directed, Germany could now claim to be unbeatable on land. Its forces were within striking range of both Paris and St. Petersburg; it had established a direct land link with its Turkish ally; its defenses had proven impenetrable to French, British, and Russian attacks. In reality, however, a German victory was far from assured.

Both alliances continued to mobilize greater resources, as more countries were being drawn into the conflict, but for both sides the conclusive defeat of the enemy remained out of reach. The tactical advantages enjoyed by the defensive side barred the way against decisive offensives on many fronts. Moreover, seemingly decisive offensives brought military advantages but nothing more. Nations committed to victory would not give up, even after suffering dramatic losses. Even Germany's deep penetration into Russian territory did not suffice to bring an end to the war on the eastern front. With the will to win undiminished on all sides, most of Europe's population was condemned to a continuing conflict.

1916: WAR OF DESPERATION

In 1916 belligerents on both sides of the battle lines launched massive offensives. They did so with greater resources than those available in 1914 or 1915. Their leaders' intentions were complex—some hoping for outright victory, some only looking to exhaust the enemy and to push him to negotiate a favorable peace—but none of those intentions were realized. The German offensive on the western front at Verdun failed to bleed the French army dry; the British advance on the Somme failed to produce the long-awaited breakthrough; the Brusilov offensive carried out by the Russian army bogged down in stalemate. In southern Europe, the Italian and Austro-Hungarian armies lunged at one another without result. Meanwhile, as the war's carnage reached unprecedented levels, the conflict continued to spread. In the Balkans, Rumania and Greece were drawn into the maelstrom. Rumania's lightning defeat at the hands of the Central Powers was a singular example of the war waged in a decisive way.

Much of what the Allied powers did started out as a plan for combined offensive operations against Germany and Austria-Hungary, offensives designed to strike more or less simultaneously. The year's fighting, however, was shaped by the clash of intentions held by leaders on both sides.

The Battle of Verdun

By 1916 the great buildup of the British army had produced a massive force designed to be thrown into action side by side with the forces of France. A potent force pushing for such a British effort was the growing feeling in France that its army was bearing the brunt of the fighting and losses on the western front. Indeed, total French casualties in 1915—killed, wounded, missing in action, and taken prisoner—reached the sickening figure of 1,549,000 men.[16] The joint offensive was scheduled to take place in spring around the Somme, but Germany struck first. The renewal of German offensive action on the western front did not aim at a breakthrough or a quick victory. In the view of General von Falkenhayn, Germany's best hope rested in a battle of exhaustion, forcing the French to fight under unfavorable circumstances in terms of terrain and supply, and inflicting intolerable losses on France's army. With France—what Falkenhayn called "Britain's arm on the continent"—crippled, the war could be brought to a negotiated conclusion favorable to Germany.

The German offensive at Verdun, a historic fortress that no French government could lightly abandon, began in the snows of winter. The carnage started in February and lasted until the close of the year: its duration of ten months makes it the longest battle in history.

German attacks hurt their own army almost as badly as they bled France's forces. Their assaults ran into tenacious French resistance. Advancing infantry found, as the Allies had in 1915, that artillery barrages left enough enemy machine guns intact to inflict intolerable casualties. Much of the fighting consisted of massive exchanges from heavy guns, and both sides inflicted comparable losses on one another. French leaders, notably General Philippe Pétain, the army's leading specialist in defensive operations, kept their heads, and Pétain maintained the army's stability by rotating units quickly in and out of Verdun.

Located in an exposed salient and supplied by a single road, Verdun appeared to be impossible to supply. Pétain found ways to bring in the needed supplies: improving the one available road (*la voie sacrée*) and

developing a massive and continuing flow of truck traffic. By the closing
months of the year, Pétain's successor at Verdun, General Robert Nivelle,
took the offensive. After the prolonged slaughter, the battle lines were close
to their starting point. Nearly 400,000 Frenchmen lost their lives in this
hellish place; the Germans emerged almost equally ravaged, with 340,000
killed or missing.

The Battle of the Somme

The British summer attack at the Somme took place while the two sides
continued to claw at one another at Verdun. Contrary to plans worked out
the previous winter, the French could not participate fully in a joint attack.
Nonetheless, the British took up their offensive with vast optimism.

The new British commander, General Sir Douglas Haig, planned a
breakthrough at the Somme based on a prolonged artillery barrage followed by a rapid advance by his forces. Hundreds of thousands of
volunteers, many from the nation's upper classes, had poured into military
service since 1914. The "New Army" they had formed consisted of raw
but enthusiastic divisions, and the Somme offensive was to be their
baptism of fire. Cavalry forces were waiting behind the lines to exploit
the forthcoming breakthrough and to take the war into a decisive phase
in open country.

Nothing of the sort occurred. Surviving German machine gunners in the
front lines combined with German artillerymen to slaughter the advancing
British. Although the first day's assault (on July 1) ended with minimal gains
and unprecedented casualties—the British loss of 20,000 killed and 40,000
wounded stands as a uniquely bloody set of casualties for a single day in
any war—Haig continued the offensive for several months. As at Verdun,
the defenders suffered grim losses while the battle line scarcely moved
forward or backward. As at Verdun, both sides seemingly absorbed their
losses and looked to another year of campaigning in 1917.

The Brusilov Offensive, Italy, and Rumania

The Russian offensive of 1916 was intended to complement the anticipated attack by French and British forces on the western front. Just as the
German offensive at Verdun disrupted the Allies' intentions in the West, so
also did it reshape the Russian role in 1916. In part to help take pressure off
Verdun, the Russians advanced sooner than planned; they also struck a lesser
blow than originally intended.

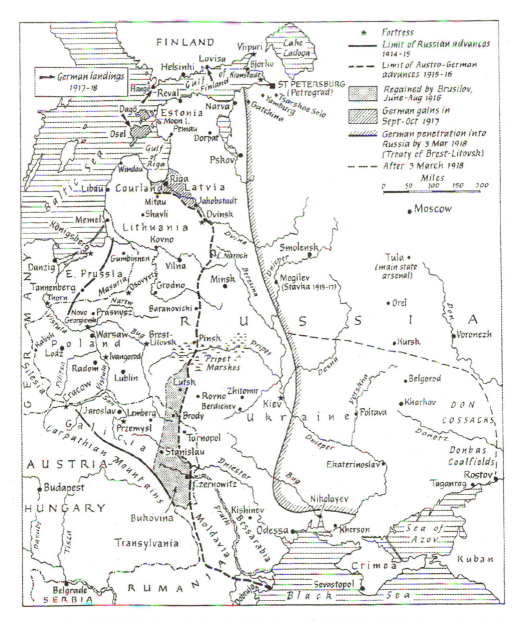

Eastern Front 1914–1918. From *The First World War*. Copyright © 1992 Joe H. Kirchberger. Reprinted with permission of Facts On File, Inc., New York.

Instead of a large-scale offensive over much of the eastern front, the Russian attack involved only a single army group (under General Alexis Brusilov) striking Austro-Hungarian forces in the southern half of the theater of operations. In short order, German reinforcements rushed to the scene (possibly taking some of the pressure off Verdun), and Brusilov's promising attack trailed off into a new stalemate. The shock of the Brusilov offensive had a notable effect on the relations between Austria-Hungary and Germany on the eastern front. The two countries now placed their forces there under a unified German-led command.

Bloody offensives took place on the two fronts on which Italy's army faced its Austrian opponents. Under Cadorna, the Italian forces continued their futile and costly offensives on the Isonzo. In a novel twist to the fighting on the Italian front, the Austrians took the offensive in the northern (Trentino) sector in May. In both sectors, as always, the defending side had the better of the fight. Operations on one front took place in the shadow of events elsewhere: Brusilov had moved up the time of the Russian army's offensive in part to aid the Italians struggling to hold on to the Trentino.

As in 1915, spectacular advances and decisive victories took place away from the quagmire of the western front. On August 27, 1916, encouraged by the initial success garnered by General Brusilov, the government of Rumania abandoned its neutrality and joined the Entente. The Rumanians made the mistake of immediately advancing westward into Transylvania, a part of the Austro-Hungarian Empire inhabited largely by ethnic Rumanians. This promising move brought no results worth the effort. The poorly trained and badly led Rumanian army advanced in halting fashion over difficult mountain roads, hindered by an increasingly effective Austrian defense. And no sooner had they begun their assault than they found their own country being attacked.

German generals showed once again what they could do against an inferior enemy in the wide spaces of the eastern front. Within a week after the start of hostilities, General August von Mackensen, Germany's leading combat commander in the east, drove northward into Rumania from bases in Bulgaria. General von Falkenhayn had been relieved as chief of staff for his failure at Verdun, but he received command of the field army that counterattacked eastward from Transylvania in mid-September. By year's end, most of Rumania, like northeastern France, Belgium, Serbia, and Russian Poland, came under German occupation. In the north, the Rumanian army, like the Belgian, was able to hold only a small sliver of the kingdom's territory.

Greece Enters the War

The new flare-up of combat in the Balkans spread the war to Greece. British and French forces had entered Greece in late 1915 in a futile effort to aid Serbia. A large contingent of their troops remained in the port of Salonika, on Greek territory, but without the consent of the Greek government. In 1916 the political establishment in Greece split: supporters of King Constantine clung to a neutrality colored by sympathy for the Central Powers. Meanwhile, former prime minister Eleutherios Venizelos and his faction favored fighting on the Allied side. Territory under the control of Venizelos joined the Allies in November while the country as a whole seemed to slide toward civil war.

Changing Leadership

The great bloodletting of 1916—Verdun and the Somme were the costliest battles of the entire war—had no apparent impact on the desire of the belligerent governments to fight to the finish. The fall of Falkenhayn in the summer led to the emergence of Paul von Hindenburg and his dominating assistant Erich Ludendorff. These German leaders were committed to an even greater national effort. An equally dynamic, determined leader emerged in Britain when David Lloyd George, formerly minister of munitions, took over as prime minister from a discredited H. H. Asquith in December.

By 1916 Kaiser Wilhelm II, the continent's most boisterous and energetic prewar monarch, had become little more than an interested observer of the operations of his armies. The generals had paid him little heed since the start of the war, and in November 1914 he told a dinner companion, "The General Staff tells me nothing and never asks my advice." With the fighting still raging at Verdun and the Battle of the Somme about to erupt, Wilhelm's conversations with his military entourage focused on the kind of social life he would permit the German aristocracy to conduct in Berlin after the war's conclusion![17]

The Strains of the War Appear

Beyond shifting personalities at the top, the third year of fighting brought more ominous developments. Verdun had, in fact, drained most of the fighting spirit from the French army; if it remained apparently intact, its cohesiveness was shaky. The discipline and organization of the vast Russian army were equally fragile. The fighting forces of Italy and

Austria-Hungary showed signs that they could not bear their share of the bloodshed much longer.

Political figures on both sides of the battle lines accepted the idea of a negotiated peace. Emperor Charles, the new monarch of Austria-Hungary, worked behind the scenes for a settlement. In France, Minister of the Interior Louis Malvy, Radical party leader Joseph Caillaux, and their coterie seemed prone not only to compromise but to defeatism. A different kind of desperation in Germany led to renewed discussion of unlimited submarine warfare. If the land offensive at Verdun had failed of results, only a new wave of attacks at sea offered the prospect of victory.

The strains on the home front in some participating countries approached the breaking point. Strikes in Germany and Russia were one sign of cracks in the determination of the warring nations' civilian population. In Petrograd, talk spread of a coup of some kind, perhaps by military leaders, to put an end to the gross incompetence of the nation's political leaders.

The Determination to Go On

Nonetheless, for those who counted in the upper circles of the belligerent countries, this was no time to make peace. In Germany, the decisive power rested in military hands, and figures like Erich Ludendorff were coming to consider renewed use of the submarine as the tool that would win the war. In Britain, the energetic and optimistic influence of David Lloyd George, the new prime minister, renewed the hope of victory. An English schoolmaster, Robert Saunders, may have captured the popular mood in a letter to his son in late December. The daily news was sad, but "public opinion is dead against Peace at present, we are only just getting our 5,000,000 Army ready for real business. . . . Fritz has got to take his medicine before we have finished with him."[18]

Thus, the belligerents readied themselves for a new year of war, their forces seemingly intact, their intentions both desperate and determined, their societies increasingly fractured.

THE WAR AT SEA

The naval war followed a vastly different rhythm from the war on land. A short spurt of violence at the start of the conflict was followed by a prolonged period in which the warring fleets merely skirmished. In stop-and-go fashion, Germany used submarines to attack merchant vessels during the first two years of the conflict. The war of surface fleets rose to a brief crescendo in 1916 with the Battle of Jutland. But the conflict's naval climax came only in 1917, when the submarine, and the war against the submarine, dominated the picture.

Prewar Naval Plans

The prewar ideas of naval planners proved even more detached from reality than those of their army counterparts. Both sides expected their battle fleets to meet in major engagements shortly after the start of the war. Germany's leading admirals expected the British fleet to do what it had done in the Napoleonic wars: move close to Germany's ports and naval bases in the North Sea in order to block Germany's maritime commerce. This seemed to offer brilliant prospects for the numerically weaker German navy. By picking its targets and times carefully, Germany could eliminate Britain's major naval units one at a time. When the strength of the British fleet had been brought within reach of Germany's High Seas Fleet, Germany would accept a general naval encounter.

Meanwhile, British leaders expected an immediate offensive by the High Seas Fleet upon the outbreak of war. The Germans would come out of their ports, face the full weight of British naval power, and suffer an early and catastrophic defeat. In Paul Halpern's description of the temper of the times in Britain, "When the war broke out, the generation that had experienced the Anglo-German naval race, read widely popular spy stories . . . and remembered the sudden Japanese attack on the Russian base at Port Arthur a decade earlier fully expected a major battle within a short period of time."[19]

The British Blockade and the First Surface Actions

German intentions were frustrated when the British instituted a novel—and technically illegal—distant blockade. British forces would not patrol off Germany's North Sea coastline as required by international law governing blockades; they would cut off Germany from the open ocean by patrolling the English Channel and the waters between Scotland and Norway. There would be few opportunities for Germany to whittle down the number of Britain's capital ships. Correspondingly, British intentions were frustrated when the Germans, expecting a close blockade, refused to challenge the Royal Navy in the open waters of the North Sea.

Small German and British task forces met off the coast of Chile and Argentina at the Battle of Coronel (October 1914) and the Battle of the Falklands (November 1914). The Germans triumphed in the first, the British in the second. But such encounters were the exception.

Instead, for the first two years of the war, the two great surface fleets dueled with one another in a number of indecisive engagements in the waters separating Germany and the east coast of England. The Germans, for example, raided Britain's coastal ports, hoping to provoke a reckless pursuit that would bring part of the British fleet into contact with superior German forces. The British set traps for the Germans, seeking on a number of occasions to get between parts of the High Seas Fleet and their home ports. Neither strategy worked.

The Battle of Jutland and Submarine Warfare

When the two fleets met for the first and only time in the Battle of Jutland off the Danish coast in late May 1916, the results were inconclusive. Battleship fought battleship only for a few hours at the close of the day. A cautious Admiral Sir John Jellicoe, acutely aware of the need to preserve Britain's existing naval superiority, rejected risky aggressive tactics. He was willing to forgo the possibility of destroying much of the German fleet in order to avoid the danger of heavy losses to the Royal Navy. Britain's command of the seas, as he interpreted it, meant reluctantly accepting an inconclusive action on the high seas.

In the aftermath of Jutland, the German navy turned its hopes away from its surface fleet. Within six months, the advocates of an unlimited submarine offensive won the day. It began promisingly in the first months of 1917 as German U-boats attacked all merchant commerce going to and from the British Isles. The crisis in the entire naval conflict now emerged: it was the war between the submarine and the weapons that could be employed against it. If the submarines won, the Allies faced the loss of their command over the sea lanes. For Britain, this meant starvation, a situation that pointed toward Germany's ultimate victory in World War I.

Although the U-boats found numerous targets down to the closing weeks of the war, Allied countermeasures, notably the use of the convoy, tipped the balance in the undersea war before the last months of 1917. Thus, both acts in the naval drama had the same result. In the first act, the surface war from 1914 through 1916, command of the sea remained unassailably in Allied hands. The second act, the undersea war of 1917 and 1918, raised the possibility of Germany's naval superiority. In the end, although after many worrisome months, the Allies prevailed here as well.

1917: THE COLLAPSE BEGINS

The fourth year of fighting brought several of the combatants to the point of collapse. France, Italy, and Russia discovered that their military forces were no longer stable organizations. Events on the home front now took on crucial significance, most notably in Russia, where the governing system itself fell victim to the strains of the fighting.

At the same time, older features of the war continued. The war spread to bring in new belligerents, the crucial newcomer being the United States. Moreover, the massive and seemingly futile bloodletting on the western front did not abate; the carnage took its most hideous form at the Third Battle of Ypres (Passchendaele).

The Fall of the Russian Monarchy and the Nivelle Offensive

Several momentous events overlapped in the first months of 1917. Germany initiated unlimited submarine warfare in early February, a policy that led directly to U.S. entry into the war. The declaration of war by the U.S. Congress on April 6, 1917, brought a train of momentous events, starting with the speedy dispatch of American naval units to British waters to help fight the submarines. The U.S. government immediately seized German merchant vessels in American ports, making them available for use against Germany; it also dispatched an advance party of senior army commanders to France to prepare for the arrival of a massive American army. In the midst of this striking development, revolution broke out in Russia: bread riots in the capital at Petrograd in early March quickly led to a breakdown in military discipline in the city's army garrison, massive street demonstrations, and the collapse of the monarchy. Meanwhile, the French prepared for an ambitious advance on the western front: the Nivelle offensive.

The Nivelle offensive of April 1917 quickly produced catastrophe. Nivelle based his plan on the view that the French army had to have a great victory to maintain its morale. His attack had the opposite effect; its visible failure led to massive mutinies that crippled the entire army for months to come. The French were successful in keeping the news from the Germans. As Pétain's biographer Stephen Ryan has put it, "At no point in the course of World War I was the military effort of the Allies in greater danger."[20] Only the restorative policies of the new French commander, Philippe Pétain, starting with better food, leave policies, and medical care, then culminating in a moratorium on costly offensives, allowed the army to recover.

Third Ypres

Haig's offensive in Flanders, a catastrophe of a different sort, began in July. Several elements shaped the Third Battle of Ypres. The most important was Haig's unbending commitment to offensive action on the western front and his belief that a decisive breakthrough was possible. That belief was bolstered by his conviction that Allied offensives were draining the Germans of men and supplies. Thus, if a spectacular victory was not yet in sight, Britain and France were nonetheless winning the war of attrition. A second element, the growing threat of the submarine, made the capture of the Belgian coast, with its nest of U-boat bases, seem imperative. Finally, Britain's still potent forces were the only means available to divert German attention from the areas held by the perilously weak French army.

As at the Somme, Haig relied upon a prolonged artillery bombardment followed by a massive infantry advance. As always on the western front, the artillery effort alerted the enemy to the area in which the assault was to occur. Beyond the skilled German defense, the British faced a still greater obstacle: the muddy terrain of Flanders. Haig had selected for his offensive a region subject to flooding. The rains of August 1917 combined with the artillery's destruction of the prewar drainage system to create a muddy hell in which effective advances were impossible and vast casualties inevitable. A temporary dry spell in September was followed by even heavier rain—and even more dismal hopes for a successful offensive—in October.

The rationale for Haig's continuing efforts became less and less convincing. By the time of the greatest losses in the fall, Pétain had gotten the French army over the worst of its indiscipline. Besides, the submarine bases were hopelessly out of reach, and the bases for the most dangerous submarines were not in Belgium but along Germany's northern coast. Unlike the French army under Nivelle, Haig's forces maintained their discipline in these impossible conditions. But the fighting capacity of the British army inevitably wavered as it suffered losses estimated somewhere between 250,000 and 400,000 men. Journalist Philip Gibbs, soon after the war's conclusion, recalled the battle's psychological cost: "For the first time the British Army lost its spirit of optimism, and there was a sense of deadly depression among many officers and men with whom I came in touch."[21]

The Bolsheviks Come to Power in Russia

As the first assaults took place in Flanders, the Russian army launched its last offensive. The driving force behind the operation was Alexander Kerensky, the war minister of the Provisional Government that had taken power after the fall of the monarchy. In later years, Kerensky remembered the combination of motives that impelled the government to take the offensive. "If Russia's present inactivity at the front and the collapse of the army's strength continued," he told one group of military planners, "the

Germans as well as the Allies would lose all respect for us and would completely disregard our legitimate interests in the future."[22] But the internal needs of Russia also dictated the summer attack. An offensive would restore the army and thus "preserve the interior of the country from the grave wave of anarchy threatening from the front."[23]

In short order, the "Kerensky offensive" failed. With it went the last fighting spirit of the Russian army. In early November, while the army stood aside, V. I. Lenin's Bolsheviks seized power from Kerensky. They had promised the Russian people they would end the conflict. Thus, one of the Great Power belligerents was now committed to deserting its former allies. Before the year was out Lenin's government signed an armistice with the Central Powers and began the negotiations that led to the Treaty of Brest-Litovsk in March 1918.

The Italian Defeat at Caporetto

During the same period in late October when Lenin prepared to push Kerensky's government aside, the Allies suffered a blow in southern Europe. It likewise pointed toward the collapse of one of their number. In late October, a combined German and Austrian army broke through the Italian front on the Isonzo. As the Italian army collapsed, huge regions of north-eastern Italy fell into enemy hands. Unlike the situation in Russia, however, the crisis in Italy was surmounted. Italian forces, under the new leadership of General Armando Diaz, set up a defensible line on the Piave. Eleven French and British army divisions rushed in to stiffen the Italian effort.

The Close of 1917

In the end, the year brought conclusive victories to neither side. The Allies were shaken and exhausted, and Russia's imminent departure from the war meant the end of the eastern front. Nonetheless, America's mobilization of its vast strength and its commitment to send a massive army to Europe rebalanced the scales. Moreover, the war against the U-boat had been contained, albeit not completely defeated. The Allies still seemed the stronger side.

But Great Britain and France had to hold on in the face of a final German offensive. Victory in the east offered Germany the opening to concentrate the bulk of its armies in France. Driven close to the limit of human and material resources, the German leaders could still spend them on a final attack in the west.

1918: THE WAR'S CONCLUSION

Before the end of the fifth year of fighting, World War I closed with a decisive victory for the Allies. Despite the elusiveness of a decision for either side before, the seemingly unbreakable stalemate finally came to a close. The addition of American strength to the Allied camp and the exhaustion of Germany and its allies brought the decision.

Woodrow Wilson and the Fourteen Points

The year began with an important step in the political course of the war. On January 8, President Woodrow Wilson issued his Fourteen Points in an address to a joint session of Congress. Without consulting the British, French, or Italian governments, the American leader set down the principles for a future peace settlement. He pointed to such goals as freedom of the seas and a postwar international organization of the world's countries. The speech likely reflected Wilson's belief that only a peace of reconciliation could be a lasting one. More immediately, however, his views countered the call by the new Communist government of Russia for an end to the war on radical terms; and Wilson may have hoped his speech could persuade Russia to remain in the war. It also served a purpose in domestic politics, providing Wilson's liberal supporters with an idealistic goal to justify the political repressions and other pains the government was inflicting on the nation in order to fight the war effectively. The speech was equally important for what it did not include. There was no mention of placing severe penalties on the Central Powers. Thus, the Fourteen Points aimed—successfully, it turned out—at undermining morale and the will to continue the war in the Central Powers. As historian Harvey DeWeerd has argued, the speech served "to prepare the minds of the German people to expect a tolerable peace despite their military defeat."[24]

The Final German Offensive

The dominant feature during the first eight months of 1918 was a series of ferocious German offensives. Empowered by the collapse of the enemy on the eastern front, Ludendorff was able to transfer the weight of his forces to the west. From March until July, Germany's armies struck the enemy lines, often with devastating effect. The German effort rested on the imaginative use of the classic tools of the war: men and guns. Superior use of artillery now combined with new infantry tactics. Specially trained assault units, for example, slipped around the enemy's defensive strongpoints to disrupt the rear. In its first appearance, against the British in Artois in March 1918, the German advance brought apparently spectacular results.

Nonetheless, the advantage remained in the weary hands of the defenders. German losses, even in victorious advances, were heavy; Allied leaders, both military and civilian, avoided panic; and under the weight of the crisis, all Allied forces were placed under a single leader, France's General Ferdinand Foch. Meanwhile, seeking a decisive kill, Ludendorff desperately shifted the weight of his efforts from one sector of the front to another. The arrival of American troops boosted Allied morale and correspondingly shook the German spirit, even though large numbers of the newcomers were not in the fight until the fall of the year.

The Allied Counterattack on the Western Front

In July and August, the tide turned with a series of French, then British, counterattacks. In September, the huge American forces recently arrived went into action. By now, the Allies, especially the British, were as sophisticated as the Germans in using their heavy guns. They approached the Germans' skill in effective infantry attacks. The most visible example of the new tools available to the Allies for successful attacks was the tank.

Nonetheless, neither side achieved a clear breakthrough in 1918. Even the spectacular feats of tank warfare on one day led to painstaking infantry advances the day following. Nothing like Erwin Rommel's thrust to the English Channel in 1940 or George Patton's breakout from Normandy in 1944 took place.

The Allied victory was based primarily on the fruits of attrition and the weight of numbers. An exhausted Germany had thrown its last resources into the contest in the spring and early summer of 1918 and suffered final and intolerable losses. German reinforcements entering the front lines found discipline in some units crumbling. As Ludendorff recorded in his memoirs: "I was told of deeds of glorious valour, but also of behavior which . . . I should not have thought possible in the German Army; whole bodies of our men had surrendered to single troopers. . . . The officers in many places had lost their influence and allowed themselves to be swept along with the rest."[25] Even so, German armies retired in good order, and the Allied advance was delayed, sometimes virtually stopped, by such effective defenses as the ones the Americans faced on the Meuse-Argonne sector in the last two months of the war. In the words of Bernadotte Schmitt and Harold Vedeler, the Germans were "a beaten army, though not a routed army, and knew it at the time."[26]

The Collapse of the Central Powers

The signal for Germany's defeat was Ludendorff's loss of heart. Pushed toward resigning by the dismal situation in France, he became even more disheartened by equally catastrophic news from other fronts. Germany's allies—Austria-Hungary, Turkey, and Bulgaria—had been worn down even more brutally than Germany by the years of fighting. Their home fronts were even more dejected, and in the Austro-Hungarian case more divided, than Germany's. Under General Louis Franchet d'Esperey—Americans who could not pronounce his name called him "Desperate Frankie"—the Allied army broke out of its pen at Salonika and produced a series of thumping victories. Franchet forced Bulgaria to ask for an armistice on September 25, liberated Serbia during October, and threatened to march on Vienna. Ludendorff stepped down on October 26, a sign that Germany was nearing the end of its role in the conflict. With the Habsburg Empire's Slavic nationalities in full revolt as well, the government in Vienna sought an armistice on October 29. The Turks found themselves in the path of a victorious British army, under the command of General Edmund Allenby, advancing northward from Palestine. After the fall of Damascus on October 1, Allenby seemed unstoppable, and on October 30 the Turks signed their armistice. With the western front collapsing as well, Germany was now exposed to invasion from the south.

The ultimate blow, although hardly the only one, came when the military calamities evoked political calamity on the home front. Told to prepare for a hopeless assault on the British fleet, the battleship sailors of the German navy at Wilhelmshaven began to mutiny on October 31. The revolt spread to Kiel, then became an urban political rebellion as hungry workers joined mutinous sailors in the first days of November. Under the weight of Allied demands, shaped by President Woodrow Wilson, Germany had already established a constitutional form of government. In the midst of the political upheaval, Kaiser Wilhelm II abdicated, Socialist leader Friedrich Ebert became Germany's prime minister, and a republic was declared. Two days later, on November 11, 1918, German delegates signed the armistice ending the war.

Germany, defeated but not invaded, plunged into political turmoil. Austria-Hungary had dissolved into smaller states based on its subject nationalities, and Ottoman Turkey was in chaos. The war was over; the uncertainties of a postwar world had already appeared.

NOTES

1. Quoted in Bertram Wolfe, *Three Who Made a Revolution: A Biographical History* (New York: Dial Press, 1948), pp. 607–8.

2. Quoted in Thomas Kohut, *Wilhelm II and the Germans* (New York: Oxford University Press, 1991), p. 184.

3. Lamar Cecil, *Wilhelm II: Prince and Emperor, 1859–1900* (Chapel Hill: University of North Carolina Press, 1989), p. 296.

4. Geoffrey Hosking, *The Russian Constitutional Experiment: Government and Duma, 1907–1914* (Cambridge: Cambridge University Press, 1973), pp. 232, 238.

5. Dennis E. Showalter, *Tannenberg: Clash of Empires* (Hamden, Conn.: Archon Books, 1991), p. 65.

6. Ibid., p. 69.

7. Quoted in Bradford Perkins, *The Great Rapprochement: England and the United States, 1895–1914* (New York: Atheneum, 1968), p. 267.

8. Gordon Craig, *The Politics of the Prussian Army, 1640–1945* (London: Oxford University Press, 1964), pp. 367–68.

9. Arno Mayer, "Domestic Causes of the First World War," in Leonard Krieger and Fritz Stern, eds., *The Responsibility of Power: Historical Essays in Honor of Hajo Holborn* (Garden City, N.Y.: Doubleday, 1967), pp. 286–300.

10. Theodore S. Hamerow, *The Birth of a New Europe: State and Society in the Nineteenth Century* (Chapel Hill: University of North Carolina Press, 1983), pp. 436–38. See also John W. Langdon, *July 1914: The Long Debate, 1918–1990* (New York: Berg, 1990), pp. 136–38.

11. For a convincing examination of the "silent war" long under way between the Central Powers (Germany and Austria-Hungary) and the Entente (Britain, France, and Russia), see Bernadotte E. Schmitt and Harold C. Vedeler, "The Plunge into War," chap. 1 in *The World in the Crucible, 1914–1919* (New York: Harper and Row, 1984).

12. Quoted in Archer Jones, *The Art of War in the Western World* (New York: Oxford University Press, 1987), p. 421.

13. Jay Luvaas, *The Military Legacy of the Civil War* (Chicago: University of Chicago Press, 1959), p. 233.

14. Phillip Knightley, *The First Casualty: From the Crimea to Vietnam: The War Correspondent as Hero, Propagandist, and Myth Maker* (New York: Harcourt Brace Jovanovich, 1975), p. 81.

15. A. Bruce Lincoln, *Passage through Armageddon: The Russians in War and Revolution* (New York: Oxford University Press, 1994), pp. 125–27.

16. Richard Watt, *Dare Call It Treason* (New York: Simon and Schuster, 1963), p. 92.

17. Gordon Craig, *Germany, 1866–1945* (New York: Oxford University Press, 1978), pp. 367–68.

18. Quoted in Trevor Wilson, *The Myriad Faces of War: Britain and the Great War, 1914–1918* (Cambridge: Polity Press, 1986), p. 407.

19. Paul Halpern, *A Naval History of World War I* (Annapolis, Md.: Naval Institute Press, 1994), p. 21.

20. Stephen Ryan, *Pétain the Soldier* (South Brunswick, N.J.: A. S. Barnes, 1969), p. 122.

21. The figures are in Schmitt and Vedeler, *World in the Crucible*, p. 180; the quotation appears in Wilson, *Myriad Faces of War*, p. 483.

22. Alexander Kerensky, *Russia and History's Turning Point* (New York: Duell, Sloan and Pearce, 1965), pp. 270–71.

23. Quoted in Richard Abraham, *Alexander Kerensky: The First Love of the Revolution* (New York: Columbia University Press, 1987), p. 193.

24. Harvey DeWeerd, *President Wilson Fights His War: World War I and the American Intervention* (New York: Macmillan, 1968), p. 384.

25. General [Erich] Ludendorff, *My War Memories* (London: Hutchinson, [1919]), vol. 2, p. 683.

26. Schmitt and Vedeler, *World in the Crucible*, p. 294.

2

Anatomy of Catastrophe:
Somme and Chemin des Dames

WAR OF STALEMATE ON THE WESTERN FRONT

In his brilliant novel of World War I, *The General*, C. S. Forester explored the thinking of one of the small group of men who commanded tens, then hundreds of thousands of soldiers in France. When Forester's fictional General Herbert Curzon first encountered the trench lines on the western front in the spring of 1915, he was struck by how fragile the enemy's defenses seemed to be. Looking past the barbed wire, "there was a strip of mud pocked with shell craters, more barbed wire beyond, and then the enemy's front line. . . . It was hard to believe that a wave of disciplined men could not sweep across that frail barrier."[1]

The seemingly endless slaughter on the western front has become the most potent image of World War I inherited by later generations. But this view of meaningless and undifferentiated carnage needs to be augmented by a consideration of individual encounters to get an accurate view of how and why the war proceeded as it did. The Battle of the Somme, for example, demonstrates, among other things, the extraordinary ferocity and human cost of the war by mid-1916. This bloodbath shows as well why no single decisive military action was possible. It further reminds us of the truth in the cliché that commanders who did not understand the conditions and tools of modern warfare wasted their men and invited disaster—a fact that takes on human form upon an examination of the role of General Douglas Haig.

Similarly, the Nivelle offensive gives a specific instance to support the commonplace, albeit accurate, view that politicians could barely control the generals who were their nominal subordinates. This tragic attack of April 1917 at the Chemin des Dames likewise illustrates how and why the war's battlefield calamities proved more than some armies could bear.

THE MACHINE GUN WAR

During 1915, the strength of the apparently frail barrier on the western front to which Forester referred had become evident. Using machine guns in combination with barbed wire and elaborate trench fortifications, the Germans repelled all attacks, often with stunning losses for the troops taking the offensive. The key weapon they employed was the machine gun. A trained team could bring it into use within four seconds. It equalled the firepower of fifty riflemen while presenting a virtually invisible target. "Six machine-guns could hold up a brigade; one gun could halt two battalions before they had got 200 yards from their front line."[2] At the Battle of Loos, a preview of the greater bloodletting at the Somme, the slaughter produced on the morning of September 26, 1915, by the deadly combination of barbed wire and machine guns horrified even the enemy. "Numbers of German machine-gunners and riflemen stopped shooting," historian Trevor Wilson writes of the attack by the British 21st and 24th Divisions "because they had not the heart to continue the massacre."[3]

THE NEED TO TAKE THE OFFENSIVE

For both French and British government leaders, taking the offensive was a necessity. In neither country could leaders permit the war to drag on endlessly without making an energetic effort to bring it to a victorious conclusion. For French leaders in particular, it was unthinkable to permit a hated enemy to occupy undisturbed and unchallenged the valuable and highly populated regions of northeastern France. There was, as yet, no unified command. Government leaders met periodically to decide matters of high strategy. The military commanders, notably Haig and Joffre, likewise held conferences to reach agreement on what to do next.

Desperate government leaders made their decisions with confident military commanders at their sides. Frederick II of Prussia and Napoleon had combined the roles of political leader and military commander. But the prime ministers and most of the war ministers of the early twentieth century had no choice, it seemed, but to take the advice of their experts. Nor did the public, since military leaders were quick to cite their special expertise. Douglas Haig's instructions to his staff prior to the Battle of the Somme on dealing with the press put such thinking in a nutshell. "Military history teems with instances where sound military principles have had to be abandoned owing to the pressure of ill-informed public opinion." And so "the nation must be prepared to see heavy casualty lists for what may appear to the uninitiated to be insufficient object."[4]

Sometimes the plight of an ally made the offensive imperative. Russia's grim condition after its retreat in summer 1915 and the failure of Joffre's assaults at Artois and Champagne pushed British war minister Horatio Kitchener to call for a British attack in France. Showing solidarity with its allies cost the British 60,000 casualties at the Battle of Loos in late September and early October.

THE SEARCH FOR A SOLUTION

British and French generals tried to solve the problem by novel uses of their infantry and artillery, but to no avail. Concentrating sufficient artillery and other forces to promise a breakthrough meant alerting the enemy to the imminent attack. This was especially so since the German positions in France lay along ridges of hills looking down on Allied forces in the flat plains below. The Germans could always prepare, not only bringing in reinforcements but sheltering their defending forces in deep, elaborate underground chambers. An attack in a limited area, where available heavy guns could be used in concentrated fashion, invited the enemy to respond by concentrating his reserves in this small segment of the front. An attack over a vast section of the front spread the available artillery too thinly to have much of an effect.

Some political leaders wondered whether there were other places to launch a decisive operation besides the densely defended western front. Winston Churchill was a fervent advocate of seizing German coastal islands in the North Sea such as Borkum or Heligoland, and Admiral Sir John Fisher, Britain's first sea lord, favored a landing on the Baltic coast. Such ideas dissolved upon close examination. The strength of German coastal defenses, and the vast mined areas in these seas, put any unit of the Royal Navy involved in such adventures in mortal danger. Apart from the peril of sending a naval force into the Baltic, the speed and efficiency of the German railroad system meant that a landing force would be outnumbered almost instantly and wiped out soon after that.

Early in the war, Lloyd George took up the cry for an offensive thrust into the Balkans. Indeed, the successful Allied offensive there in the fall of 1918 had vast strategic consequences, one of them being to expose southern

Germany to invasion. But for most of the war, the prospects in this region were dismal. In 1916, 300,000 Allied troops were held firmly in the bridgehead at Salonika in what the enemy called "the greatest Allied internment camp." Attempts to move northward failed repeatedly so long as the Bulgarians, buttressed by the Germans, remained firm. Cadorna's repetitive efforts to break through Austro-Hungarian defenses on the Isonzo from 1915 to the last months of 1917 showed how little could be done in such terrain.

STAGNATION IN TECHNOLOGY AND IDEAS

There were no great innovations in technology in sight. The tank was the most promising offensive tool, but it remained a primitive weapon with great potential but no proven value. Generals like Douglas Haig and Robert Nivelle had to rely on a mixture of infantry and artillery. Even by the standards of the first two years of the war, the failures of 1916 and 1917 and their consequences were unprecedented.

A striking fact is the lack of development in the minds of senior commanders. In May 1917, after two years of futile and bloody efforts, Haig wrote to his army commanders, "We are now justified in believing that one great victory, equal to those already gained, may turn the scales finally." As his biographer Gerard De Groot has pointed out, "The memo was a virtual carbon copy of those issued before and during the Somme offensive."[5]

It should be noted that the Germans too had an offensive mentality, and their leaders were willing to suffer huge casualties to use it in the search for a decisive victory. The assault on France through Belgium in 1914 was an example of Napoleonic principles at work: Germany hoped to annihilate the French army and to drive France from the war in less than two months. In the closing months of 1914, Falkenhayn conducted his assault on the British at Ypres with the same reckless loss of life the French were to suffer the following year. During four days of the carnage in northwestern Belgium, the Bavarian regiment in which young Adolf Hitler served lost 3,000 men killed or wounded from its total strength of 3,600.[6] In the east, Hindenburg and Ludendorff repeatedly badgered Falkenhayn for the troops that would make a decisive assault on the Russians possible. The brilliant advance that began with the breakthrough at Gorlice-Tarnow in May 1915 seemed evidence that German arms could drive Russia from the war.

But Germany's inferiority in numbers kept its forces mainly on the defensive in the west between November 1914 and March 1918—with the important exception of the battle of attrition Falkenhayn conducted against the French at Verdun. The Germans nonetheless excelled at the ferocious counterattack. At Loos, in October 1915, on the Somme in 1916, at Passchendaele and Cambrai in 1917, Allied advances routinely faced immediate and devastating return blows from the enemy. The spirited German counterattack at Loos, which recaptured the key Hohenzollern Redoubt, prompted even British General Sir Henry Wilson to comment, "Stout fellows those Boshes."[7]

THE FINAL GERMAN OFFENSIVE

The victory over Russia allowed Ludendorff to take the offensive on the western front in spring 1918. The failure of the submarine offensive and the imminent arrival of a huge American army made such an effort seem imperative. Using novel tactics such as brief, precisely targeted barrages and swift infiltration, the German effort got off to a brilliant beginning. But as spring turned to summer, the cost of the offensive became unbearable. Allied defenses hardened, and both the French and British deepened their defensive lines to absorb and repel enemy attacks. Between July 15 and August 2, as Ludendorff's troops faced Allied counterattacks on the Marne, the Germans lost 110,000. Allied losses were 160,000. The Allies, of course, could easily replace such losses as American reinforcements arrived, while the Germans were quickly running out of fighting men.

Thus, the answer to the stalemate was to do what had been done before—but more imaginatively and with greater resources. The twin bloodbaths show how decisively technology had come to favor the defensive side—and how the need to win nonetheless pushed generals and politicians to attempt to break through the limits of technology and terrain.

GENERAL DOUGLAS HAIG AND THE NEW ARMY

The driving force behind the attack at the Somme in the summer of 1916 was General Sir Douglas Haig. A friend to the royal family and a scion of the Scottish aristocracy, Haig was a supremely confident commander whose resolute conduct of the war was buttressed by a deep religious faith. Wedded to offensive operations at almost any cost, Haig's philosophy of war had been formed in the pre-1914 environment of the army's Staff College. The goal of operations was to defeat the enemy decisively on the battlefield, with infantry as the key to success. Then the victorious general was to exploit that success with cavalry operations. As historian Tim Travers has put it, Haig considered the role of modern fire power but believed that "it

THE BATTLE OF THE SOMME GRINDS ON

The failure of the first day was followed by four months of more limited attacks, met by the usual German counterattacks. In these fierce follow-ups to the slaughter of July 1, the two sides bled more evenly. In the end, German casualties at the Somme numbered approximately 465,000 compared to British losses of 500,000. The British had dented, but not broken, the German defensive line.

By the time the fighting eased in this corner of northeastern France, the German high command had gone through its last great change of the war. Having failed at Verdun, suffered a drain on his manpower at the Somme, and been shaken by Rumania's entry into the war, Falkenhayn was compelled to resign. The eastern generals, Hindenburg and Ludendorff, now took command. One of their first actions was to visit the western front and to order the retraining of German combat troops. Their efforts would come to fruition in the smashing German offensive of 1918.

PRESSURE ON THE FRENCH TO ATTACK IN 1917

The French need for a brilliant victory in 1917 stemmed in part from long-standing humiliation over the German occupation of a substantial part of the nation. Beyond that, however, the shakiness of France's allies, Russia and Italy, seemed to require decisive action on the western front.

Finally, the possibility that the French army itself was being worn to a nub was frightening. The causes of discontent were easy to see. Entitled to seven days' leave every four months, soldiers went a year or more without getting away from the combat area. Even the lucky soldier who got his leave found that the army had made no provisions for transportation to get him home. At the same time, supervision over troops once they reached rear areas was lax; drunkenness and indiscipline were one consequence, but so too was the soldier's vulnerability to pacifist and defeatist propaganda commonly available by the middle of the war. Despite the national passion for food, rations for front-line soldiers were poor. Rest camps near the front lines were shabby and dangerously close to the fighting. The ready availability of alcohol at local cafés further undermined discipline.[11]

GENERAL ROBERT NIVELLE

The possibility of victory was personified by General Robert Nivelle. He had taken command at Verdun during the last phase of the fighting there in the closing months of 1916. In carefully planned and rehearsed offensives, albeit on a small scale, he had won notable victories at minor cost in lives. Forced to choose a new commander-in-chief to replace Joffre, who had been discredited by the lack of preparation at Verdun, the French government picked the relatively junior general, Nivelle, jumping him over the heads of more experienced commanders.

Nivelle offered spectacular results. He claimed that the techniques perfected in the fighting at Verdun would permit the longed for breakthrough into open country, outflanking the enemy, and producing decisive victory. With his unaccented English—he was the child of a French father and an English mother—he was even more impressive for the leaders of the British government than he was for French politicians.

Nivelle worked with the two tools available: the heavy guns of the artillery and the striking force of the infantry. Like other generals before him, he hoped they could be used together in a new and effective way. Concentrate enough artillery, he said, to bombard the enemy lines from the immediate front to rear area regions; then send in infantry trained to move forward at rapid speed to penetrate all layers of the German line. His attack, unlike earlier ones, would be characterized by (his words) violence, brutality, and rapidity. It would bring the essential, illusive breakthrough.

THE POLITICIANS FACE NIVELLE

The politicians who heard Nivelle's proposals stood in no position to control him closely. By now the war had gone on for two and a half years, and both Britain and France had suffered millions of casualties. Yet no political leader had the popular support or the military expertise to disregard the advice of his country's military experts. The weak French government, headed by the aged Alexandre Ribot, was one in a series of cabinets that had let military leaders conduct the war more or less as they chose.

The British government was a new one. Its ambitious leader, David Lloyd George, had just come to power pledging that the war would be conducted more vigorously and decisively than it had been under his predecessor. Douglas Haig was pushing for an attack in Flanders, but Lloyd George had no enthusiasm for the British commander who had performed so badly at the Somme in 1916. Stretching for an alternative to Haig's plan, the British prime minister showed that he too was susceptible to Nivelle's optimism.

For his political audiences, Nivelle pointed to the map. The German front in northeastern France, with all its strengths, had a conspicuous flaw: a bulge stretching from Arras in Artois to Reims in Champagne. Let the British strike the northern face of the bulge to distract and unsettle the Germans;

then the French would launch their war-winning offensive against the southern face. Victory would come in the form of a breakthrough on the River Aisne near Soissons, followed by a general offensive on much of the western front.

THE PREPARATIONS ON BOTH SIDES FOR THE NIVELLE OFFENSIVE

As at Verdun, but now on a huge scale, Nivelle trained troops to carry out his plans to a glittering conclusion. The battering force of French artillery shells would move forward rapidly ahead of the troops in a "rolling barrage." The infantry would follow with equal speed, with fresh troops brought up continually to move through the positions taken by the first waves.

As the French forces concentrated, the elements that destined them to failure began to appear. Through a variety of sources—spies, captured field orders, but also just by observing the masses of French forces—the Germans learned Nivelle's intentions. They responded with a defensive measure just as novel as Nivelle's plan of attack: they withdrew from their salient. Destroying everything behind them and leaving thousands of booby traps, they pulled back between March 15 and 19. The vulnerable salient no longer existed. Ludendorff had reduced the length of his front by almost thirty miles. Thirteen divisions had been removed from the front line to constitute a potent reserve. Beyond these measures, the Germans embarked on a sophisticated reconstruction of their battle line aimed at multiple networks of defensive lines and groups of strongpoints. Mobile defensive forces would be able to avoid enemy artillery fire, abandon unpromising sectors of the line, and then counterattack to retake crucial areas. As this formidable system was taking shape, Nivelle prepared his attack for early April.

Despite the renewed strength of the German defenses, the need for a victorious offensive persisted, and Nivelle promised one. The attack would go ahead as planned. In the north, the British were to make their diversionary assault eastward. The main thrust was still to take place in the south: even after the German withdrawal, part of their line still rested along the Aisne River. Here the French would carry out Nivelle's design.

APRIL 1917: THE FINAL DEBATE

Nivelle now faced the doubters: leaders of the French government, notably Minister of War Paul Painlevé, as well as his own generals, including Alfred Micheler, who was scheduled to direct the major portion of the attack. A particularly cogent criticism came from General Pétain, Nivelle's superior at Verdun. He pointed to the insuperable, unavoidable twin problems of the western front. First, the Allies lacked the huge number of heavy cannon needed to bombard the entire area Nivelle planned to assault. Second, the Germans had created a defensive network of surpassing strength.

Nivelle had answers. The situation of France's allies was desperate, and the German defenses were hardly as strong as some believed. His method of attack was novel—and it would succeed. In a final meeting with his critics close to the day of the assault, Nivelle added some final elements to his argument: national morale would never support another large-scale attack; France must move now or, presumably, never to liberate its territory. Besides, if the offensive failed, he would break it off within forty-eight hours. There would be no repetition of the prolonged bloodletting at the Battle of the Somme. Nivelle had the advantage of momentum: now that the French had made extensive preparations for an attack, the vast gathering of men and matériel, combined with fervent hopes for a huge victory, made a force that was virtually unstoppable.

THE NIVELLE OFFENSIVE AND CATASTROPHE

The attack began on the morning of April 16. In a matter of minutes, Nivelle's plans proved faulty. As at the Somme, machine guns and machine gunners survived the bombardment and cut down the attacking forces. More and more French troops were sent forward—Nivelle's plan had called for fresh forces to pass through the ranks of those who had exhausted themselves in the first attack—and newcomers and the day's veterans were packed together.

As Pétain had predicted, the French lacked enough heavy guns (would even twice as many have been enough for a full-fledged breakthrough?) to bombard all of the enemy's positions in the attack zone. Bad weather made it impossible for airplanes to direct artillery fire. The rolling barrage, designed to strike the areas directly in front of the attacking infantry, was transformed into random firing. In the end, the French attackers barely penetrated the German defenses.

This futile battle at the Chemin des Dames brought nothing of what Nivelle had pledged. The promise of winning a decisive victory sank without a trace into no man's land. So too did Nivelle's pledge to break the fighting off in forty-eight hours. His scattered forces, many of them placed in perilous positions along the front, could not simply pull back. And the fighting went on.

THE COST OF OFFENSIVE WARFARE

Failure came at a high price. For the British army, bloody and shaken but still intact, the Somme was a way station to equally great sacrifices in Flanders in 1917 as the army survived as a fighting force. In the long run, however, the losses were irreplaceable: the educated and socially prominent volunteers who had rushed to the colors as volunteers in 1914 and 1915 were the leaders of the next generation. At the Somme they died in droves. For the French army, the Chemin des Dames had more immediate consequences, namely, the collapse of the French army. Nivelle had argued correctly that the morale behind the French war effort was precarious. French losses in the battle were modest by the measures of trench warfare: 144,000 killed and wounded. He discovered, however, that his failed offensive began the collapse: much of the French army plunged into mutiny in May and June.

As a result of the disaster, a new kind of French general, Philippe Pétain, now took command. He shot the leaders of the mutinies, but he won over the rank and file of the army with an improved system of leaves, better rest camps and food, and a policy of remaining temporarily on the defensive. Since 1915 Pétain's style of waging war had emphasized small-scale attack and vast artillery preparation. That now became the style of all French operations until, under the urging of Foch and Clemenceau, Pétain joined in the vast summer and fall 1918 offensive that closed out the war.

THE MEMORY OF CATASTROPHE

Both the Battle of the Somme and the Nivelle offensive (the Battle of the Chemin des Dames) illustrate the deadly dilemma of the western front. Each can represent a score of similar, if less costly and less well-known encounters, in which troops were thrown in hopeless attacks against powerful defenses manned by a determined enemy. But in a war marked by futile offensives, these two tragic encounters have come to symbolize the pain and loss of the entire war for two nations. The Battle of the Somme is the portion of the war's carnage that has held the British imagination most tightly during the course of the entire century. For decades after July 1, 1916, for example, the *Times* of London published poignant memorial messages, placed each year on the anniversary of the battle by the loved ones of individuals who fell that awful morning.

For Frenchmen, the Battle of the Chemin des Dames remained an unbearably painful memory for decades. The futility and horror of the Nivelle offensive were captured vividly in the 1957 American film *Paths of*

Glory, which the French government did not permit—perhaps could not permit—to be shown to its own people four decades after the tragedy. The gripping battle scenes picture only French soldiers dying. The audience never sees the implacable and well-entrenched enemy shooting them down.

In such ways is the war remembered by generations fortunate enough not to have fought in it. War had indeed become modern, terribly so, with faceless machines destroying all before them. In that way, these battles became a metaphor not only for modern war but for the brutality and inhumanity of impersonal bureaucratic society, where, in the acid words of Georges Clemenceau, it is the privilege of great men only to stand on the terrace to observe the slaughter below.

NOTES

1. C. S. Forester, *The General* (Harmondsworth, Eng.: Penguin, 1936), p. 143.

2. Denis Winter, *Death's Men: Soldiers of the Great War* (Harmondsworth, Eng.: Penguin Books, 1979), p. 112.

3. Trevor Wilson, *The Myriad Faces of War: Britain and the Great War, 1914–1918* (Cambridge: Polity Press, 1986), pp. 258–59.

4. Quoted in Gerard De Groot, *Douglas Haig, 1861–1928* (London: Unwin Hyman, 1988), p. 242.

5. Ibid., p. 324.

6. Robert Asprey, *The German High Command at War: Hindenburg and Ludendorff Conduct World War I* (New York: William Morrow, 1991), p. 123.

7. Wilson, *Myriad Faces of War*, p. 263.

8. Tim Travers, *The Killing Ground: The British Army, the Western Front and the Emergence of Modern Warfare, 1900–1918* (London: Allen and Unwin, 1987), pp. 89, 96.

9. Martin Middlebrook, *The First Day on the Somme: 1 July 1916* (New York: W. W. Norton, 1972), p. 245.

10. John Keegan, *The Face of Battle* (London: Jonathan Cape, 1976), p. 245.

11. Richard Watt, *Dare Call It Treason* (New York: Simon and Schuster, 1963), pp. 219–23.

3

Anatomy of Success: The War Against the Submarine

At the start of 1917, the Allies, most notably Great Britain, were threatened with the full force of a devastating weapon. The Germans decided to use unrestricted submarine warfare against merchant shipping. In order to capitalize on the submarine's advantages of stealth and surprise, the Germans attacked, without warning, both Allied vessels and ships bearing the flag of neutral countries. The Germans concentrated their effort in a wide zone around the British Isles, hoping to close off shipping lanes and to shut down Britain's ability to wage war. The use of the new technology of the submarine raised new questions about the rights of neutrals and the "rules" of the sea. It also led to rethinking the nature of naval warfare in the modern age.

For all the vast expenditures of 1914, the huge naval armadas and even their individual vessels only rarely saw action. To the surprise of all authorities, the naval war took a novel turn. The submarine war—as the Germans used the new weapon to strike at Allied commerce, and their opponents sought desperately to find effective countermeasures—became the centerpiece of naval operations for the final two years of the war. As U-boats hunted their prey and Allied surface forces sought to combat the Germans, the course of the entire war at sea hung in the balance.

SUBMARINE WARFARE AGAINST THE ENEMY'S FLEET

Few naval leaders had seen the potential of the submarine before World War I. But the British Grand Fleet was the first to feel the deadly force it could wield. On September 1, 1914, Admiral Sir John Jellicoe received word of submarine sightings near the main British naval base at Scapa Flow. His battleships were forced to flee, in humiliating fashion, to the open waters of the North Sea, where destroyer flotillas could protect them. Until anti-submarine defenses could be put into place at Scapa Flow, Jellicoe was compelled to use Lough Swilly on the Irish coast as his main base. But disaster struck soon. At the close of September, three obsolete armored cruisers, which the Admiralty leaders had carelessly placed near the Dutch coast without destroyers to shield them, fell victim to a single submarine within less than an hour. Jellicoe soon got word that 1,400 officers and men, most of them recently mobilized naval reservists, had perished. The danger became even more clear on October 27, when a German submarine sank the ultramodern battleship *Audacious* off the northern coast of Ireland as it sailed to engage in target practice. The loss was considered so catastrophic that the Royal Navy throughout the war denied that the *Audacious* had been more than damaged.[1]

In response to these calamities, Jellicoe conducted all major operations with an eye to the danger from the submarine—and also from enemy minefields. He refused to send his ships deep into enemy waters, and, notably at the Battle of Jutland in May 1916, he turned away from the enemy rather than risk exposing his precious battleships to mortal danger. Thus, the nature of naval warfare changed early in the war. The ultimate weapon, reluctant as the admirals of the day were to admit it, was no longer the battleship but the tiny underwater vessel that could put a torpedo into a great vessel's hull below the waterline.

To be sure, there were British submarines at work as well. They served as a scouting force for the Grand Fleet, and they found an occasional victim in the form of a war vessel, like the German light cruiser *Hela*, which a British submarine sank off the coast of Heligoland on September 13. But they had few German merchant ships to target outside the Baltic.

THE GERMANS ATTACK MERCHANT SHIPPING

The Germans' war on merchant shipping began in less spectacular fashion than their attacks on the Royal Navy. There was no comment at the Admiralty after a British steamer, SS *Glitra*, went to the ocean bottom on October 20, 1914, off the coast of Norway. When the German war on civilian vessels began in earnest in early 1915, it provoked a dangerous political rather than military response. And it came from the world's most important neutral power, the United States. Following the sinking of the British liner

Lusitania with a massive loss of civilian life, including 128 Americans, President Woodrow Wilson made it clear that such war measures might bring the United States into the conflict. For the next year and a half, German military authorities kept the submarine war against civilian shipping on a tight chain. The exception was in the Mediterranean, where there were few American vessels to sink. In general, as one naval historian has put it, "As a military weapon the submarine proved itself a far more versatile warship than had been foreseen before the war."[2]

GERMANY'S USE OF UNLIMITED SUBMARINE WARFARE

But desperation at Germany's failure to win the war on land in 1916 pushed leaders like General Erich Ludendorff to adopt a policy of unrestricted use of submarine warfare. There seemed little choice. German forces were outnumbered on the western front, where 150 of their divisions faced 190 Allied divisions. British artillery production was in full swing, and the Germans defending the lines in Belgium and France would soon be facing twice as many British cannon as they had in the Battle of the Somme. Russia's Brusilov offensive in the summer of 1916 indicated only dim prospects for an early victory on the eastern front.[3]

The prospects of winning the war via the submarine were mixed. On February 1, the Germans began their unrestricted campaign with 111 operational U-boats. Fewer than half were at sea. The submarines of the time required extensive maintenance: thus, for much of the war more than half of the fleet was in home ports for refurbishing at any given time. The army put so many demands on Germany's efficient but badly strained industrial system that the production of new submarines lagged. The shortage of skilled factory labor was a principal problem. Thus, even at the close of the war, due to losses at sea and a sputtering production program, Germany had only 179 vessels; the need for maintaining the vessels kept the number actually on combat stations to about 120.[4]

For all its deadly striking power, the submarine was a fragile weapon of war. Hit by a single cannon shell, or even rammed by a merchant ship, the thin-skinned submarine was likely to be crippled if not destroyed. Even the concussion from the explosion of a near miss might crack the thin skin of the U-boat's hull. The tactics of striking without warning while the German attacker was submerged came from the U-boats' vulnerability. But this mode of conducting naval operations necessarily put noncombatants traveling on civilian ships at risk. In this way, the Germans committed the politically disastrous step of provoking neutrals like the United States.

The German move to unlimited submarine operations changed the entire nature of the conflict on the ocean in 1917, and it raised the strong possibility that Germany would bring the war to a successful conclusion. By the third year of the war, Britain was the mainstay of the Allied side; Britain's defeat meant Germany's victory in World War I; and Britain faced defeat in its most vital effort: at sea.

THE ALLIED NEED TO RESPOND

On land, novel factors in the war had created a dilemma that stood for years beyond the ability of military leaders to solve. Machine guns, barbed wire, and modern transportation networks combined to form a defensive system that an advancing enemy could not break through; indeed, attempts to do so led to hideous casualties. A lack of imagination on the part of the generals combined with an absence of effective countertechnology and a failure of will on the part of political leaders to produce prolonged catastrophe. In contrast to that grim record, the Allies, led by Britain, were able to devise a successful response—and in a timely way—to the threat of the submarine. As on land, military conservatism at the highest levels stood in the way of an effective solution, but, in the end, a new generation of navy leadership emerged that proved less hidebound than the military brass in adapting to the new technology of war.

The first hint of severe crisis came in the fall of 1916. The German navy had failed to alter the balance of power in the North Sea when it met the British Grand Fleet at Jutland. Now, within a few months, the authorities in Berlin turned to an intensified form of submarine warfare against merchant vessels. Some restrictions remained, but the upward trend in Allied losses suggested what a potent weapon the submarine might become. In October 1916, for example, German submarines sank 175,000 tons of Allied shipping, a peak so far in the war.

Britain stood as the chief target of the submarine offensive. Since the last decades of the nineteenth century, there had been a steady rise in the amount of food the country needed to import from abroad. By the start of the war, fully 80 percent of the bread consumed, along with vast quantities of other foods, came from foreign sources. An effective submarine blockade promised to drive Britain quickly to the brink of starvation.

Apart from Britain's food needs, the nation's war effort, from shipping armies to France to supporting far-flung operations from the eastern Mediterranean to the Persian Gulf, depended upon an unbroken stream of merchant traffic. Statistical analysis showed the German High Command that Britain could be knocked out of the war within six months if German submarines disrupted the island nation's sea traffic. The Germans hoped to destroy 600,000 tons of British shipping per month. Neutral countries like Norway whose ships played a crucial role in the carrying trade with Britain would become too frightened to continue.

EARLY BRITISH COUNTERMEASURES
AND THEIR LIMITATIONS

The first British response to the submarine, dating from the start of the war and intensified in 1916, included a number of measures. The British navy set down extensive minefields to block German submarines from leaving their harbors. A barrier based on nets as well as mines was set up in the English Channel. Merchant ships received naval guns to defend themselves, and the navy employed decoy vessels known as Q ships. These appeared to be merchant ships, but they were actually vessels designed to attack U-boats; manned by naval crews with hidden armaments, they tried to make the submarines surface and approach so that the hunter could be transformed into the hunted.

Nonetheless, the lords of the Admiralty and most combat commanders favored a different countermeasure: patrolling key sea lanes with warships. This requires some explanation. For centuries, the island nation's navy had protected wartime commerce by a different method: escorting convoys of merchant vessels. But this practice had fallen into disfavor during a century without naval warfare after Britain's 1805 victory over France at Trafalgar. Doctrines of free trade made ship owners reluctant to put their vessels under government control, even in moments of peril. The speed of merchant vessels in the new era of steam power seemed to offer adequate protection against attack. Most important of all, the offensive naval doctrines of theorists like American admiral Alfred Thayer Mahan proclaimed that the duty of a fighting navy was to seek out and destroy the enemy's main fleet. Patrolling the sea lanes to seek out the submarines appeared consistent with this offensive mind-set.

Thus, the navy discarded the protection of commerce, and it did so for reasons of doctrine, even for reasons of psychology. To hunt the enemy down was proper; to shield merchant convoys was almost cowardly. As Trevor Wilson has remarked, British leaders failed to see that "the way to counter submarines was not by going in search of them but by standing between them and their quarry."[5] Unfortunately, the patrols encountered few submarines, and sank even fewer, as losses of merchant ships continued to mount. Even the most aggressive patrolling amounted to nothing more than watching the ocean. As the war went on, the navy accepted a limited use of convoys, especially for transporting troops and particularly valuable individual ships. But most naval authorities rejected their wider use.

THE DEBATE OVER CONVOYS

The arguments against change seemed compelling: convoys would make a bigger target for submarines, and they would have to travel at the speed of the slowest vessel. According to international law, convoys could not be formed in neutral ports. Allied port facilities would be overwhelmed by the arrival of numerous ships at once. Merchant captains were not trained to sail in convoys. And, of course, there was an insufficient number of naval vessels to provide adequate escorts.

Pointing to a shortage of escorts clinched the argument for many admirals. The most effective escort, due to its speed and armament, was the destroyer. But these vessels were essential for the operation of the Grand Fleet: destroyers provided the protective screen behind which the invaluable battleships traveled. Thus, the need for the Grand Fleet to be prepared for operations in the North Sea at a moment's notice clashed with the need to provide adequate escort vessels.

THE ESCALATING CRISIS

The crisis was solved in the first half of 1917. Several factors contributed to the Allies' hairbreadth escape from mortal peril. First, the issue was so pressing that political leaders, notably David Lloyd George, demanded a quick solution. Second, the chief method to combat the danger was a traditional one; it needed only to be revived (and expanded) as well as updated. Third, some military leaders in responsible positions, supported by maverick officers at lower levels, accepted and promoted the new measures.

Nonetheless, even Admiral Sir John Jellicoe, who took command of the entire British navy in late 1916 primarily to deal with the submarine war, remained committed to patrolling as the basic response to the U-boat. To his credit, he immediately set up an Anti-Submarine Division under Admiral Alexander Duff to plan and coordinate this part of the naval war. Nonetheless, even while losses escalated dangerously in the first part of 1917, he refused to move energetically to adopt convoy tactics.

During these bloody months, merchant ships were being sunk faster than they could be replaced. In January, while the submarines still operated with some restrictions, Britain alone lost 49 merchant vessels. In February, with the Germans now uninhibited in their attacks, total British losses amounted to 105; by March the toll rose to 147. The losses of other countries on the Allied side as well as those of neutrals more than doubled these terrifying figures.[6]

Allied sea captains saw their friends sail into the open ocean—to disappear without a trace. But the totals were the most disturbing news for those who had access to these figures. In April 1917, German submarines sank almost 900,000 tons of Allied shipping. One of every four merchant ships voyaging to or from Britain was destroyed. Such carnage was beyond the country's ability to sustain. Jellicoe told Admiral William Sims of the United States Navy as much in April; he noted that the submarine threat could not be contained and that the war was being lost. By the summer, at the present rate of loss, supplies to the British Isles would be reduced below the point at which the war could be continued.

THE ADOPTION OF THE CONVOY SYSTEM

The staggering losses of April evoked a decisive sense of urgency in people who could make a difference. In his memoirs, written in the 1930s, Lloyd George put his personal intervention at the center of the change. Indeed, on April 30, he made a well-publicized visit to the Admiralty to investigate the situation and presumably to push for the adoption of a convoy policy.

The appearance of the prime minister in this dramatic fashion had less of an impact than he claimed. For one thing, the situation had become so critical by the middle of April that naval authorities like Duff had already begun to adopt the convoy system. Moreover, employing convoys in an efficient, effective, and widespread way had to wait until summer 1917. The most promising results were evident only in the fall. Unenthusiastic commanders and the lethargic practices of the naval bureaucracy continued to delay things well beyond Lloyd George's dramatic drop-by.

One element that promoted convoys was the initiative of relatively junior officers. Individuals like Captain Herbert Richmond and Commander Reginald Henderson committed themselves to the adoption of the convoy, and they provided civilian leaders like Lloyd George with the information needed to overcome the military conservatives. For example, hidebound admirals had argued that the number of ships traveling to and from British ports each week was so great that they could never be properly escorted. Henderson demonstrated—and informed Lloyd George—that the calculations were faulty. They should have been based only on the number of ocean-going ships, discounting voyages by small coastal vessels. By that standard, the current percentage of losses was appalling. On the other hand, the number of escorts available would be adequate to protect these imperiled ships.

The success of relatively junior naval officers in convincing key political leaders to adopt a winning strategy had no counterpart, of course, in land operations. The discipline in both services militated against such detours around the chain of command; but naval men took the risk, while their comrades in the army did not. A partial explanation can be found in the solutions offered. Officers like Richmond and Henderson could point to an old and traditional tool of warfare merely waiting to be adopted. The objections of senior admirals that sea traffic around the British Isles was too extensive to be put into convoys could be refuted easily. Knowledgeable naval men had the facts and figures they needed in hand. On land, there was no such packaged solution available. Officers could point to the promise— still basically untested—of the tank, but its early trials on the battlefield hardly made it a convincing solution to the blood-soaked stalemate.

The strongest tribute to the success of the convoy came from the opposing side in the words of Admiral Karl Doenitz, a submarine officer in World War I, then commander of the German U-boats from 1936 to 1943, and leader of the German navy from 1943 to the end of World War II. As he put it in his memoirs, "The German U-boat arm achieved great success; but the introduction of the convoy system in 1917 robbed it of its opportunity to become a decisive factor."[7]

WHY THE CONVOYS SUCCEEDED

Convoys worked for a number of reasons. Concentrating vessels in convoys made them less visible to a submarine than they would have been as individual travelers, and submarine commanders complained that the ocean now seemed empty. There was little visibility from a submarine's periscope, and, instead of an endless stream of individual ships to watch for, the captain of the submarine now had the far less frequent opportunity of spotting a convoy. When German attackers encountered convoys and their armed escorts, only a brief assault was possible before the submarine itself was placed in deadly peril as several enemy destroyers pummeled it with depth charges. Contrary to the view of conservative British admirals, the convoy forced the submarines to fight the British navy—and on highly unfavorable terms. The best German commanders, or at least the most aggressive, suffered the highest losses.

The Germans discovered that the entry of the United States into the war—a certainty once Berlin ordered unrestricted submarine warfare—injured their efforts quickly and painfully. The rapid arrival of more than thirty American destroyers in Europe was a key factor in supplying an adequate number of escorts. The United States seized interned German cargo vessels when war was declared: thus, half a million tons of shipping from the merchant German fleet shored up the beleaguered Allied forces.

By September 1917 the tide had turned. Most shipping in the busy North Atlantic corridor went by regular convoy. Each month, more of the Allied sea traffic came under the convoy system. Losses to the submarine continued, but at a sharply reduced rate. By the war's last months, German submarines were sinking only one merchant vessel for every four they had destroyed in spring 1917. Frustrated commanders returned to port with most of their torpedoes still on board.

OTHER MEASURES AGAINST THE SUBMARINE

Although the convoy was the crucial innovation, the danger faded away for other reasons as well. The establishment of a more effective mine barrier both across the English Channel and between northern Scotland and Norway hindered the passage of U-boats. In an important advance in technology, the ineffective mines Britain used during the first years of the war had now been replaced with more deadly varieties. Under First Lord of the Admiralty Sir Eric Geddes, a dynamic businessman who had organized the railroad system in France, British shipbuilding led the Allied side in replacing lost ships. By March 1918, the number of newly constructed vessels exceeded the continuing losses to the U-boats.

Advances in technology produced mixed results. Efforts to locate submarines using sound-detecting devices ("hydrophones") proved unsuccessful. It happened that these primitive instruments worked best only when all ships in the area had stopped, a deadly move to make when U-boats were present. Depth charges, however, became steadily more potent weapons against the U-boat, and the imaginative use of the airplane grew in significance. Aerial patrols did not sink large numbers of U-boats, but they forced German sub commanders to remain submerged—meaning that the submarines had to travel at slower speeds—to avoid aerial attack. During the last months of the war, the Germans concentrated their operations in coastal waters, and here aerial patrols played an even larger part in harassing the submarine.

By the beginning of 1918, under the leadership of the new commander at Dover, Admiral Roger Keyes, a more effective combination of mines, nets, and bright nighttime lighting hindered U-boat traffic through the Dover Strait. Large U-boats coming from German ports found it almost impossible to pass the new barrier and were forced to take the lengthy northern route around Scotland to reach the open Atlantic. These vessels had a cruising time of only about a month. The additional six to ten days required to take the northern route slashed the time they were available to attack Allied shipping lanes. For smaller U-boats stationed in Flanders, sailing through the Channel became far more dangerous than heretofore. By midsummer 1918, it had become impossible.

An even more ambitious plan was put into effect to block the northern route between Scotland and Norway. Promoted and carried out largely by the United States Navy, this mine and net barrier was in place only in the last months of the war. It probably made the route more dangerous for the large U-boats that used it, although it could not stop the underwater traffic. British intelligence, centered on the famous Room 40 at the Admiralty, intercepted and interpreted German radio traffic, allowing Admiralty officials to learn the approximate location of U-boats. Convoys, whose escorts all had radios, could be warned and rerouted.

The Allies were able to block the effort to terrorize neutrals. Britain had potent tools to use in dealing with the Scandinavian countries, for example. If they wished to trade anywhere on the globe, they needed coaling facilities that only Britain could provide. Even in the face of huge losses in early 1917, these neutral countries continued to carry goods to Britain.

Britain's new Ministry of Food acted to make the production and distribution of food more efficient. Farmers were encouraged to put their land back into the production of cereal grains (as opposed to less productive use for pasture). Government bureaucrats rationed the food available, and they saw to it that grain once used for beer now became flour for bread. They also made sure that shipping became more efficient under the threat of the U-boat. Available vessels now concentrated on carrying foodstuffs across the relatively short North Atlantic passage instead of sailing to Australia or Argentina for the same kind of cargo.

Direct attacks on the Flanders bases turned out to be the least useful of all possibilities. Encouraged by the navy, but also impelled by the need to take pressure off the mutinous French army, General Sir Douglas Haig launched his 1917 Flanders campaign, aimed, in part, at retaking the coasts holding U-boat bases. It was a bloody failure that never came close to its objectives. Aerial attacks and long-distance shelling of bases like Ostend and Zeebrugge proved ineffective. In April 1918, a daring and memorable direct attack was made by an amphibious force of sailors and marines commanded by Keyes. It aimed at blocking the U-boats' passage from Zeebrugge and Ostend to the open sea by sinking British ships in the area's narrow coastal channels. Despite the bravery of the force involved, the British attack put in place only a partial and temporary barrier. Its main effect was to raise British morale, at home and on the western front, during the grim days of the Germans' spring offensive.

In the end, Britain and its allies had a range of resources upon which to draw in defeating the submarine. The imminent nature of the crisis and the clear-cut danger that failure meant losing the war in a measurable period of time assured that all those resources would be employed.

THE FUTURE OF SUBMARINE WARFARE

Over the longer run, the Allies' terrifying experience with the submarine in 1917 enriched the warfare of the future. Submarine development continued among all the main belligerents in the two decades after the war. The potential of that weapon was now evident, and when war broke out again in 1939, the British and German submarines of the day went into action immediately and with crushing effect. The Germans made the biggest headlines. The sinking of the battleship *Royal Oak* early on the morning of October 14, 1939, when a German U-boat penetrated the defenses at Scapa Flow, was Jellicoe's nightmare of 1914 turned into grim reality. But Berlin made its greatest commitment of underwater forces to snap the "Atlantic Bridge" connecting Britain and the Western Hemisphere in 1942; it was the linear descendant of their earlier effort in 1917. Here Admiral Karl Doenitz, a veteran of World War I, initiated wolf pack tactics in an effort to counter the defensive power of convoys. This technique had been used briefly in May 1918; it involved several U-boats striking simultaneously at the ships of a single convoy. At that time, the tactic failed, partly because British intelligence learned of the danger and rerouted vulnerable vessels.[8]

Allied countermeasures also drew on the experience of 1917–1918. The British government applied the same system of food rationing and promotion of agriculture in the second war that they used in the first. And the military countermeasures likewise took up the earlier pattern. Convoys were the norm from the start of the war, and aerial patrols played a key part in harassing and sinking the submarine. The depth charges and location devices, such as sonar, were modern versions of those tools applied or tried in the earlier war.

Nonetheless, during the interwar period, navies continued to center their strategy and building programs on the battleship. In a plea to the United States secretary of the navy, the navy's General Board wrote in August 1937: "The battleship is the basic instrument of naval warfare. . . . An orderly program of replacement must be instituted . . . to prevent our battle line strength from falling to a third rate status." The plea was based on concern that the United States would be left behind as Germany, Japan, France, and Italy were busy building their great ships of the line.[9]

It took World War II and the lessons of both the submarine and the aircraft carrier to change this emphasis. For example, when the United States joined the war against Japan in December 1941, both belligerents made the submarine a key weapon in the Pacific. The ability of the United States Navy to cut off naval traffic to and from the home islands of Japan by the late spring of 1945 was the dream of World War I submariners transformed into successful reality. The subsequent history of the submarine, now nuclear-powered, has made it the premier weapon in naval warfare.

THE IMPORTANCE OF THE UNDERSEA WAR

In the first two years of World War I, the basic pattern of prewar naval power remained intact. A superior British fleet dominated the world's strategic oceans without facing a serious challenge. By the winter of 1916–1917, however, Germany's use of the submarine threatened to upset a naval balance in favor of Britain that dated from the Battle of Trafalgar in 1805. Used principally against merchant vessels, Germany had hopes—and the Allies had fears—that the submarine would starve the British Isles into submission and deliver victory in the entire conflict to the Central Powers.

At what can now be seen as the critical moment of the naval war, the Allies responded. The victory over the submarine fended off one of the few means by which Germany could prevail in battle. It may, indeed, have been Germany's only realistic hope of outright victory—and it faded in the wake of the convoys that dominated Allied shipping by the close of 1917.

NOTES

1. Paul Halpern, *A Naval History of World War I* (Annapolis, Md.: Naval Institute Press, 1994), pp. 33–34.

2. Arthur Hezlet, *The Submarine and Sea Power* (New York: Stein and Day, 1967), p. 80.

3. Laurence Moyer, *Victory Must Be Ours: Germany in the Great War, 1914–1918* (New York: Hippocrene Books, 1995), p. 181.

4. Hezlet, *The Submarine and Sea Power*, pp. 87, 97.

5. Trevor Wilson, *The Myriad Faces of War: Britain and the Great War, 1914–1918* (Cambridge: Polity Press, 1986), p. 92.

6. Ibid., pp. 428–29.

7. Quoted in Arthur Marder, *From the Dreadnought to Scapa Flow: The Royal Navy in the Fisher Era, 1904–1919*, Vol. 5, *Victory and Aftermath (January 1918–June 1919)* (London: Oxford University Press, 1970), p. 77.

8. Halpern, *Naval History*, p. 427.

9. Robert L. O'Connell, *Sacred Vessels: The Cult of the Battleship and the Rise of the U.S. Navy* (Boulder, Colo.:Westview Press, 1991), pp. 303–4.

4

The United States in World War I

WAR COMES TO THE UNITED STATES

In November 1917, a young American prep school teacher named William Langer enthusiastically joined the army in order to fight in World War I. Langer, later one of his country's most distinguished historians, noted in his memoirs of the war how he and his comrades in Company E, First Gas Regiment—"several college graduates . . . and for the rest an odd mixture of older men, young lads, mechanics, salesmen and what not"—had all volunteered. They went willingly into a conflict they knew was characterized by "the murderous fighting on the Somme and around Verdun." Motivated perhaps by patriotism, although they never discussed such feelings, they were, as Langer recalled, drawn to the fight "simply fascinated by the prospect of adventure and heroism."[1]

Over the next twelve months, 2 million young men, volunteers and conscripts, took the long voyage across the Atlantic, and, like Langer and his buddies on July 13, 1918, landed in France. Members of the first American army to fight on the continent of Europe, they personified the vast changes that the United States brought to the war—and the changes the war was bringing to the United States.

World War I brought the most dramatic and significant intersection of American history and European history since the era of the American Revolution. The great republic of North America had entered world affairs tentatively at the turn of the century, but it now marched, in less than three years from the outbreak of World War I, to center stage in this epochal struggle. The course of the war, and especially that of its final two years, is comprehensible only with an eye to the role of the United States.

Moreover, war often accelerates existing trends in the life of a country, and it can also turn a nation in a new direction. The American experience in World War I stands as an intriguing example of such rapid transformation. When war broke out in Europe, the huge country across the Atlantic was in the midst of a great surge of industrial and urban growth, and it continued to face traditional problems of racial division and the absorption of waves of immigrants. Suddenly, these changes intersected with a novel involvement of the United States in the affairs of Europe—with momentous consequences for both Americans and Europeans.

AMERICA'S INITIAL RESPONSE TO THE WAR

Despite its neutral status during the first two and a half years of the war, the United States early on cast a substantial shadow over the conduct of the conflict. Although President Woodrow Wilson in 1914 asked Americans to maintain a genuine feeling of neutrality, to be "impartial in fact as well as name," he himself, like most leaders of American opinion, was more sympathetic to the cause of the Allies. Many Americans viewed Germany as the homeland of a disreputable, even dangerous militarism. Its brutal invasion of the neutral country of Belgium necessarily made American leaders wonder how the United States, another neutral country, would fare in a world dominated by German power. Wilson personally admired the British system of government and thought that a victory by the Central Powers in the war would set back democracy everywhere.

American commercial and cultural ties with Great Britain and France were stronger than those to Germany, and the British had worked hard to cultivate good Anglo-American relations since the late nineteenth century. The British also had the advantage of controlling the flow of information from Europe to America. On the day they entered the war, the British cut the German undersea cables linking that country to the Atlantic, establishing an Allied monopoly over news from Europe. American policy tilted toward the Allies. Indeed, some of the president's key advisers, notably Colonel Edward House, openly declared their support for the Allied cause early in the conflict. Secretary of State William Jennings Bryan, the administration's most vocal advocate of avoiding support for either side, resigned over that issue in June 1915.

America's trade links to some of the countries of Europe swelled as a result of the fighting. With Britain's blockade of Germany, only the Allied

powers could buy and deliver the products of the United States; thus, American commerce with Britain and France grew vastly, more than tripling in value by the close of 1916. Meanwhile, commerce with Germany virtually disappeared. In October 1915, fear that a halt in Allied purchases in the United States would trigger a recession pushed the administration to end a ban on private loans to Britain and France.

THE ISSUE OF THE SUBMARINE

One development after 1914 brought a direct confrontation between the governments in Berlin and Washington: the German use of submarine warfare. Americans expected to be able to trade and travel in wartime under the protection of neutrality. Submarine warfare placed American lives in the line of fire, and the inevitable crisis with Berlin soon arrived. When a German submarine sank the British liner *Lusitania* on May 7, 1915, killing 128 Americans, the United States took a direct diplomatic part in the war. American pressure forced Germany to limit its use of the submarine, and the United States now assumed the role of a potential adversary if Germany's leaders renewed the submarine campaign of early 1915. Earlier frictions and irritations with Britain had arisen over American trade with the continent. The British navy, for example, diverted or detained American ships bound for Scandinavian ports to make sure they were not carrying strategic goods that could be sent on to Germany. Such concerns now faded. Americans distinguished between the minor irritations of British restrictions on the shipment of goods and the German willingness to take American lives.

AMERICAN PREPAREDNESS
AND THE ELECTION OF 1916

The war impelled Americans inside and outside government to lay a base for future military activities. In late 1915, Wilson called for preparedness measures such as the expansion of America's armed forces. In February 1916, he pointed specifically to the need for the United States to have the most powerful navy in the world, and the Naval Act of 1916 authorized the construction of ten battleships and a number of smaller vessels. Meanwhile, starting at Plattsburg, New York, in 1915, wealthy young men had paid their own way to attend privately operated officer-training camps.

The presidential election of 1916 showed how the war loomed over American life. Wilson's opponent, Supreme Court Justice Charles Evans Hughes, claimed that the president had been weak in defending American

rights in Europe. A belligerent Theodore Roosevelt was disgruntled with both candidates, seeing Hughes as insufficiently warlike and Wilson as downright cowardly in his refusal to confront imperial Germany, and calling Wilson "yellow." By the final weeks of the campaign, Wilson's reelection effort hung on his party's slogan, "He kept us out of war." Democratic orators stated simply that a vote for Hughes was a vote for war, and in the end, Wilson won by a narrow margin. With America committed to act if the submarine war resumed, the president himself knew the hollow nature of the election slogan. As he put it privately, "Any little German [U-boat] commander can put us into the war at any time by some calculated outrage."[2]

WILSON HOPES TO MEDIATE

A less obvious link between the war and American policy was Wilson's hope of playing a major role in ending the war and shaping the peace settlement. Wilson, a Progressive Democrat who abhorred war as wasteful, believed in the rule of law and the power of diplomacy. He also believed that the United States had a moral obligation to extend its democratic principles to the world, if not by example, then by more visible engagement in world affairs. Wilson preached an internationalism that argued that American interests were not confined to the Western Hemisphere. From 1914 onward, using Colonel House as his emissary, the American president promoted contact with the warring parties to further this goal of positioning the United States as a mediating power.

EARLY 1917: UNLIMITED SUBMARINE WARFARE AND THE ZIMMERMANN TELEGRAM

Following the election of 1916, as hopes for a negotiated settlement faded, Wilson apparently concluded that only as a belligerent could the United States play its appropriate role in constructing the postwar world. In any case, events forced America's hand by 1917. Whatever the president's exact intentions, in the first months of that year, relations between the United States and Germany crumbled. The military leaders in Berlin renewed unlimited use of the submarine, gambling that Germany could win the war in Europe before the United States could mobilize its vast latent human and industrial resources.

Moreover, with American intervention in the war growing likely, Germany made a clumsy appeal to the government of Mexico: in return for Mexico's military support against the United States, Berlin would help

Mexico regain the territory it had lost to the Americans in the war of 1848. When the Wilson administration made the offer known to the American people on March 1—British intelligence had intercepted a key message known as the Zimmermann telegram, and passed it to Washington—this helped stifle opposition to war in the western United States, one of the bastions of isolationist sentiment. On April 2, President Wilson addressed the recently elected Congress on the first day of its new session. He requested and quickly got a declaration of war.

THE PROGRESSIVE MOVEMENT
AND WARTIME SOCIAL CHANGE

In the nineteen months during which the United States was fighting the war, a wave of social and political change swept across the country. As American soldiers went "over there," the nation "over here" went through a dramatic transformation that touched most of the population of 100 million. A major force promoting and shaping this transformation was the Progressive current that had been evident in the United States since the turn of the century. Progressives believed that society could be reformed: it was possible to attack vices deliberately and systematically; it was possible as well to promote social and economic justice. Using the techniques of the social sciences and the power of enlightened government, Progressives believed that they could identify, address, and solve many of the problems of a rapidly growing industrial society. Thus, the war effort offered an opportunity to attack alcoholism and prostitution through government action. Recently arrived immigrants could be brought into the mainstream of American life and taught middle-class values through systematic Americanization campaigns, including encouragement to support the war effort.

AMERICAN WOMEN AND AMERICAN BLACKS

Consider some of the rapid, far-reaching effects that came from transforming the American economy to produce the goods needed for a modern war. Two groups, for example, previously on the fringes of the workforce—women and African Americans—now found unprecedented opportunities open to them. Some women who had not been employed before 1917 now took jobs, but a far larger group took new and better-paying positions. In all, 1.5 million women took jobs in industries connected to the war effort. In addition, countless numbers of women supported the war by staffing and organizing relief agencies, selling war bonds, and promoting patriotism in school and at work. In a war that moved toward "total mobilization," women further helped the cause by conserving food at home. As an editorial in *Life* magazine during the war reminded mothers, everyone in the household could contribute to American victory: "Do not permit your child to take a bite or two from an apple and throw the rest away; nowadays, even children must be taught to be patriotic to the core."

For African Americans, the change was more sweeping still. Employers' long-standing preference for native white or immigrant workers had to be put aside in a country in which millions went into the military and in a world in which emigration from Europe had halted. As the number of jobs in factories expanded, African-American men were permitted, even encouraged, to obtain them. Since most members of this minority group lived in the rural South at the start of the war, economic opportunity meant geographic exodus. Approximately 400,000 blacks went north to the major industrial cities of the Northeast and Midwest; 60,000 migrated to Chicago alone. Black newspapers, such as the *Chicago Defender*, reported on employment opportunities, and northern black churches sent letters to southern congregations inviting their members north to find jobs and share fellowship.

Prospective employers and railroads recruited blacks and channeled their movement northward. The immediate reception for blacks was sometimes hostile as white Americans reacted angrily to a black presence. Starting in East St. Louis, Illinois, in 1917, then spreading to Chicago in 1918, race riots erupted across the urban North. An ever growing roster of fatalities marred the country's domestic peace and reminded blacks that leaving Jim Crow in the South did not mean finding peace and freedom in the North.

AN EXPANDING ROLE FOR GOVERNMENT

The size of the federal government doubled during the course of the war as the hand of government reached into most areas of national life. And not since Abraham Lincoln's years in the White House during the Civil War had the country's chief executive stood so evidently at the center of the national government. Wilson's appointments of George Creel, Herbert Hoover, William McAdoo, and Bernard Baruch personified the new force of government activity. These talented and energetic individuals now took control over vast areas of national life in a way that would have seemed unimaginable in 1914. Men now spoke casually of spending millions—anything to win the war.

The Propaganda War

In a country as large and varied as the United States, shaping public opinion was a massive task, especially when it came to overcoming opposition or indifference to the war effort. More than 13 percent of the population was foreign born, and the United States contained 8 million Americans of German descent, over 4 million with roots in Ireland, and 2 million Swedish Americans. All of these groups were traditionally hostile to Entente countries like Britain and Russia or else emotionally linked to Germany. Led by former journalist George Creel, the government's Committee of Public Information (CPI) set out to arouse and maintain support for the war. Creel moved to sell the war by mobilizing a corps of 75,000 public speakers—the "Four Minute Men"—to address crowds in places like movie theaters. Creel's moviemakers produced propaganda films with titles like *Pershing's Crusaders* or *The Prussian Cur*. Specially written articles went to elementary and high schools and to local newspapers for reprinting on their own pages. Immigrant communities found Creel's articles appearing in their own languages in their own newspapers, and Creel's staff, including many university professors, watched those same newspapers to ferret out antiwar sentiments.

The Food War

For Americans at home, the war and the vast expansion of government were felt every day at mealtime. Under the direction of Food Administrator Herbert Hoover, one of a number of Americans elevated to national prominence by the war, authorities in Washington set out to match the country's food supply to the demands of the war. Rejecting outright rationing, Hoover relied instead on appeals to the public to conserve food and to farmers to produce more of it. A massive publicity campaign set a pattern of "meatless" and "wheatless" days, and 20 million Americans, the majority of them women with families, pledged to run their households in accord with Hoover's directives. By setting the price of wheat at a high level, however, Hoover used direct government power to boost production.

The Federal Government and the Wartime Economy

No economy can remain untouched by the claims of large-scale modern warfare, and the United States, like the European belligerents, saw the role of government swell. For example, authorities in Washington took over the operation of the nation's railroads. On December 26, 1917, President Wilson named his secretary of the treasury, William G. McAdoo, head of the federal government's Railroad Administration. With Hoover in charge of the food supply, there remained only the country's industrial system to bring, at least temporarily, under government direction.

On March 4, 1918, in order to direct war production, President Wilson appointed Wall Street financier Bernard Baruch head of the War Industries Board. Armed with only limited legal powers, Baruch nonetheless got the cooperation of industry in providing goods of the highest priority for the war effort. The War Industries Board successfully put pressure on steel executives to limit prices, and it promoted measures to conserve vital commodities and freight capacity. It increased industrial efficiency by encouraging the standardization of products—everything from steel plows to baby carriages to coffins. Promoting the substitution of paper wrappers in place of pasteboard cartons and wooden boxes for civilian clothing, the board freed over 17,000 freight cars for vital wartime use. The board served as well as the purchasing agent for America's wartime partners. Its most important task was allocating scarce resources. Thus, the board induced the automobile industry to lower production of pleasure cars by threatening to cut off its supplies of coal and steel.

INDUSTRY RESPONDS TO THE WAR

The nation's industry also moved toward greater concentration. For one thing, the Department of Justice limited the activity of its Anti-Trust Division during the wartime years. Bernard Baruch and the War Industries Board encouraged cooperation among individual companies operating in a single industry, and the government favored large enterprises over small ones in granting war contracts. While the owners of industry prospered during the war, many workers also did well. The eight-hour work day was now becoming the norm throughout the country. In industries where unions were powerful, such as coal mining, wages rose as much as 20 percent over the levels of 1914.[3]

Unlike World War II, in which American industry produced mountains of war matériel for itself and its allies, the mobilization of the economy in World War I brought disappointing results. Matching industrial production to the needs of the military brought frustrating bottlenecks in a country in which government and private industry were unaccustomed to working together. For example, a massive program to build merchant ships, employing almost 400,000 workmen, produced few vessels before the Armistice. American military men had to rely on supplies of French artillery pieces and airplanes to wage the war. Had the war lasted another year, however, the power of American industry would have been visible in a flood of military equipment. Still, the war did bring to Washington a small army of businessmen, who learned to work with the military in matters of purchasing and supply. Business and military officers discovered a common language of scientific management and the benefits of cooperation. In a sense, then, the foundation of America's "military-industrial complex" was laid in World War I rather than in World War II.

BUILDING THE ARMED FORCES

Unlike the other belligerents, the United States had made virtually no military preparations for war on the scale that armed conflict developed starting in 1914. The country not only lacked a large army, it also had no plans for massive mobilization, and even the small army it had in hand—less than 130,000 officers and men augmented by 180,000 in the National Guard—was scattered and poorly trained. Only in the navy, comprised of some 60,000 men and 300 ships, did the United States have a force capable of rapid application.[4]

The need to man a large army and navy, and to do it quickly, convinced a reluctant President Wilson to adopt conscription. In a major policy shift from the traditional American reliance on voluntarism to fill the ranks, Congress passed the Selective Service Act authorizing a universal conscription policy to meet any manpower needs during war or a national emergency. Through local draft boards, the government registered 24 million men between the ages of eighteen and forty-five. Almost 3 million American males found themselves called into military service. More than 1.5 million more volunteered. For most of them, military service brought a new acquaintance with distant parts of the country and fellow soldiers from other groups in the population. In the 42nd (Rainbow) Division, for example, troops from twenty-six states and the District of Columbia served together. The army also was the venue for furthering Wilson's and the Progressives' social reforms. The anti–venereal disease and anti-prostitution campaigns the Progressives had launched in American cities now went to the army camps. Soldiers were warned that "a German bullet is cleaner than a whore."

To the consternation of segregationist politicians from the South like Senator James Vardaman of Mississippi, roughly 400,000 African Americans served in the military. Although blacks were confined to segregated units and often left to do fatigue duty such as hauling goods and trash removal, two black divisions did reach the front. The 92nd Division fought as a unit under

American command. Its performance was roundly condemned by white senior officers, although its problems stemmed in part from poor training and inadequate leadership. Regiments of the 93rd Division, however, saw combat as part of the French army and fought valiantly.

For over 2 million young Americans, conscription meant a personal encounter with European life as well as the threat of death or injury in combat. Processing young Americans for military service produced information on the population that no one had possessed before. Some was highly disturbing: doctors examining the recruits found that almost 30 percent were physically unable to meet the standards for military service. During World War I social scientists and medical doctors conducted the first mass testing of Americans as to "intelligence." Using the recently developed Binet intelligence test—which later scientists showed to have been skewed in favor of western European cultures, among other defects—the testers "confirmed" many popular stereotypes about the "inferiority" of blacks and southern and eastern European groups. Armed with such "scientific" data, racists and nativists called for restrictions on blacks and limits on immigration.

THE WAR AGAINST DOMESTIC DISSENT

Once the United States declared hostilities, opposition to the war got little sympathy from the government and most Americans. The government imposed harsh measures to squelch criticism. Laws like the Espionage Act (June 1917) and the Sedition Act (May 1918) penalized heavily not only actions in opposition to the war effort, such as obstructing conscription or the sale of war bonds, but also speech and writing that criticized government policies. The Supreme Court upheld the laws, which were applied widely. Justice Oliver Wendell Holmes defended restrictions on free speech in time of national danger by noting that no one had the right to cry "fire" in a crowded theater. The laws inflamed fears of enemy sabotage and led to excessive reprisals against imagined threats to security. More than 2,000 Americans had to defend themselves against prosecution under the Espionage Act, and half of those accused were convicted.

Americans outside government acted in even more sweeping fashion. The government's "Hate the Hun" campaign rapidly spread into a popular crusade against all things German. Superpatriots tried to shut down school and university courses in the German language and to ban the performance of German music, and they invaded the offices of the German-language press. Anything German became suspect in a climate where German-haters spread rumors that Germans put ground glass in Red Cross bandages or worse. Sauerkraut became "liberty cabbage," and German-American companies changed their names to English-sounding ones. In Indiana, East Germantown was renamed Pershing; in Iowa, Berlin was transformed into Lincoln. Both the Philadelphia Orchestra and the Metropolitan Opera Company banned German music. Violence against individuals of German ancestry, against spokesmen for pacifism, and against labor leaders and politicians opposed to the war stained American life. Unofficial groups operating with government sanction, such as the American Protective League, spied on their neighbors. Wilson did little to check the excesses, which served to fuel the anti-German crusade.

More important, as the war revealed the divided loyalties in an immigrant society, with Old World hatred carried to New World settings, efforts to promote nationalism gained force. Businesses instituted "Americanization" programs to teach their foreign-born workers English and to impose a uniform set of rules in the workplace. Many social reformers shifted their emphasis from encouraging gradual adaptation to American ways to calls for more aggressive Americanization in adult education programs and in the schools.

WOMAN'S SUFFRAGE IN THE UNITED STATES

If American involvement in the war constrained the freedoms of German Americans, pacifists, and anyone else labeled as disloyal, it enlarged the liberty of women. The most salient consequence was woman's suffrage. The campaign to obtain the vote for women went back to the mid-nineteenth century, and suffragists had become a powerful lobby in cities and several states by the early twentieth century, but even a Progressive leader like President Wilson had opposed a national suffrage amendment. In the course of the war, with women playing a crucial and visible role in national life, that position became untenable. Wilson shifted to support woman's suffrage in January 1918. He was, he claimed, motivated by the support women had given to the war. Meanwhile, the influence of other opponents faded. The amendment giving women the vote passed Congress in June 1919; the states ratified it in fourteen months.

PROHIBITION

The war also helped advocates of prohibition. The spirit of wartime sacrifice, in particular the need to conserve food, delivered new support to opponents of making and consuming alcoholic beverages. Prohibitionists also played on nativism, arguing that "disloyal" Irish and German immigrants wasted valuable American resources by drinking gallons of whiskey and beer. And the Progressives' efforts to clean up the corrupt saloon politics received a boost from a war effort cast as a crusade for good government everywhere. Congress responded to the well-organized temperance lobby by passing a temporary ban on the production of intoxicating liquids in the summer of 1917. In January 1919, the Constitution was amended to make the ban permanent.

AMERICA'S INTERNATIONAL ECONOMIC POWER

In 1914 the United States, for all its industrial power, played a limited albeit expanding role in world economic affairs. It remained a debtor nation, dependent on Great Britain in particular as a source of capital. Britain and Germany as well had a greater share of international trade, and the two still dominated the markets of Latin America. The wartime years changed all that and dramatically accelerated the rise of the United States as the center of the global economy.

Immediately after the outbreak of war, the British and French governments began massive importation of American goods. With Americans making few purchases from a war-torn Europe, the United States soon transformed itself from a debtor into a creditor nation, taking up the duties and privileges of lender to the world. During the course of the conflict, American business interests also moved aggressively to dominate international trade with the countries south of the Rio Grande. The physical and financial exhaustion of all the European powers—winners and losers alike—at the close of the conflict kept the United States at the center of the global economy long after the Armistice and the peace treaties had been signed.

AMERICAN FORCES IN ACTION

America's military impact on the war was uneven, though in the end the U.S. presence would prove critical in the Allies' push to victory. The first six American destroyers arrived in European waters on May 4, 1917, less than a month after the declaration of war. They went into action immediately—and in close cooperation with Britain's Royal Navy—to help stop the devastating German submarine campaign. But American soldiers arrived in large numbers only after a year's delay. U.S. participation was weakened by problems in command. Reluctant to become too entangled in European affairs even as American troops were dispatched overseas, the

United States technically did not join the Allied alliance or integrate its armed forces into a unified command. The American army, under the command of General John "Black Jack" Pershing, was engaged as the American Expeditionary Force (AEF) and sought to operate in its own sector of combat. The American forces would not be incorporated into a coordinated Allied military front until late 1918.

The importance of the American army's role in the war remains controversial. As the last German offensive took place in June 1918, bringing General Ludendorff's troops dangerously close to Paris, first five, then five more American divisions went into action in the Second Battle of the Marne. That they helped to stop the enemy advance is beyond dispute. Nonetheless, some historians consider that the Germans already had overextended themselves, and that even in the absence of American reinforcements the British and French could have held them.

Similarly, the greatest American operation of the war, the Meuse-Argonne offensive from September to the November Armistice, had ambiguous results. General Pershing's hopes that Americans could achieve the breakthrough that had eluded Anglo-French forces for four years proved false. The slow and costly advance by his two field armies served instead to pin down German divisions while the French and British thrust forward in other sectors.

Thus, both the American naval effort and the American role in the land war were less decisive than U.S. leaders might have wished. Nevertheless, the psychological effect of a growing American military presence on Germany's armed forces and its home front was inevitably weighty. And, unlike the countries alongside which it fought, the United States found its military strength growing explosively as the war ended. In the final months of the war, for example, more than a quarter million American troops were arriving in France each month—with millions more ready to follow. The AEF had forty-two divisions at the close of the war; in 1919 that number was slated to rise to eighty divisions, surpassing in size both the British and the French forces on the western front.

AMERICAN WARTIME DIPLOMACY

In contrast to its military role in 1917 and 1918, the United States stood at the pivot of the Allies' diplomatic effort. Wilson's slogan of a war that would "make the world safe for democracy" set a goal and a tone for American diplomacy. The United States, more than any other participant, committed itself openly to fundamental changes, not only in the international order, but in the way in which international relations were to be conducted. Thus, in January 1918, President Wilson set down the framework for negotiations leading to both the Armistice and subsequent peace treaties in his Fourteen Points. He pressured Britain and France to accept, at least nominally, ideas like public diplomacy and a reordering of the map of Europe on the principles of nationality. A striking idea the American president presented in his Fourteen Points was a League of Nations that would help regulate international affairs after the war had been concluded. Wilson argued that World War I thus would be the "war to end all wars."

Wilson's ideas resonated in the enemy camp. When Germany began to negotiate for an end to the fighting, it addressed its requests to the United States and called for a peace settlement along the lines of the Fourteen Points. Thus, with defeat imminent, Germany's new prime minister, Prince Max of Baden, cited the Fourteen Points as he proposed an immediate armistice to the German Reichstag on October 5. For the remainder of the negotiations leading to a cessation of hostilities, the lines of communication ran from Berlin to Washington—and then to London and Paris.

WILSON AND THE PEACE CONFERENCE

Unwilling to entrust peace negotiations to subordinates, Wilson took the unprecedented and controversial step of assuming direct control of the U.S. mission. He left for Europe on December 4, 1918, to attend the peace conference in person. This meant that his ideas about the shape of postwar Europe would be heard, and signalled the importance of America's claim to a central place in any settlement. Enthusiastic crowds greeted Wilson in Paris and London and inflated his hopes for a peace along the lines of his Fourteen Points. But, in the end, Wilson misread public opinion in Europe and the history of European rivalries. Wilson's proposals prevailed only in part, generally where dismantling empires and disarmament meant breaking up the might of the defeated Central Powers. What had been the Austro-Hungarian Empire and the western part of the Russian Empire were reorganized on the basis of nationalities, and the Versailles conference recognized the final collapse of the Ottoman Empire. Newly independent countries like Poland, Czechoslovakia, and Yugoslavia—still ethnically mixed but designed to satisfy the national allegiances of most of their populations—fulfilled Wilson's hopes. And the major powers committed themselves to a League of Nations. He failed, however, to prevent Britain and France from requiring Germany to pay heavy reparations to the victorious powers. The French, moreover, got the right to occupy the Rhineland for fifteen years. He failed likewise to win the United States Senate over to his project for a League of Nations.

THE COST OF THE WAR

The war cost the American people 125,000 of their sons. Fifty thousand men died in combat. Another 75,000 died from other causes, notably the influenza epidemic that struck in the closing months of the war. In eight weeks starting in September, influenza caused 300,000 deaths in the United States. A total of 479,000 Americans died in 1918 and 1919, including 2,000 troops en route to Europe. An American Army of the Rhine, 16,000 strong in 1920, remained in Germany in the region around Trier and Coblenz to help enforce the peace treaty, its last unit leaving only in January 1923.

Many Americans who had served in the war returned with lasting psychological difficulties. "War neurosis" (commonly known as shell shock) led to disability discharges for almost 42,000 servicemen. In early 1922 veterans' hospitals contained 9,000 patients suffering from service-connected psychological difficulties. Eighteen years later, the number of individuals hospitalized or otherwise being treated for this injury to the emotions remained the same. This suggests that there were vastly more former servicemen who suffered in silence or got care outside government channels.[5]

THE CHANGING EXPECTATIONS
OF BLACK AMERICANS

African Americans returned from the war with a range of new experiences. Many had found their contacts with the French people free from the racism of their own country. They returned with military training that made it possible to resist white violence, as in the Tulsa, Oklahoma, race riot of 1921. Perhaps most important of all, many African Americans now expected better treatment in the United States as a result of their service for their country. They found little if any tangible change around them, but their strengthened hopes and expectations were expressed by W.E.B. Du Bois: "Make way for Democracy! We saved it in France, and by the Great Jehovah, we will save it in the United States of America or know the reason why."[6]

WAR AND THE INTELLECTUALS

The war influenced the attitudes and perspectives of many American writers and intellectuals. Ernest Hemingway, William Faulkner, and e. e. cummings were three major writers who went to war and incorporated their experiences in their fiction. Hemingway was wounded while serving with an ambulance unit in Italy, Faulkner was hurt in a plane crash while training with the Royal Canadian Air Force, and cummings had an offbeat encounter with the war when he spent four months in a French detention center as a suspected subversive. The restless Hemingway, like many American intellectuals in the 1920s, went to Europe as a long-term refugee from his own society. And the trauma of the war led to what literary critic Frederick J. Hoffman has called "an almost obsessive preoccupation with wounds and death," visible in Hemingway's fiction down to *Across the River and into the Trees* in 1950.[7] Even more distilled and prolonged bitterness toward the army, the U.S. government, and the country's entire participation in the war can be found in the works of John Dos Passos starting with *Three Soldiers* in 1921.

THE PEACE SETTLEMENT

The central role that the United States had played briefly on the global diplomatic scene faded quickly. The Senate's rejection of the Treaty of Versailles and its clause establishing the League of Nations foreshadowed the prolonged period of isolation that followed. While polls had shown that much of the public favored the League, Republican senator Henry Cabot Lodge delayed the process of ratification in summer 1919 until opponents of the League could rouse popular feeling against it. President Wilson tried to win over the public, but was paralyzed by a stroke during a train tour across the country. Back in Washington, he rejected changes in the treaty clauses pertaining to the League that might have overcome opposition in the Senate. In the end, the Senate rejected the entire treaty on November 19, 1919. Disillusionment with the war, fed by artists and writers in the 1920s who criticized the loss of American innocence and the pointlessness of machine-age slaughter, added to the rush to turn inward and to abandon Wilson's internationalism. American economic strength, however, continued to play a dominant global role, even during the 1920s.

A VARIETY OF CHANGES AT HOME

In the United States wartime changes varied from the permanent to temporary to transitory. The swollen power of the federal government shrank back to its prewar size. The railroads, for example, returned to private management, and the War Industries Board was abolished. Nonetheless, the memory of government expanding to meet the needs of 1917 and 1918 remained—perhaps for use again in time of international or even domestic emergency. The black migration to the industrial North forever changed the demographic landscape and the shape of American race relations; for one thing, African Americans now had a new political role that came from the relative ease with which they could organize and vote in regions outside the South. Women, however, despite their visible success in the political realm, saw only modest economic progress. Most of the jobs that opened up for them during the wartime period went back to male hands after the war had ended. For immigrants, the war signalled a major shift in national policy. Although immigration swelled to prewar levels immediately after the war, the nativism of 1917–1918 did not subside. Fearing an invasion of political and biological "contagions"—from communism to the flu—coming from Europe, and invoking the license to hate that the wartime "Hate the Hun" campaign and Americanization programs had fanned, nativists won a major victory in the various National Origins acts of the 1920s. These used supposed social science classifications of "national origins" to limit the number of southern, central, and eastern Europeans who could legally enter the United States.

Thus, in many respects, the war provided a preview of future change. It would take another great conflict, in which the United States played an even more substantial role, to make some of the changes foreshadowed by World War I permanent. Looking back from a vantage point decades after World War II, one can see in the America of 1918 suggestions of what was to come: the United States as international superpower, an American society in which women's roles differed drastically from the pattern of the nineteenth century, a racial distribution in which the problems and possibilities of black-white relations involved the entire country, and a federal government that played an ever widening role in American social and economic life.

For Europeans, American power and American ideas had played an unprecedented role in the course of events on their continent. Little more than two decades after the end of World War I, in the circumstances of a still greater conflict, but in a fashion foreshadowed by events seen from 1914 through 1919, the United States would again assert its influence in immeasurably more potent and lasting fashion.

NOTES

1. William L. Langer, *Gas and Flame in World War I* (New York: Alfred A. Knopf, 1965), pp. xii, xviii.

2. Quoted in John Garraty and Robert McCaughey, *The American Nation: A History of the United States since 1865*, 6th ed. (New York: Harper and Row, 1987), p. 700.

3. David Kennedy, *Over Here: The First World War and American Society* (Oxford: Oxford University Press, 1982), p. 258.

4. Robert H. Ferrell, *Woodrow Wilson and World War I, 1917–1921* (New York: Harper and Row, 1985), p. 14; Edward M. Coffman, *The War to End All Wars: The American Military Experience in World War I* (New York: Oxford University Press, 1968), p. 91.

5. Ronald Schaffer, *America in the Great War: The Rise of the War Welfare State* (New York: Oxford University Press, 1991), pp. 202, 209–10.

6. Quoted in ibid., p. 89.

7. Frederick J. Hoffman, *The Twenties: American Writing in the Postwar Decade* (New York: Viking Press, 1955), p. 74.

The War's beginning: German cavalry passing through Berlin on the way to the front, 1914. Photograph number 111-SC-89398. Courtesy of the National Archives.

Gas and flame attack on the western front. Photograph number 111–SC–10879. Courtesy of the National Archives.

Wartime refugees in Russian Poland, 1915. The Hoover Institution, Stanford University.

Warbond rally put on by the Provisional Government in Russia, April 1917. The Hoover Institution, Stanford University.

The war at sea: Destroyers escort a convoy, 1917. Photograph number 111–SC–7145. Courtesy of the National Archives.

The machine gun war: A captured German machine-gun nest in France, 1918. Photograph number 111-SC-28573. Courtesy of the National Archives.

American troops in combat in a French village, 1918. Photograph number 111–SC–44308. Courtesy of the National Archives.

The nightmare of the supply line: American trucks in Meuse-Argonne, 1918. Photograph number 111-SC-44308. Courtesy of the National Archives.

The War's end: Crowds celebrate Armistice in Paris, 1918. Photograph number 111–SC–28573. Courtesy of the National Archives.

The War's aftermath: American officers in German territory on the Rhine, 1919. Photograph number 111–SC–44308. Courtesy of the National Archives.

From the left: David Lloyd George, Vittorio Orlando, Georges Clemenceau and Woodrow Wilson at the Versailles Peace Conference, 1919. The Hoover Institution, Stanford University.

5

The Home Front

World War I brought unprecedented demands on the civilian populations of the warring nations. Once the initial campaigns of the war had produced stalemate, the conflict grew in scope and intensity. The need to supply the fighting forces, to produce the arms and the food supplies required by armies of unprecedented size, meant mobilizing entire societies. Thus, the story of events on the home front constitutes a crucial portion of the war. No country could hope to see the war to a successful conclusion without such an effort.

The forerunners of such activity on a national scale can be seen in French history: in the *levée en masse* in 1793 to defend the imperiled revolution from outside invasion and domestic insurrection and in the subsequent national mobilization of 1870–1871 as France struggled to defend its territorial integrity in the Franco-Prussian War. But such earlier efforts paled in comparison to the way in which the resources, energies, and enthusiasms of several entire societies were conscripted during World War I.

The systems of transportation and communication produced by the Industrial Revolution, the expansion of the right to vote, and the establishment of sweeping, if not universal, obligations for young men to perform military service tied individuals intimately to their governments as never before. World War I shows those governments, often in desperation, calling on their citizens for unprecedented massive efforts. In a real sense, this war now demonstrated how much a government could demand, not only from its fighting men, but from its civilians as well.

Besieged from the outside and faced with demands from their governments for ever increasing sacrifices, the societies of Great Britain, France, and Germany heaved and buckled under the strain. Social pathologies proliferated, ranging from increased juvenile crime to slackening standards of sexual morality. Nonetheless, during a seemingly endless conflict, the basic elements of social cohesion remained intact. In this way, World War I demonstrated how great a strain modern industrialized societies could bear. Death from enemy action, life under enemy occupation, and shortages of food and other necessities afflicted millions. Nonetheless, the bonds of patriotism bolstered by expanded government power held the home front together in nations like these three until—or in the case of Germany almost until—the war's close.

CIVILIANS GREET THE WAR

The first reaction for many on the home front was a surge of patriotism. One of the most eloquent commentators on this emotion was Stefan Zweig, a leading Austrian author and a widely traveled member of Europe's intellectual elite. He found himself in a Belgian seaside resort as war approached, and he left Belgium on the last train for Germany. Upon returning to his native Vienna, even this cosmopolitan writer discovered that he had been caught up in a wave of popular patriotic emotion that affected his countrymen at every level of society. Zweig's distaste for war and superheated nationalism soon reasserted itself, but he found, to his horror, that most of his fellow writers, like the poet Ernst Littauer, were busy producing diatribes against enemy countries. In Littauer's case, patriotism brought forth nothing less than the poem "Hymn of Hate" against Great Britain.

But the hardships of war arrived soon enough. For many Europeans who had established personal ties across national borders, the war created deep personal conflicts. Before 1914, marriages between citizens of different countries were common. The mother of Theobald von Bethmann Hollweg, Germany's prime minister during most of the wartime years, was a Frenchwoman. The brother of Georges Clemenceau, France's prime minister during the final year of the war, was married to an Austrian. One of the most famous people caught between two sets of loyalties and identities was Princess Daisy of Pless (1873–1943). Born into an upper-class English family, Mary Theresa Olivia (Daisy) Cornwallis-West married a prominent German aristocrat, Prince Henry of Pless, in 1891. Her husband and one of her three sons served in the German army in World War I, and she herself tried to balance her mixture of loyalties. In the end, her marriage could not survive the strains brought on by the war, and she was divorced from her husband in 1922.

CIVILIAN CASUALTIES

The war soon struck vast numbers of Europeans in more deadly fashion. The range of modern military forces and new weapons made civilians the direct targets of military action. In December 1914, for example, the German navy slipped past British defenses in the North Sea and bombarded three towns along the Yorkshire coast. In Hartlepool, Scarborough, and Whitby more than 100 civilians died and 600 were wounded. German Zeppelins began to strike southeastern England in January 1915; they bombed London in May and eventually reached much of the southern half of the country. This World War I version of "the Battle of Britain" was a preview of the greater aerial struggle that began a quarter century later. In 1917 the Germans began to rely mainly on bombing planes. Their entire aerial assault on Britain caused about 1,500 deaths and 3,400 injuries between 1915 and the close of the war.

Paris, too, fell victim to a range of enemy assaults. The Zeppelins appeared in March 1915 and again in 1916, and enemy bomber attacks, notably in the first eight months of 1918, caused hundreds of casualties. In March 1918, the German army began to use massive naval guns to shell France's capital from the northeast. Fired at a distance of seventy-five miles, the shells struck at random at the city's civilian population for forty-four days. Two hundred fifty-six Parisians died and 625 were wounded, with shells landing on churches and in the lovely city's main squares.

On the other side, in 1917 and 1918, British and French bombers made numerous raids on the cities of western Germany—Mainz, Cologne, Karlsruhe, and Trier—hitting as far eastward as Stuttgart. More than 700 Germans were killed and more than 1,800 injured in these attacks.

Civilians died as well at their newly dangerous workplaces. In December 1916, for example, thirty-five women munitions workers in Britain were killed in an accident in a plant near Leeds; in January 1918, a worse catastrophe killed sixty-nine workers and injured hundreds more when their factory in East London exploded.

Starting in October 1914, German submarines began their attacks on Allied merchant ships. They were soon, deliberately or by accident, sinking neutral vessels as well. Allied submarines sank German vessels in the Baltic, but the German attacks in the Atlantic and the Mediterranean shaped the reaction to this novel form of warfare. The civilian passengers and seamen who died on torpedoed ocean liners and merchant ships—3,000 Norwegian seamen among them—were the most significant noncombatant casualties of the war. Such deaths pulled the neutral United States first to the brink of war, then into the maelstrom.

BEREAVEMENT

Families in all of the belligerent countries learned of the death of relatives and friends. For many women, this was their first and most direct contact with the reality of the fighting. No class escaped such losses. The experience of Vera Brittain, a young English university student and subsequently a nurse's aide, was all too common. She suffered one tragic loss after another. By the close of the war, her fiancé, her brother, and two close male friends had all been killed in action.

ENEMY OCCUPATION

Civilian populations on the side of the Allies felt the direct hardship of enemy occupation. The vast majority of Belgians and many of the residents of northeastern France spent the war under German military administration. In Poland, western Russia, and the Balkans as well, the violence of the war pushed a multitude of European civilians from their homes. Fleeing battered cities and hostile armies, entire families took to the roads to find shelter elsewhere. Out of Belgium's population of 7.6 million, 1 million fled their country, taking refuge in the Netherlands, France, and Britain. In the fall of 1915, the full force of the war struck the population of Serbia, as the country was flooded with Austrian, German, and Bulgarian troops. Large numbers of civilians accompanied the remnants of the Serbian army, escaping from their beleaguered country westward over the mountains of Montenegro and neutral Albania to the Adriatic Sea. Out of a force of 170,000 soldiers, 30,000 did not live to reach the ports of Valona and Durrazo for evacuation. An equal number of civilian refugees died in the harsh journey through the mountains.

Sometimes occupation brought massacres. As German forces pushed through Belgium in August 1914, they often responded in a brutal and massive way to suspected civilian snipers. In the province of Brabant alone, for example, 839 Belgians were executed and the center of the historic city of Louvain was burned. Even as the enemy pulled out, the cost to civilians was high. The German army's strategic retreat on the western front in spring 1917 was accompanied by a wave of destruction of French territory; wells, orchards, mines, and houses were systematically wrecked.

FOOD SHORTAGES AND RATIONING

But hardship came most broadly due to the shortages of food, clothing, and other necessities imposed on the civilians of the belligerent countries. Germany was the first to face the problem of food shortages, then suffered the most. Before the war, that country had produced most of its own food, even exporting large quantities of foodstuffs like rye and beet sugar. But the needs of the army soon meant lesser supplies of things like meat for civilians, and the British blockade deprived German agriculture of vital fertilizers. By late December 1914, voluntary food conservation gave way, at least in Berlin, to food rationing. Within a year, British naval power was having a sharp effect on Germany's food supply.

Throughout 1915, German civilians felt the pressure of the war in the bread supply. Bread rationing was established in Germany in the first January of the war. By the end of 1915, it was set in many regions at half a pound daily per person, one-third less than what Germans had consumed in peacetime. The bread itself was "war bread," adulterated with potato flour. In 1916 most foods were rationed, especially staples such as meat, potatoes, and milk. From May onward, the director of the newly established War Food Office had increasing authority over what every German ate. The supply of milk dwindled, and fats like butter and cooking oil, consumed generously in all German homes before the war, became increasingly hard to obtain. Ersatz (substitute) foods, many of them hideously unappetizing, appeared and took the place of real coffee and real eggs.

Civilians wandering the countryside in search of food became a common sight in Germany and in Austria as well. Buying directly from farmers was one way to circumvent rationing. The practice became so widespread that officials in some regions refused to allow outsiders to visit their farm villages. Another way was to patronize the black market or high-priced restaurants. Germany's population buzzed with stories of the unfairness of a system that allowed the rich to evade the worst effects of the food shortage.

In the last two years of the war, food shortages became critical. A witness to the food crisis in the Central Powers was George Abel Schreiner. A naturalized American citizen who had been born in Germany, Schreiner served as a war correspondent for America's Associated Press. He arrived in Germany at the start of the conflict and remained in central Europe until the United States entered the war. Schreiner's picture of deprivation in Germany and Austria included a discussion of how the food supply was distorted from early in the war as the well-off hoarded as much nourishment for themselves as possible. His description of food lines—

"to eat under government supervision," as he put it—showed the anguish of people dependent upon seemingly callous governments for their meager nourishment.[1]

A poor potato harvest deprived Germans of their staple food in the winter of 1916–1917. It was replaced by turnips, even as the bread ration was reduced and fruits and vegetables nearly disappeared. The government lowered the bread ration again in May 1918. Two months later, the equally crucial potato ration was reduced by half. When the Armistice arrived in November 1918, it was greeted by a nation in which everyone was hungry and most were malnourished. The effect of years of poor food raised the mortality rate in the elderly. Poorly nourished youngsters were vulnerable victims to diseases like tuberculosis.

By contrast, the populations of Britain and France avoided serious food shortages during the first three years of the war. France was Europe's most prosperous and self-contained agricultural nation. Britain, so long as it controlled the sea lanes, could be assured of a food supply, even though British agriculture had so dwindled since the 1870s that it provided only 20 percent of the wheat and something more than half the meat the population ate. The major concern at first was the rise in food prices: meat, for example, cost 40 percent more in Britain after the war had gone on for just a year.

Food difficulties appeared in Britain only at the close of 1916. Adulterated "war bread" now replaced the standard loaf in the shops, and the government made appeals for a cut in meat consumption and for the cultivation of private food gardens. Alcoholic beverages were weaker than their prewar counterparts, and brandy was obtainable only if your doctor prescribed it.

As the submarine menace began to sever Britain's sea links with the world in 1917, the government moved rapidly to arrest the danger. Bread consumption fell, not as a result of formal rationing but in the wake of a government propaganda appeal. British agriculture revived under a system of government subsidies. Compulsory rationing—with only tea, cheese, and bread excepted—was put in place early in 1918.

In France, the food shortage also arrived only late in the conflict. War bread, called "national bread," appeared in May 1916. By year's end, however, lines in front of grocery stores were lengthening, and the government began to plan heavier restrictions. In 1917 they arrived as France also began to suffer shortages and price rises. Sugar was rationed, milk was often unobtainable in cities at any price, and, in a blow to every French home, "national bread" became even less palatable than the version of the previous year. In November even this had to be rationed.

IMPROVED LIVING STANDARDS IN WARTIME

Britain and France won the war in part because they were able to assure the health and well-being of their population. Fair systems of rationing saw the living standard of elites fall, but the living standard for much of the population rose. For those who were not in the age group that went to war, life expectancy, at least in Britain, went up. Restrictions on the consumption of alcohol—the potency of beer was reduced by law, as were the hours when alcoholic beverages could be served—prolonged the lives of those accustomed to drink to excess. But it also meant more money left over to provide for their families. Even more important, the wartime prosperity resulting from the boom in factory jobs meant more money for children's clothes and shoes. Ironically, war bread provided more nourishment than the kind most Britons ate in normal circumstances.

OTHER WARTIME SHORTAGES

In these three countries, other shortages made life shabby and grim. Civilians in Germany, for example, cut off from the outside world by blockade, found clothing difficult to come by. The lack of cotton and leather meant paper garments and wooden shoes. Soap as well became a precious commodity for Germans. Shortages of coal meant that cities were increasingly dark at earlier and earlier hours, and private homes were barely heated. Both Germany and France felt this bite acutely. Most elementary schools in Berlin had to close during the harsh winter of 1916–1917 because they could not be heated. Even in Britain, with its vast coal resources, the shortage of manpower for the mines meant a pinch followed by rationing at the close of 1917.

ECONOMIC HARDSHIPS

The initial impact of the war was ruin for many. Shops in deserted garrison towns found their customers gone. French winemakers, their workers gone to more lucrative employment, were pressed to stay in business. Middle-class businessmen whose enterprises had no link to the war found themselves without customers; few Europeans were able to spend money on furniture or other relics of a peacetime world. Where civilian factories closed, unemployment soon escalated. Paper mills and hatmakers' workshops shut their doors in France in the last months of 1914. Inflation cut deeply into the buying power of civil servants and others on fixed incomes. By the war's conclusion, many German civil servants found that

their salary had lost more than half its 1914 buying power. Real wages may
have dropped as much as 20 percent in France between the war's beginning
and the Armistice, chiefly due to inflation.

CENSORSHIP AND THE WAR AGAINST DISSENT

A more universal hardship also came as governments curtailed the rights
of their citizens in order to fight the war more effectively. On August 8, 1914,
four days after Britain had entered the conflict, Parliament passed the Defense
of the Realm Act (or DORA). Its original aim was to protect the country
against espionage, but it expanded as the war went on, and the British
population was increasingly limited in what it could say, where it could travel,
and how much restraint it could expect from its policemen. Such a suspension
of the population's civil liberties for the duration of the conflict was only one
product of DORA, which was expanded to regulate the operation of industry
and to control Britain's food supply. The need to boost ammunition production
led to unprecedented restrictions on workers. David Lloyd George, Britain's
new minister of munitions, used the Munitions of War Act (July 1915) to
discipline his labor force. Strikes were outlawed, and the right of the individual
to seek another job elsewhere was curtailed.

In both France and Germany, countries where individual liberties were
less rooted in national traditions, measures like DORA, declaring the
country in a state of siege, had much the same effect. In Germany, the entire
civil administration, including supervision of newspapers, came under
direct military control with the start of the war. For military news, the
approved sources were statements given out twice weekly at the General
Staff's Press Department meetings with editors. Civilian government officials provided directions for the coverage of other issues. A similar system
carried the day in France. In Britain, the military role in censorship was less
in evidence. The government's Press Bureau issued official war news and
censored other stories on the war that newspapers proposed to print. The
incentive to submit stories for clearance was strong: the sanctions of DORA,
including suspension of publication, could fall on any newspaper that
printed a story that was later disapproved.

Newspapers and magazines joined voluntarily in the effort to promote
the war. As J. M. Winter put it, "For the duration of the war most editors
and their staffs were willing to forgo the critical function of the press"; he
cites "the German satirical magazine *Simplicissimus* [which] shelved its
traditionally acerbic wit and adopted a patriotic line."[2] On the other side of
the lines, British newspapers likewise became cheerleaders for the war

effort, according to Winter using euphemisms so that "a retreat was called a rectification of the line" to soften the impact of bad news.[3] When Lord Lansdowne, a prominent former cabinet minister now horrified by the human cost of the war, tried to appeal publicly for a negotiated peace, the *Times* of London refused to publish his letter on the subject. But the *Times* enthusiastically reported wild stories of German atrocities.

In Britain, restrictions on passing information to the press concerning government activities preceded the war; the Official Secrets Act was passed in 1911. When DORA lapsed after the end of the war, however, the government perpetuated some of its wartime powers to restrict the flow of information with the additional provisions of the Official Secrets Act of 1920. It was necessary to have such a law against leaking official documents, as one government spokesman argued in the parliamentary debate of 1920, because "experience during the war has made it quite plain that a provision of that kind is necessary if the work of foreign agents is to be checked."[4]

WOMEN IN WARTIME

World War I also brought a tidal wave of social change, evident most immediately as many of the young men in society marched off to war. A disproportionately female population inhabited the home front everywhere, and this led to substantial changes in the work force. Most countries experienced a wave of unemployment followed by a surge in the need for labor. Young people, but especially women, entered the factories in large numbers. The world's most famous armaments plant, the Krupp works at Essen, Germany, employed 12,000 women in 1916; none had been employed there at the outbreak of the war. In the entire machine industry, women employees rose from some 75,000 before the war to nearly 500,000. In French munitions factories, women made up 25 to 30 percent of the work force by 1918.

In France in 1914, and in Britain two years later, the government called on women to work as agricultural laborers. France's mobilization at the war's beginning drained the countryside of men at harvest time; the government asked farm women to step into the breach. In February 1916, the British government asked for 400,000 women to volunteer for work on the country's farms.

WORKERS AND EXPANDING INDUSTRY

The production of armaments became the highest economic priority in the belligerent countries, and the need for factory workers in such industries exploded. Enemy occupation of France's great industrial bastion meant that new centers of heavy industry had to be created in Paris and in the central and southern provinces. By the close of 1915, the population of Paris stood at nearly double its prewar size. A belt of cities stretching from Rouen in the north to Marseilles and Grenoble in the south now provided much of France's industrial strength. In the southern city of Toulouse the prewar gunpowder factory employed 100 workers; by November 1918, it required 30,000. In Britain the population of London swelled steadily, and the new munitions centers set up by Lloyd George in 1915 continued to draw in workers. But the flow of migrants moved in other directions as well: the call for agricultural workers drew Englishwomen out of the cities and onto the land. In Germany, industrial centers like Essen and Dortmund and shipyard cities like Danzig and Kiel grew. Meanwhile, the call-up of men reduced the population of Berlin and Hamburg.

France became, next to the United States, the most important destination in the world for foreign migrants. A flood of laborers, half a million strong, poured in, the majority coming from Spain, China, and the Asian and African portions of France's empire. In the small industrial town of Le Creusot, the working population in the spring of 1918 included 1,700 Chinese, 240 Algerians, and over 400 workers from the Iberian peninsula. Without counting prisoners of war, also an outside presence in the community, the total foreign work force reached 2,770.

CIVILIANS AND THE PROPAGANDA WAR

The war was fought in the realm of words and the arts. In Germany, scholars like the theologian Adolf von Harnack and the economist Werner Sombart as well as literary giants like Thomas Mann asserted the need for Germany, with its superior culture, to triumph on the battlefield over enemies like Great Britain. Mann, along with the English poet Rupert Brooke and other writers throughout the continent, hailed the war as a purifying experience that would wash away the meanness and routine of peacetime life. In Britain, H. G. Wells took up the pen with equal vigor. "There shall be no more Kaiser, there shall be no more Krupps; we are resolved. That foolery will end," he wrote in August 1914.[5] British and German clergymen were equally enthusiastic. Arthur F. Winnington-Ingram, the Lord Bishop of London, stated the issue clearly: "We are on the side of Christianity against anti-Christ." Pastors like Otto Zurhellen responded by accusing Germany's enemies of striking at it due to envy.[6] Even in the face of the blood spilled in torrents on the Somme, A. Conan Doyle could write in spring 1918: "Those young lives were gladly laid down as a price for final victory—and history may show that it was really on those Picardy slopes that final victory was in truth ensured."[7]

In the hands of patriots, the visual and performing arts likewise contributed to pumping up the war effort. A poster entitled "The U-Boats Are Here" by the German artist Hans Rudi Erdt showed the home front that the British were paying a price for the war. Meanwhile, the posters of English artist Frank Brangwyn condemned German Zeppelin raids and urged civilians to stand behind the men in the trenches by buying war bonds. As late as October 1918, Britain's official war artist, James McBey, could paint a glamorous painting, *Lawrence of Arabia,* to show the legendary hero victorious in Damascus. At the other end of Europe, Russian artists joined in to celebrate the war. Hubertus Jahn concluded his study of "patriotic culture" in that country by noting, "Postcards, posters, and films [all] played important roles in the distribution of patriotic motifs and in wartime entertainment in general."[8] Anti-foreign feeling flourished among civilian populations from the start of the war. In Berlin the popular Hotel Westminster now welcomed guests as the newly named Lindenhof. German music was banned from public performances by many orchestras in Britain and France. The sinking of the civilian liner *Lusitania* in May 1915 led to a wave of violence against naturalized British subjects who had been born in Germany. Englishmen with German-sounding names were harassed, and many English families hurriedly anglicized their names at the start of the war. By the close of 1916, American embassy personnel in Berlin found themselves in danger of assault when speaking English on the street.

NEW MORAL STANDARDS

The war brought the threat, and sometimes the reality, of a sudden loosening in sexual customs. It drew millions of women out of their households and into the work force, and wrenched an even greater number of men from their homes for military service. Placing the threat of death or injury in the minds of soldiers and civilians alike, the conflict shook the existing moral order.

In Britain, for example, the huge influx of women into well-paid jobs in munitions plants led to public conduct that shocked observers. Working women used their new freedom to drink in public, to dress in provocative new styles (short skirts and even trousers), and to purchase luxury goods with their newfound affluence. For many, these were unwelcome departures from the country's traditions of proper behavior. A rapid increase in the number of divorces likewise seemed a clear sign of society's decay.

In all the warring countries, the dangers faced by the fighting man made hanging on to traditional sexual morality difficult at best. Men on leave or in rest areas near the front found prostitutes readily available. Unmarried women at home found it harder to deny sexual favors to a boyfriend who might never return from his next turn in the trenches. Married women, out of loneliness or financial desperation, were tempted to ignore their obligations to their spouses.

George Abel Schreiner, who observed the growing hunger in the Central Powers, watched the changes in moral behavior as well in wartime Germany and Austria. As a widely traveled war correspondent, he found signs of a sliding moral order from the cafés where combat soldiers gathered in brief leaves from the fighting front to homes where women without their husbands could no longer govern the behavior of their children.

By the close of 1916, the cost of the war in manpower in Germany and Austria meant that marriageable women now outnumbered eligible men by a ratio of five to four. British observers grew alarmed about a rise in illegitimate children. The number of divorces in England and Wales increased 500 percent between the last year of peace and 1919. The increase in male drunkenness, and the new phenomenon of widespread drunkenness among women, seemed direct results of the high wages paid in the buzzing economy.

Illegitimate births rose sharply in Germany, too—so much so that most areas of Germany ended the practice of indicating illegitimacy on birth certificates. With families facing the stress of a father at the front and a mother in the arms factory, juvenile delinquency escalated. Restrictions on adolescents also faded as the wartime economy offered them jobs and high wages and undermined traditional systems of apprenticeship. After two years of war, Germany saw a 50 percent rise in crime among male teenagers. It went up another 25 percent in 1917. German authorities pointed to theft as a particular concern, attributing it largely to the lack of a parent in the home. In Berlin in 1917, for example, the authorities noted that only 8 percent of teenagers working in industry were under the supervision of both parents; only 20 percent had even one parent present.[9] They were also alarmed by "licentiousness," that is, improper sexual behavior, among female adolescents. The suggested remedy was "corrective education," probably meaning confinement in a state-run juvenile home.

In Britain, the authorities likewise faced frightening changes. Children only thirteen or fourteen years old were, like their German counterparts, earning enough in the wartime economy to cause them to shake off parental supervision. A consequent concern was the jump in the level of juvenile crime, especially for children ages eleven to thirteen. Theft was the most common offense, with consignment to a reformatory or industrial school the most common remedy. Teenage girls were seen as victims of "khaki fever," an attraction to young men in uniform expressed in loitering around army bases and dispensing sexual favors. The resulting threat to social stability involved both the spread of immorality among lower-class girls who participated in this infatuation and the spread of venereal disease. Members of the middle class responded to the danger by forming groups like the Women Patrols Committee to help supervise public places where such girls congregated. These unofficial organizations sometimes got the sanction of local government and operated in conjunction with police constables.[10]

LABOR UNREST

The most visible sign of changing public attitudes toward the war came in the form of labor unrest. Labor leaders in all three countries, as well as most leaders of Socialist and labor parties, supported the war in 1914. But as the war dragged on in bloody fashion, conflict behind the screen of unity became more evident.

Although labor unrest rose and then subsided in Britain and France in 1917, tensions escalated steadily and most significantly in Germany. By the spring of 1917, some members of Germany's Socialist party (SPD), led by Hugo Haase, broke away to advocate an end to the war without "annexations or indemnities." More radical Socialists, following future Communist leader Karl Liebknecht, had been arrested the year before for agitating openly against the war. As Germany moved into 1918, labor unrest began in a fashion that stretched down to the Armistice. Strikes in the first months of the year threatened arms production in Berlin and affected 250,000 workers there, as well as other workers in Hamburg and Leipzig. Miners struck in Silesia in July, and in the fall months the entire nation was engulfed in worker unrest compounded by military mutinies. The collapse of order on the German home front, including military mutinies, combined with the deteriorating position of the German army on the western front to force the government to end hostilities.

TEMPORARY AND PERMANENT CHANGES

Changes on the wartime home front did not always translate into permanent shifts in European society. Many of the women who went into factory work during the war in Britain, France, and Germany returned to their homes following the Armistice. The expanded role of government in such areas as censorship went back to peacetime norms.

However, inflation and, for a time, food rationing continued into the postwar years. After the war, France found itself with a permanent immigrant presence that had begun with the foreign laborers brought in to help run the wartime economy. The moral laxity of the wartime years was evident—at least to many worried observers—in areas like the divorce rate in the 1920s. The effects of prolonged malnutrition were evident in the German population long after the war had ended.

The experience of factory workers in the war did not lead to the postwar upheaval some feared. Despite instances of labor unrest as the war went on, high wages and plentiful jobs eased the discomforts of working in a semi-militarized environment, and patriotism remained a powerful adhesive force. In Britain, organized labor enthusiastically supported the war effort even at the close of the long conflict. Moreover, the presence of Labour party officials like Arthur Henderson in the wartime cabinet from spring 1915 onward probably encouraged workers to believe that their party might some day take power. In the postwar period, the growth of unemployment removed much of the unions' bargaining power, and the basic structure of Britain's industrial society remained intact. In Germany as well, unions cooperated with the wartime government even as it became a military dictatorship. When Germany passed into revolution in the final months of 1918, the unions took an equally moderate stance vis-à-vis the country's industrial leadership. Here too the old social order survived. In France, as well, a surge of labor militancy during and immediately after the war soon gave way to relative peace in industrial relations. The rivalry between France's Communist and Socialist parties divided the political influence of even militant labor groups. A conservative majority in the postwar French parliament stood firm against the wave of strikes that hit the country in late 1919 and the spring of 1920, and French labor unions, swelled by new recruits during the wartime years, declined in strength equally fast as the newcomers abandoned them.

WOMAN'S SUFFRAGE

In one clear instance the wartime role of women led to a substantial result, the end of a long-standing quarrel over women's rights in Great Britain. In March 1918, with prominent opponents of woman's suffrage like former prime minister H. H. Asquith now removing their objections, Parliament approved giving women the vote. The decision was anything but close, with seven "ayes" recorded for every "nay."

In Germany, the same result came in a different fashion. It was not as a reward for service within the existing system granted while the war went on but rather a consequence of the collapse of the old order. The only large-scale group in favor of woman's suffrage before World War I was the German Socialist party. Despite women's contributions to the war effort, there was no move to grant them the vote during the conflict. In January 1918, two months before British women received the vote, the Prussian Diet refused to grant German women voting rights even in local elections. The participation of Anita Augspurg and other leaders of the prewar women's movement in pacifist meetings like the Hague Congress of April 1915 served instead to retard progress toward woman's rights. Women received the vote only after the war, and then as a result of the revolution of November 1918. Prince Max of Baden's government introduced universal male suffrage in late October, and, as unrest continued, the majority coalition in the Reichstag, represented by the Joint Parliamentary Committee drawn from the Center, Progressive, and SPD (Socialist) parties, was pushed to call for this further extension of voting rights. As historian Gordon Craig concluded, "The acquisition of political rights for women was not, therefore, the result of pressure or persuasion . . . but rather of military defeat and the collapse of the German Empire."[11]

In France, women did not find that the war brought them lasting political or social change. Frenchwomen entered the labor force in large numbers. They entered politics as well, serving as mayors in some rural communities. But the movement for woman's suffrage ceased to operate in wartime circumstances, and its most prominent leaders, Hubertine Auclert and Eliska Vincent, died during the conflict. France's loss of population during the war gave conservative opponents of woman's suffrage a powerful argument seen in the title of an article published in 1919: "France has more need of children than electors."[12] As men reclaimed their jobs, most women returned to their homes.

Thus, both winners and losers found themselves shaken by the wartime experience. But as Europe's peoples settled back into their peacetime pursuits, a complex picture of the continent emerged of newly initiated changes, older changes accelerated, and previous patterns persisting.

Nonetheless, the war the civilians fought was unprecedented in its scope and significance for the conflict's outcome. Not since the Thirty Years War (1618–1648) ravaged central Europe had so many wartime hardships been placed on so many European civilians. But this time the power of the modern state to control, direct, and alleviate those hardships had been an important part of events. The war saw civilians play a key role, because the belligerent governments needed them to do so. Governments did what they could to maintain the energies on the home front. The civilians' ability to endure and to contribute to the war effort—even as their societies were being shaken by the conflict's cost—was a critical element in the hopes on each side of the battle front for ultimate victory.

NOTES

1. George Abel Schreiner, *The Iron Ration: Three Years in Warring Central Europe* (New York: Harper and Brothers, 1918), pp. 215–19.

2. J. M. Winter, *The Experience of World War I* (London: Macmillan, 1988), p. 166.

3. Ibid., p. 186.

4. Quoted in David Hooper, *Official Secrets: The Use and Abuse of the Act* (London: Secker and Warburg, 1987), p. 36.

5. Quoted in Dominic Hibberd, *The First World War* (Houndmills, Basingstoke, Hampshire, Eng.: Macmillan, 1990), pp. 43–44.

6. Quoted in A. J. Hoover, *God, Germany, and Britain in the Great War* (New York: Praeger, 1989), pp. 24, 57–58.

7. Hibberd, *First World War*, p. 104.

8. Hubertus F. Jahn, *Patriotic Culture in Russia During World War I* (Ithaca, N.Y.: Cornell University Press, 1995), p. 172.

9. Richard Bessel, *Germany after the First World War* (Oxford: Clarendon Press, 1993), p. 24.

10. On khaki fever, see Angela Woollacott, " 'Khaki Fever' and Its Control: Gender, Class, Age and Sexual Morality on the British Homefront in the First World War, " *Journal of Contemporary History* 29 (1994): 325–47.

11. Gordon A. Craig, *The Germans* (New York: G. P. Putnam's Sons, 1981), p. 161.

12. Steven C. Hause, "More Minerva than Mars: The French Women's Rights Campaign and the First World War," in Margaret Randolph Higgonet, Jane Jenson, Sonya Michel, and Margaret Collins Weitz, eds., *Behind the Lines: Gender and the Two World Wars* (New Haven, Conn.: Yale University Press, 1987), p. 111.

6

War and the Collapse
of the Old Order:
Russia and Austria-Hungary

On March 8, 1917, a demonstration in the Russian capital, Petrograd, marking International Women's Day soon grew into full-fledged urban insurrection. The police failed to restore order, and army troops mutinied instead of firing on the crowd. Vasily Shulgin, a Nationalist deputy in Russia's Duma (parliament), recoiled from the spectacle of revolutionary masses in the streets of the capital: "Only hot lead could drive this terrible beast, that had somehow burst free, back into its den."[1] Instead, the unrest spread, and the monarchy collapsed within a matter of days. Tsar Nicholas II abdicated, and no ranking member of his family was willing to succeed him. After celebrating its three hundredth anniversary only a year before the outbreak of the war, the Romanov dynasty abruptly left the seat of power.

WAR SHAKES THE OLD ORDER

In the classic formulation of nineteenth-century Prussian general and military theorist Karl von Clausewitz, war is an instrument of national policy by which states pursue their interests using force and violence. This picture presumes that the governmental system wielding such an instrument will be able to control it and, more important, will survive to see the armed conflict brought to a conclusion.

For some countries, World War I developed into a test their systems of government could not endure. An essential feature of the conflict—and a measure of its intensity—was the way in which World War I overturned

venerable monarchies, and how prominent and long-established multinational states dissolved.

World War I helped to bring on upheavals in Russia and a number of other
major European countries. Political and social tensions existed everywhere
in the Europe of 1914, and in the following wartime years all of the great
European belligerents experienced events that shook the old order. But
neither the war alone nor prewar tensions alone brought on revolution. Irish
nationalism, for example, as demonstrated in the uprising of Easter 1916,
could not yet dissolve the unity of Great Britain. Nor did the army mutinies
in France in 1917 undermine domestic stability.

In imperial Russia in 1917 and in Austria-Hungary in 1918, where the
strains and traumas of the war combined with existing problems, dramatic
breaks with the old order occurred. Russia's debased, unpopular monarchy
and inept bureaucracy, its impoverished rural population, and its alienated
urban working class had already shown how they could threaten national
stability. In addition, talented and determined revolutionary leaders were
either on the scene or only a short distance away in foreign exile. Finally,
an imperial population in which only half the tsar's subjects were ethnic
Russians added an explosive nationalities problem. In Austria-Hungary, the
most volatile internal conflict also turned on the question of nationalities,
and led finally to the collapse of the old order.

Drastic and dramatic change came to the two great powers at different
points in the war, and came about in different ways. The two countries'
peacetime circumstances varied, and so too did their wartime experiences.
In each country, the role of the monarch, the radicalism practiced by leaders
of the domestic opposition, and the success of the armed forces and their
state of discipline all played a role. There were also important differences
concerning the presence or absence of enemy armed forces on the country's
soil and the relationship each country had with its wartime allies. Most
important in the short run—when the discontented had to decide whether
or not to take to the streets—was how well the government functioned in
maintaining public order and in guaranteeing an adequate food supply.

THE RUSSIAN MONARCHY

For the quarter century before crowds took to the streets in March 1917,
Russia's problems had begun at the top with an inept and imperceptive
monarch. In the words of historian Hugh Seton-Watson, "Nicholas was
brought up to believe that it was his sacred duty to uphold the principle of
autocracy."[2] Thus, in January 1895, only two months after taking over the

throne, Nicholas rejected a call by liberal landowners serving in the zemstvo (local governing body) in the province of Tver for some form of popular representation in the making of national policy. He dismissed this notably moderate proposal as "senseless dreams about participation . . . in the affairs of internal government."[3] Such statements set the tone for the next two decades.

In early 1905 the country plunged into revolution. The war against Japan, begun in February 1904, had brought a grim series of defeats for both the Russian army and the Russian navy. The strains the war placed on the civilian population brought unrest to a boiling point, first among the country's factory workers, then among the peasants and the military rank and file. The brutality of the government was on open display on January 22, 1905, the starting point for the revolution, when the workers of St. Petersburg and their families, marching to petition the tsar, were shot down on their way to the imperial palace. The toll of men, women, and children probably reached 200, with another 800 wounded. This barbarous treatment of Nicholas's subjects stripped away the traditional loyalty of the population to the country's crowned head. The Revolution of 1905, which the government managed to quell only in the last months of the year, forced the tsar to relax his opposition—albeit merely for tactical purposes—and he granted the Russian population a constitution and a Duma, a nationally elected representative body with limited powers of legislation. As late as the summer of 1914, however, he was openly in favor of turning the clock back by abolishing the Duma.

The public image of the empress also speeded the decline of the monarchy's popularity and prestige. A German princess by birth, Alix of Hesse-Darmstadt, renamed Alexandra in 1894 when she adopted Eastern Orthodox Christianity and married Nicholas, was even more opposed to political change than he. She detested public appearances and saw to it that the imperial family was isolated in the summer palace at Tsarskoe Selo outside St. Petersburg. Dominating her husband, whom she sometimes called "darling boysy" in their private correspondence, she offered him reactionary political advice in a frantic voice. During World War I, for example, she used her typical tone in urging him to appoint certain officials despite opposition by the Duma: "Be Peter the Great, John [Ivan] the Terrible, Emperor Paul—crush them all under you."[4] Officials of the imperial government such as Prime Minister Ivan Goremykin saw themselves as the tsar's servants rather than as independent political figures. In all, the people surrounding Nicholas were a strong force encouraging him to keep all the safety valves closed as political tensions grew.

THE RUSSIAN POPULATION
AND INDUSTRIAL GROWTH

Prewar Russia contained a rapidly growing population, 130 million people according to the census of 1897, most of whom lived in rural poverty. Serfdom, which tied the rural population to the land, had been abolished in the 1860s. But this halfway reform had left the peasantry dissatisfied. Forced to pay exorbitant prices for the land they received, they saw an equal share of the land given to their former overlords, the local nobility. The terms of the emancipation also tied the peasantry to their local villages, perpetuating most of the personal restrictions of serfdom.

The country's ethnic mixture merely added to such tensions. Since the middle of the seventeenth century, Russia had acquired a large non-Russian population. Constituting 55 percent of the population in 1897, the nationalities included ethnic Germans in the Baltic provinces, Moslems in Central Asia, non-Russian Slavs such as the Ukrainians, and a host of tiny groups ranging from the Chechens of the northern Caucasus to the Khants of northwestern Siberia. Nicholas continued a campaign of Russification begun under his father, Alexander III, who ruled from 1881 to 1894. This effort to force the Russian language and culture on other nationalities within the country served to sharpen the discontent of dangerously large groups like the Ukrainians.

Humiliated by military defeat in the Crimean War (1854–1856) the government by the 1890s had embarked upon a program of rapid industrial growth with little thought to the social or human costs involved. This added factory slums to Russia's major cities, as well as producing millions of urban industrial workers, most of them recently uprooted peasants. The grim nature of life in the new industrial slums was reflected in workers' health. One of every seven factory workers fell ill each year; one in two died before reaching the age of forty-five. Most children in the workers' quarters of the burgeoning industrial centers never lived to become adults.[5]

Industrialization also helped produce a Marxist revolutionary movement to compete with the Populist revolutionary movement that had existed since the 1860s. Both the Populists, with their faith in peasant revolution, and the Marxists, with their expectation of a revolution by factory workers, consisted of urban intellectuals. The Marxists included talented leaders ranging from radicals like Vladimir I. Lenin and Leon Trotsky to more moderate figures such as Julius Martov. All worked confidently to produce the revolution that their German mentor, Karl Marx, called inevitable in an industrial society.

MILITARY DEFEAT AND FORCED EVACUATION

Russia's entry into the war placed unmanageable strains on this rickety system. Military catastrophe came within the first weeks of fighting, with one army annihilated and a second badly mauled at the Battle of Tannenberg (August 1914). Starting in May 1915, the sweeping German-led offensive at Gorlice-Tarnow allowed the Central Powers to occupy the western portion of imperial Russia. Apart from the military debacle, the economic consequences were grave: Germany now held some of the most important of Russia's agricultural and industrial regions, and had captured much of the rolling stock of Russia's barely adequate prewar railroad system.

A measure of the foolishness of Russia's military leadership was the policy of devastating and forcibly evacuating areas the Germans were about to occupy. This produced hundreds of thousands of refugees from these western regions who poured into the major cities of Moscow and Petrograd. Even government officials were appalled at the sight. "People were torn away from their homes with but a few hours in which to settle their affairs. Their stores of food and at times even their houses were burned before their very eyes," recorded one observer.[6]

THE TSAR TAKES COMMAND OF THE ARMY

Military successes against the Turks and the Austrians barely budged the scale of public opinion, and the prestige of the government sank steadily. Nicholas made the questionable decision to take direct command of the army after the summer 1915 retreat. This left Alexandra in charge in the capital, Petrograd. Suspected by many of being a traitor due to her birth and upbringing in Germany, she and the entire monarchy were even more discredited by rumors about her liaison with Rasputin. This self-proclaimed holy man and notorious libertine had gained entry into Alexandra's circle around 1907 due to his apparent ability to treat her son's (the tsarevich Alexis) hemophilia. Even before the war he had meddled in political affairs. After the tsar's departure for the front, Rasputin's psychological hold on the empress gave him crucial influence in appointing his incompetent cronies to lead key government ministries. Such a dismal picture led the tsar's cousin to note, "The government itself is the organ that is preparing the revolution."[7]

In June 1916 the army showed its mettle in the early stages of the Brusilov offensive. General Alexis Brusilov, the dynamic commander of the southwestern front, led four field armies in crushing the Austro-Hungarian forces in this sector. But a more important factor was the overall decline in military discipline as seen in an exploding desertion rate. The situation was particularly dangerous in Petrograd, which was not only the capital and a major industrial center, but also a major military center containing large numbers of troops scheduled for shipment to the grim prospects of the fighting front.

Imperial Russia's ties to its allies in western Europe brought few benefits. Turkey's entry into the war prevented Britain and France from supplying Russia's beleaguered military system via the Mediterranean. Even if the route to the Black Sea had been open, the shortage of ships and the distance involved would have limited direct aid. There was never any prospect that large numbers of French or British troops could be sent to Russia as they were to Italy to bolster that weak ally after its defeat at the Battle of Caporetto in October 1917.

CIVILIANS' HARDSHIPS AND THE OUTBREAK OF REVOLUTION

Meanwhile, the urban population was tormented by raging inflation and the breakdown of the food and fuel system. In Petrograd at the start of the revolutionary year 1917, bread prices rose 2 percent each week, and one agent of the political police warned that "children are starving in the most literal sense of the word."[8] The food shortage was due partly to the disintegration of the railroad system, and it also showed the government's ineffectiveness in dealing with the rural masses. There was plenty of food in the countryside. But with no consumer goods available from Russia's wartime factories, peasants hoarded their grain harvests rather than selling for no real return.

Thus, when the Women's Day demonstrations escalated into massive unrest in March 1917, the monarchy had little to fall back on. The new year had begun with large and ugly strikes that commemorated the anniversary of the massacre in front of the Winter Palace twelve years earlier. An ominous sign for the government was the lack of enthusiasm displayed by the Cossacks in putting down labor unrest. Drawn from the southern and eastern border-lands of Russia, the Cossacks were traditionally the most reliable troops the monarchy possessed for subduing domestic strife. As disorder spread in Petrograd, first the Cossacks, then army units wavered. A key event took place at a public meeting on March 10 at Znamenskaya Square in the capital city. When an army lieutenant drew his revolver to silence a radical orator, a Cossack rode forward to kill the officer with his saber.[9]

THE TSAR'S ABDICATION AND THE FORMATION OF A PROVISIONAL GOVERNMENT

This sign of a disintegrating monarchy soon became the norm. Isolated at Russian central military headquarters at Mogilev, Nicholas tried in vain to reach his capital. A railwaymen's strike diverted him to the headquarters of the northern front. There his generals persuaded him to abdicate.

The Provisional Government took power in the wake of the tsar's departure. Drawn from members of the Duma, it was a self-appointed body whose members were acutely aware that they held no formal popular mandate. Nonetheless, they proclaimed freedom of the press and the right of workers to strike and granted amnesty to all political prisoners. The traditional police force was abolished in favor of a new, supposedly less repressive militia. Perhaps due to its high ideals, perhaps due to hopes it might wage the war more effectively, the postrevolutionary government enjoyed a brief period of popularity. Initially, the dominant figure was Paul Miliukov, the foreign minister and a western-style liberal. A rising figure who came to direct the Provisional Government by early summer was the more radical Alexander Kerensky. Both leaders, however, were committed to remaining in the war and postponing radical social and political change. Events soon outran their control.

The delay in carrying out basic reforms such as distributing land to the peasantry undercut the government's authority. Peasants soon took over lands without waiting for the government's approval. The decision to remain in the war proved even more unpopular. Desertion rates, high even in 1914, now threatened the very existence of the armed forces. Moreover, since the start of the revolution, the Provisional Government had been forced to share power with the Petrograd Soviet. This group of revolutionary intellectuals claimed to represent the interests, not of the entire nation, but of the peasants, workers, and soldiers. Its leadership grew increasingly radical, especially by the fall of 1917.

THE BOLSHEVIK REVOLUTION

The collapse of the monarchy had sparked an upheaval among the former empire's non-Russian peoples as well as a rural uprising. The arrival home of genuinely radical leaders like Lenin and Trotsky committed to removing Russia from the war opened the way to a second upheaval, the Bolshevik Revolution of November 1917. In exile in Switzerland, Lenin had been a vocal critic of the war since August 1914, and he had called for Russia's defeat as a positive step toward revolution. Once back in Russia—he arrived on April 16—he condemned the Provisional Government, pledged to remove Russia from the war, and promised land to the peasants and control over the factories for the workers.

Bolshevik leaders took advantage of Russia's continuing turmoil and the ineptitude of the Provisional Government to move toward power. In late

June the Ukraine broke most of its ties with Petrograd, a sign that the minority peoples of the former Russian state were moving toward outright independence. Early the next month Kerensky, now minister of war and soon to be prime minister as well, conducted a disastrous offensive on the eastern front. Its failure accelerated the collapse of the army. In September Kerensky destroyed the last remnants of his authority by a clumsy effort to bring army units into Petrograd to help him crush the Bolsheviks and establish an authoritarian government. Growing suspicious of the army's commander, General Lavr Kornilov, Kerensky reversed himself and turned to the Bolsheviks for help in stopping Kornilov. In consequence, Kerensky alienated the army's commanders, boosted the power of the Bolsheviks and the workers' militia they dominated, and set the stage for his own downfall.

Lenin saw the opportunity to seize power in Petrograd acting in the name of the Soviet. Using his formidable powers of persuasion, he won over a majority of his fellow Bolshevik leaders. Trotsky demonstrated his tactical brilliance in directing the seizure of key locations in Petrograd on the night of November 6–7.

Thus, in a second revolution—the Bolshevik Revolution of November 1917—Lenin and his party took power in Petrograd and, a few days later, in Moscow. Although the Bolsheviks had not yet extended their power to the countryside, control over the industrial and political centers gave them virtual power to command the Russian government. The Bolsheviks' unity, discipline, and even ruthlessness also gave them a tactical advantage over their rivals, who remained divided in purpose and limited by their own scruples or self-interest. Thus, fully a year before the war ended for the other belligerents, Russia had a radical government that moved rapidly to pull that country out of the war. Even more significantly for Europe's future, the war had opened the way for Marxist radicals to control one of the continent's Great Powers. They now had the opportunity to change the shape of the economy and society of Russia—and, as time would prove, for the next seven decades to promote radical change elsewhere in the world.

NATIONALISM IN THE HABSBURG EMPIRE

Revolution came to Austria-Hungary only in the closing days of the war. The country was a multinational empire with numerous restless groups within it, but it survived more than four years of costly fighting. The empire suffered shortages of food, fuel, and clothing, but even without using armed force to maintain stability at home, the country's basic framework remained solid until the fall of 1918.

The major source of tension within the empire of Franz Joseph was the nationalities question. Constructed in the late seventeenth century, the empire linked the historic German and Czech possessions of the Habsburg family with newly acquired regions—inhabited by Hungarians and south Slavic peoples—taken from a fading Ottoman Empire. Over the centuries, Habsburg diplomacy and military efforts brought Italians and more south Slavs like the Bosnians under the flag of the double eagle.

In 1867, in the last of the empire's configurations, the system was split in two. In the western, or Austrian, half, the dominant role was occupied by the German minority presiding over such restless groups as the Czechs and Bosnians. In the eastern half, Hungarians ruled, implementing frequently harsh policies of cultural assimilation directed at peoples like the Slovaks.

Up to 1914, even the most vocal representatives of the nonruling groups spoke, at most, of shifting the system into federal form. Autonomy rather than independence was the maximum program, with the Hungarians, jealous of their status as co-rulers of the empire, the most immovable obstacle to such a shift. As C. A. Macartney describes the situation before the war, "It was still true that only a relatively small fraction of the peoples of the Monarchy wanted to leave. In the great majority of cases they were still manoeuvering for position within the existing Monarchy."[10] Moreover, Austria-Hungary lacked the massive, alienated masses of peasants recently removed from serfdom who made up the bulk of the Russian population. Similarly, the country had made a slow, and not disastrously disruptive, transition toward becoming an industrial power. Macartney says of the first years of the twentieth century, "Materially, these were the most prosperous years that the Monarchy had ever known." Industrial production was increasing rapidly, emigration was draining off the excess population of rural areas, and "the general material condition of most of the Monarchy could be regarded as at least one of dawning well-being."[11]

THE HABSBURG MONARCHY

The monarchy provided a potent rallying point for the diverse peoples of the empire. Franz Joseph had been the ruler since 1848, and he stood as the most senior monarch in Europe. He had presided over his country's affairs as it lost most of its Italian possessions in the war of 1859 with Piedmont-Savoy and France. He also had seen the Habsburg Empire lose its influence in German affairs following its defeat in the Seven Weeks' War against Prussia in 1866. The empire, which had been reconstituted repeatedly over the centuries, now took its final shape in 1867 as the German leaders in

Vienna compromised with the Hungarians, who had been such dangerous rebels, to create the new Dual Empire.

The monarchy, with Franz Joseph as emperor of Austria and king of Hungary, was one of the institutions, along with the national army, that held the system together. Rising at dawn and laboring on state business throughout the day even as he grew aged, Franz Joseph was a model of crowned industriousness. One scholar describes him in these decades as a monarch whose "very being somewhat attenuated the asperities and animosities of peoples in the multinational realm . . . he embodied the common concern for law and order."[12]

Unlike in Russia, during the war there were no suggestions that the monarch or members of his family were dangerously sympathetic toward the enemy; nor were there charlatans with crucially important influence on the order of Russia's Rasputin. Convinced that victory was unlikely, the old monarch nonetheless played the same role—symbol of imperial unity—that he had played since 1848. He claimed little influence in making policy, but as Edward Crankshaw has put it, he was "the living symbol of the reality of the Dual State."[13] The death of Franz Joseph in 1916 brought his attractive young great-nephew to the throne as Emperor Charles. The new monarch's efforts to remove his country from the war soon became public knowledge. They probably added to his popularity.

THE WAR AND THE WARTIME ALLIANCE
WITH GERMANY

The country's performance on the battlefield offers a partial explanation for the persistence of the ancient regime in this era of unprecedented strain. To be sure, the war began badly for Austro-Hungarian arms, as its forces were humiliated in operations against both Serbia and Russia. Two efforts to advance into Serbia—one in August 1914 and the other that December—resulted in decisive Serb victories. The empire's armies staggered back in the face of their smaller but highly motivated adversary. In advancing against the Russians in Galicia, the results were even worse. Austro-Hungarian troops were stopped, then pushed backward. An army of 120,000 men was besieged at Przemysl, which fell in March 1915. The Polish provinces of the empire now rested in enemy hands, Russian troops were advancing on the passes through the Carpathian Mountains, and the plains of Hungary lay open to invasion.

The following year brought a decisive reversal of fortune in both areas. With the aid of their powerful ally Germany, Austrian troops took the offensive against Russia at Gorlice-Tarnow in May 1915, driving the enemy out of Galicia and deep into Russia's home territory. In October, aided by Bulgaria as well as Germany, Austrian troops overran all of Serbia, then turned to occupy Montenegro as well. The pattern of critical help from Germany available to produce important Austrian victories held for the remainder of the war.

In the summer of 1916, Russian troops under General Alexis Brusilov penetrated the Austrian lines and advanced into Volhynia, a part of the Habsburg lands. Once again, German forces were immediately available to lead a successful counteroffensive. When Rumania entered the war and invaded the Habsburg holdings in Transylvania, Germany stepped in still another time to invade Rumania and turn around the direction of the campaign. In August 1917 General Luigi Cadorna's Italian army achieved a victory of sorts on the Isonzo, advancing at heavy cost on the Bainsizza plateau. German troops then provided the edge of the sword for the Central Powers' devastating counterattack on Italy in October 1917, leading to the decisive victory at Caporetto.

Without German aid, Austria's military successes—and even its security against Russian invasion—were uncertain. If Russian troops had penetrated to the center of Hungary in the spring and summer of 1915, the consequences would have been profound. But Germany's interest in preserving its only ally and its ready ability to do so staved off this as well as lesser crises. During most of the war, and especially at the time of Caporetto, when the Central Powers broke through the Italian defenses on the Isonzo in October 1917, Austrian authorities had the prestige of military successes to offset the difficulties on the home front.

THE AUSTRO-HUNGARIAN MILITARY FORCES

One of the great surprises of the war was the stability of the Austro-Hungarian army. In Crankshaw's words, "The army was at first wholly loyal, and the greater part of it was to remain loyal, in the teeth of fearful punishment, for the next four years, justifying all the claims that had been made for its supranational quality."[14] Together, Austro-German and Hungarian troops—representing the two dominant ethnic groups in the empire—composed only 26.7 and 22.3 percent, respectively, of the army's total strength.[15] Nonetheless, Hungarians, Czechs, Slovenes, Croats, and other nationalities fought side by side. In one famous case of desertion, the Czech 28th Infantry Regiment abandoned its position in the Carpathian Mountains and went over to the Russians in April 1915; but it was an isolated event in this early stage of the war. For Hungarians, traditional enmity toward the Russians helped hold them loyally in place. For most of the south Slav nationalities, the campaigns defending the empire against the Italians proved a popular effort. The army likewise remained a force for stability within the empire. In January 1918, for example, reliable troops still stood ready to put down workers' unrest in Vienna.

The mutiny of naval crews at the Gulf of Kotor in early February 1918 was a sign of danger, "the first serious disturbance among the Austro-Hungarian armed forces." It was in part the result of prolonged inactivity on vessels that had been pinned to shore by the Allied blockade of the Adriatic. But it reflected both nationalist sentiments and the sailors' awareness of the recent revolutions in Russia. Military authorities were able to put it down without difficulty.[16] Only in midsummer 1918 did mutinies, refusals to go into combat, and desertion en masse become common.[17]

NATIONALIST LEADERS AND THE EMPIRE'S ENEMIES

The ability and even the willingness of national leaders to undermine the prewar system turned out to be highly limited. Figures like Thomas Masaryk, a Czech university professor and political leader who had escaped to Italy early in the war, tried to raise support abroad for an independent Czechoslovakia. But meanwhile, leaders in the Czech regions of the empire continued to profess (and practice) loyalty to the empire. Edward Crankshaw sums up the situation: "Until 1917 every anti-Habsburg gesture was regularly condemned by the local Czech authorities and countered by formal declaration of solidarity with the Monarchy and loyalty to the throne."[18]

Austria-Hungary's enemies showed little interest in subverting the basic structure of the empire until 1918. It still seemed that, in the postwar world, Austria-Hungary might be a useful counterweight to revived German power in central Europe. In his Fourteen Points, U.S. president Woodrow Wilson spoke only about greater autonomy for the subject peoples of the empire, and as late as January 5, 1918, Prime Minister David Lloyd George of Great Britain hedged his call for "genuine self-government on true democratic principles" for the peoples of Austria-Hungary by stating that "a break-up of Austria-Hungary is no part of our war aims."[19]

THE FINAL YEAR OF THE WAR AND THE EMPIRE'S COLLAPSE

Political discontent at home remained, with one notable exception, within peaceful limits. In Austria—but not in Hungary—the parliament was not allowed to meet until early 1917. In a dramatic act of protest, Friedrich Adler, the son of a leading Socialist politician, assassinated Count Carl Stürgkh, Austria's prime minister, in October 1916. Nonetheless, the intense political ferment visible in Russia in 1917 was not to be seen. When Vienna's workers, pushed by a cut in the bread ration, went on strike in January 1918, government leaders met with them, worked out a compromise, and ended the crisis peaceably.

The empire's collapse came suddenly: in the face of military invasion, in the face of a dramatic shift in the policies of the empire's adversaries, and as a result of a relatively recent surge in the militancy of the non-German and non-Hungarian nationalities. Meanwhile, conditions for the civilian population grew impossibly difficult.

The population of the empire had long borne the hardships of hunger and inflation. The German ambassador reported starvation in Vienna in 1916, and in 1917 the harvest was poor, cutting yields by as much as one-half in some regions.[20] By the fall of 1918, the situation for the civilian population almost everywhere was desperate. C. A. Macartney sums up the situation thus: "In the big towns and industrial centres, queues waited all day for the miserable pittances to which their ration cards entitled them, and even those were often not available."[21]

When the Austrian parliament was recalled in May 1917, delegates representing the national minorities began to call for reforming the system to create a federation. The following year Czech leaders went further, adopting on January 6, 1918, a resolution calling for an "independent Czecho-Slovak nation." After Caporetto, the desperate Italian government sought to ease friction with its nominal Serb ally and unofficially accepted the creation of a Yugoslav state as a war aim. That goal would mean tearing away the south Slav lands of the empire. With the final German offensive of the war threatening to defeat the Allies, and the Dual Empire clearly a German satellite, the attitude in Washington, London, and Paris toward Austria-Hungary changed. The government in Washington took the lead, expressing its sympathy for the "nationalistic aspirations of the Czecho-Slovaks and Jugoslavs for freedom" on May 29, 1918.[22] In early June 1918, at Versailles, the prime ministers of Britain, France, and Italy also expressed their sympathy for these goals. Next, Britain took the lead. On August 9 it recognized "the Czecho-Slovaks as an Allied nation" and "the Czech-Slovak National Council as the supreme organ of Czecho-Slovak national interests."[23] On September 3, the United States followed as the Wilson administration officially recognized the National Council as a legitimate government.

Coupled with political changes abroad were shifts in the empire's military fortunes. The advance of General Louis Franchet d'Esperey's Allied army northward after its breakout from Salonika cut into the heart of Austria-Hungary. And in late October, the final Allied offensive in Italy at last shattered the tough skeleton of the military system.

In rapid-fire fashion, representatives of the national minorities now took charge in one area after another. On October 6, for example, a council of Serbs, Croats, and Slovenes had convened in Zagreb calling for a single independent nation. In his imperial manifesto of October 16, Emperor Charles, trying to stem the tide, announced that the nationalities of the Austrian portion of the empire were free to form their own states within a federal system. On October 28, nationalist leaders in Prague did precisely that and proclaimed the formation of a Czecho-Slovak republic. As the war ended, the Habsburg state ended as well.

THE AFTERMATH

Revolution in Austria-Hungary brought profound changes to eastern Europe. Out of the map of the old empire, territories went to form—or to help form—the new states of Czechoslovakia, Poland, and Yugoslavia. Rumania doubled its size as a result of lands it carved from the former Habsburg possessions. But these newly formed states were economically weak and mutually hostile. By the end of the 1920s, with the exception of Czechoslovakia, all were headed toward dictatorship. And their dismal future was compounded by their vulnerable position between two once powerful neighbors, Germany and Russia, who were certain to regain that power in the decades to come.

Both the Russian and the Austrian cases show the dynamic power of World War I to alter the map and the reality of European life. Whatever the intentions of the statesmen and generals, the course of the conflict and the strains it imposed on European life upended much of the old political order.

A witness to this grim new world was the Austrian writer Stefan Zweig. In the winter of 1918–1919, he returned to his home in Salzburg to face the fact that his former country, the old Austro–Hungarian Empire, had ceased to exist, that he now lived in the midst of mass hunger and poverty, and that Salzburg was now located in a shrunken, newly created Austrian state, a small German-speaking republic centered around the immense old imperial capital of Vienna.

Zweig shared an experience common to millions of Europeans. They returned from the battlefield or from foreign exile to find the political world they had known permanently obliterated. In the same way that the war had demanded the lives and health of so many fighting men, so also had it made casualties of entire systems of government. For the Russian soldier returning to find tsarism replaced by communism, for the Bosnian soldier returning to learn he was a citizen of the heretofore unknown country of Yugoslavia, and for Zweig returning to a weak, poverty-stricken Austria, the war had created a new political world.

NOTES

1. Quoted in W. Bruce Lincoln, *Passage Through Armageddon: The Russians in War and Revolution, 1914–1918* (New York: Oxford University Press, 1994), p. 336.

2. Hugh Seton-Watson, *The Russian Empire, 1801–1917* (Oxford: Clarendon Press, 1967), p. 547.

3. Quoted in ibid., pp. 548–49.

4. Quoted in W. Bruce Lincoln, *In War's Dark Shadow: The Russians Before the Great War* (New York: Oxford University Press, 1983), p. 278.

5. Ibid., p. 121.

6. Quoted in Lincoln, *Passage Through Armageddon*, p. 156.

7. Quoted in John M. Thompson, *A Vision Unfulfilled: Russia and the Soviet Union in the Twentieth Century* (Lexington, Mass.: D. C. Heath, 1996), p. 113.

8. Lincoln, *Passage Through Armageddon*, p. 315.

9. W. Bruce Lincoln, *The Romanovs: Autocrats of All the Russias* (New York: Dial Press, 1981), p. 718.

10. C. A. Macartney, *The Habsburg Empire, 1790–1918* (New York: Macmillan, 1969), p. 804.

11. Ibid., pp. 755–57.

12. Arthur J. May, *The Passing of the Hapsburg Monarchy, 1914–1918*, 2 vols. (Philadelphia: University of Pennsylvania Press, 1966), vol. 1, pp. 425–26.

13. Edward Crankshaw, *The Fall of the House of Habsburg* (New York: Viking Press, 1963), p. 408.

14. Ibid., p. 412.

15. Gunther E. Rothenberg, "The Habsburg Army in the First World War," in Robert A. Kann, Belá K. Király, and Paula S. Fichner, eds., *The Habsburg Empire in World War I* (Boulder, Colo.: East European Quarterly, 1977), pp. 74–75.

16. Z.A.B. Zeman, *The Break-up of the Habsburg Empire, 1914–1918: A Study in National and Social Revolution* (London: Oxford University Press, 1961), pp. 140–41.

17. Rothenberg, "Hapsburg Army," pp. 81–82.

18. Crankshaw, *Fall of the House of Habsburg*, p. 413.

19. Quoted in Zeman, *Break-up of the Habsburg Empire*, p. 178.

20. Macartney, *Habsburg Empire*, pp. 818, 824.

21. Ibid., p. 830.

22. Quoted in Victor S. Mamatey, *The United States and East Central Europe, 1914–1918: A Study in Wilsonian Diplomacy and Propaganda* (Princeton: Princeton University Press, 1957), p. 261.

23. Quoted in ibid., p. 302.

7

Consequences of the War: A Contemporary Perspective

On the eightieth anniversary of the Battle of the Somme, Clarrie Jarman, aged 100, was able to recall for the benefit of the *Times* of London his brief part in the events of July 1, 1916. Then a young private in the Queen's Royal West Surrey Regiment, Jarman rose out of his trench at 7:30 A.M. and was hit by enemy fire almost immediately. After suffering for fourteen hours where he lay, the young man was carried off by his army's Medical Corps; a few days later, Jarman's leg was amputated. The elderly Englishman is one of the dwindling set of former combatants alive to remember the war and their role in it. Martin Middlebrook's feat in interviewing over 500 veterans of the battle for his splendid 1972 book *The First Day on the Somme* can no longer be repeated; the men with firsthand experience of the war have mostly vanished from our midst.

But others, who were not a part of the war, have taken pains to remember it in a symbolic way. On September 22, 1984, for example, President François Mitterand of France and Prime Minister Helmut Kohl of West Germany together visited the battlefield of Verdun. Their purpose was to emphasize how their two nations have since put aside the old hatreds that showed themselves with such force at Verdun—and again between 1939 and 1945. Kohl took care to see one part of the battlefield where his father fought.

As Jarman, Mitterand, and Kohl show, those who lived through the slaughter between 1914 and 1918 and survived to old age, as well as their descendants, have inhabited a century marked by World War I. In international relations and domestic politics, in intellectual life and in science and economics, understanding the course of events in the past eight decades must begin with an understanding of the war and its impact. Even as the last few veterans die off, the war's force continues to be felt in many ways.

HISTORIANS' RETROSPECTIVE

Some historians, among them George Kennan, see the war as the source from which flowed all of the violent calamities of the twentieth century. It helped produce the Russian Revolution and the prolonged separation of the greatest power in eastern Europe from the rest of the continent. It embittered the German people, opening the way for Adolf Hitler's rise to power and thus making World War II virtually inevitable. It shattered the political and economic stability of eastern Europe, creating a battleground for both the Nazi regime of Hitler and the Communist dictatorship of Joseph Stalin.[1] Economic historian Patrick O'Brien adds the quieter but likewise painful consequence of chaos in the world's markets and stagnation or decline in the prosperity of nations. "The war and its aftermath," he notes, "seriously disrupted a highly successful liberal international order that took about three decades to put together again."[2] John Steele Gordon puts the same catastrophic story in a larger scheme. He calls the war one of the great discontinuities in world history, devastating European culture and destroying any sense of confidence in the future. It split the eras before and after it in a way comparable only to such sweeping calamities as "the volcanic explosion that destroyed Minoan civilization on the island of Crete about 1500 B.C. or the sudden arrival of the conquistadors in the New World three thousand years later."[3]

To that doleful list, Arthur Marwick has added another large element. For decades after the Armistice, the war "bulked large in everyone's minds as the inescapable *universal analogue*. The war provided both precept and practice."[4] Thus, not only fascists and communists used the lessons the war taught about how entire countries could be reorganized in time of real or ostensible emergency. Democratic governments could tap the same vein of experience in crises like the Great Depression of the 1930s.

THE WAR'S COST

The immediately destructive impact of the conflict is easily recounted. The war cost an estimated 10 million lives and produced another 20 million or so crippled or seriously wounded. Not physically hurt but scarred nonetheless were 5 million widowed women, 9 million orphaned children, and 10 million individuals torn from their homes to become refugees.[5] The four great prewar empires present on the European continent—the German, the Russian, the Austro-Hungarian, and the Ottoman—had all been destroyed. Millions of men were demobilized and sent back home to make their way as best they could in a Europe whose old patterns of life had been shaken and sometimes completely destroyed. The losers were penalized, and the victors rewarded themselves.

THE PEACE SETTLEMENT

The peace settlement left a sad weight on Europe. The war ended formally with a series of peace treaties among the victorious Allies and Germany, Austria, Bulgaria, and Turkey. Of these agreements, the most significant and the most controversial was the Treaty of Versailles, which German representatives signed on June 28, 1919. The terms of the treaty came as a harsh shock to many Germans who had hoped the influence of President Woodrow Wilson would help bring about a lenient settlement. Among a host of onerous provisions, Germany had to limit its army to 100,000 men, give up its colonial possessions, permit the Rhineland to be occupied for fifteen years, and accept the obligation to pay reparations to countries on the winning side. The exact sum due for reparations debt was to be settled only in the future, but it was certain to be a heavy burden on the prospects for Germany's economic recovery. Moreover, Article 231 of the treaty compelled Germany and its allies to accept full responsibility for the outbreak of the war. The German government, led by Prime Minister Philipp Scheidemann, indicated at first that it would not sign the treaty, but signing was unavoidable if Germany was to survive as a unified country.

By the close of 1919, the English economist John Maynard Keynes prophesied in *The Economic Consequences of the Peace* that placing of heavy reparations on Germany would block the entire continent from enjoying a prosperous future. And Adolf Hitler, the most talented demagogue of the nationalist right in Germany, would soon rail against the treaty as a horror perpetrated by vicious foreigners against the German people and accepted by German leaders who were nothing more than traitors and criminals.

The peace settlement produced a permanent international organization, the League of Nations. Woodrow Wilson enthusiastically promoted the idea of such a body at the peace conference, and the Covenant of the League was inserted into the Treaty of Versailles. The organization's membership consisted of the victorious nations who signed the treaty and neutral countries whom the victors invited to join. But the League of Nations lacked worldwide scope due to the refusal of the U.S. Congress to accept the treaty and the accompanying obligation for its signatories to participate in the international body. Initially, Germany and the Soviet Union were also absent from the League, since powerful members like Great Britain and France blocked their admission.

THE VICTORS' SIDE

The victors were not immune from unwelcome political change. Soon after the end of the war, the British government found itself confronting a determined movement for Irish independence. The London government faced Irishmen embittered, not only by four years of wartime inaction in response to Ireland's claim for home rule, but also by Britain's bloody repression of the 1916 Easter uprising. Open hostilities between Irish rebels and a specially formed and brutal British force—the "Black and Tans"—ordered to suppress them broke out in 1919 and stretched on for two years. In 1921, Britain gave in, granting most of Ireland self-governing status as the Irish Free State.

Both Britain and France sustained blows to the confidence of traditional governing groups. The death at the Somme in 1916 of Raymond Asquith, the son of the prime minister and broadly recognized as one of the rising young men of his generation, illustrates the caliber of future leadership lost in the conflict. As Trevor Wilson has noted, while all social groups in Britain lost large numbers of men, fighting men from the peerage, from boarding schools, and from Oxford and Cambridge universities—invariably serving as officers—were two or sometimes three times as likely to be killed in action as men from more modest backgrounds.[6] In France as well, educated members of the middle and upper middle class fell in heavily disproportionate numbers. Prime Minister Neville Chamberlain of Britain, in the appeasement era of the 1930s, expressed the implications of such losses when he asserted that the preservation of peace was essential, because European civilization itself could not survive another such calamity.

In the short run, however, the massacre of those destined by birth and education for leadership positions did not make itself felt in public affairs. Both Britain and France returned to apparent stability in the 1920s under mainly conservative governments. As historian Gordon Wright has noted: "One effect of the conflict was to reassure Frenchmen about their government system. . . . it had survived and beaten the great autocracies and had managed to turn up abler leadership than did the authoritarian regimes."[7] The deeper wounds to national stability and confidence, expressed in the title of Gabriel Marcel's 1933 play, *A Broken World*, would appear, inflamed by the Depression, in little more than a decade.[8]

Disappointment and disillusion were soon in evidence in the United States following the close of the war. For most Americans, continued involvement in Europe's political affairs seemed pure folly, and the United States quickly returned to a stance of isolationism. The fear that the United States would again be drawn into a European conflict was expressed in the neutrality legislation of the 1930s. The view that the United States could stay out of Europe's quarrels prevailed among the American public until Pearl Harbor. Even then, it took Hitler's declaration of war against the United States on December 11, 1941, to swing American public opinion behind participation in the European war.

POSTWAR INTERNATIONAL RELATIONS

International affairs moved along new paths for a substantial time after the war's conclusion. Germany, the rising power of the late nineteenth and early twentieth centuries, was reduced in size and power in the aftermath of World War I. The Treaty of Versailles ended the German overseas empire, and it restricted the size and nature of the German military system. While neighbors such as France and Poland could have armies as large and as well equipped as they wished, Germany was compelled to limit its force to 100,000 men and to renounce the era's most potent weapons, such as the submarine and the combat airplane. The surrender of the great ships of the German navy after the November 1918 Armistice, and their scuttling by their own crews at Scapa Flow on June 21, 1919, to prevent them from being transferred to British hands, ended the threat of Germany as a naval power. The territory of imperial Germany was reduced by 15 percent as it lost lands to Belgium, France, Denmark, and Poland. For the next decade and a half, countries along Germany's borders were able to breathe more easily at the sight of their mammoth neighbor reduced to second-rate military status.

THE PROBLEM OF NATIONAL MINORITIES

In accordance with Woodrow Wilson's Fourteen Points, an independent Poland emerged after the war, ending a situation dating from the partitions of Poland in the late eighteenth century that had placed the Polish people under Russian, Austrian, and Prussian (later German) rule. To fulfill Wilson's pledge that Poland have "free and secure access to the sea," the victorious powers compelled Germany to surrender an area known as the

Polish Corridor to the newly created state. This step promoted Poland's economic stability, but at the cost of embittering German public opinion and providing a potent theme for Hitler's propaganda. The Corridor not only cut East Prussia off from the rest of postwar Germany; it also meant that 1 million Germans were to be incorporated into the Polish state. In fact, hundreds of thousands chose instead to flee across the new border into Germany. The decisions of the peacemakers likewise returned Alsace-Lorraine to France, with a consequent exodus of Germans from this region.

The creation of Poland, with its substantial German minority, illustrates how difficult it was to realize the principle of national self-determination that Woodrow Wilson saw as a key to a stable and secure European order. The same explosive minority issue was also on display in Czechoslovakia. To provide that newly created country with a secure western border, Czechoslovakia received the Sudetenland, a territory with more than 3 million ethnically German inhabitants. These Germans were former subjects of the Habsburg Empire and had never lived in a united Germany, but Hitler was to make their supposed plight under foreign rule into a potent weapon for his expansionist plans in 1938. The refusal of the victorious Allies to permit the rump state of Austria to form a union with postwar Germany likewise raised the explosive issue of ethnic Germans stranded outside Germany proper.

The peace treaties violated the principle of national self-determination for numerous groups besides the Germans. For example, Rumania was rewarded for being on the winning side with vast territorial gains such as Transylvania; consequently, its population of 16 million now included 1.5 million Hungarians. The Kingdom of the Serbs, Croats, and Slovenes (soon renamed Yugoslavia), with 12 million inhabitants, likewise included some 400,000 Albanians, nearly 500,000 Hungarians, and half a million ethnic Germans. Nearly 4 million Ukrainians and more than a million White Russians found themselves, willing or not, made citizens of Poland.

REVOLUTIONARY RUSSIA AND THE NEW NATIONS OF EASTERN EUROPE

The war had equally immediate and spectacular consequences for imperial Russia. World War I led directly to revolution. Removed from the international system by the Bolshevik Revolution of November 1917, Russia (soon reshaped into the Soviet Union) was transformed for several decades into an inwardly looking country wrestling with the domestic problems of forced industrialization and the perfection of a Communist dictatorship. Under the dictatorship of Joseph Stalin, the turmoil of World War II and its aftermath allowed the Soviet Union to expand into eastern Europe. Communism, established in one country as a result of World War I, now entrenched itself in half a dozen more.

Other products of the war were the new nations of Yugoslavia and Czechoslovakia. As the fighting came to a close, a victorious Serbia with a winning army at its disposal controlled the construction of a Yugoslav (meaning "south Slav") state. The prestige of Thomas Masaryk and the leadership of other Czech intellectuals and politicians brought together Czechs and Slovaks—as well as numerous other groups—in a united Czechoslovakia. Both of those states survived the turmoil of the twentieth century to last through the 1980s. Dominated for decades by Serbs, Yugoslavia was destroyed during World War II, then reconstituted under the Communist leadership of Marshal Tito (Joseph Broz). Czechoslovakia was dismembered starting with the Munich Pact of 1938, then restored after World War II, only to find itself in the Soviet sphere.

THE DISAPPEARANCE OF THE OTTOMAN EMPIRE

The war brought the Ottoman Empire crashing down after more than five hundred years. Stretching from southeastern Europe to the Arabian peninsula, it now faced threats from within and without. Russian operations in the Caucasus in 1915 were matched by the British assault at Gallipoli and British offensives from the Persian Gulf toward Baghdad. In 1917 a revolt of the Arab population brought the war home as the entire Arabian peninsula threatened to break away from the control of Istanbul. The revolt, which included the efforts of the charismatic British leader T. E. Lawrence, was doubly dangerous because it corresponded with General Edmund Allenby's offensive through Palestine toward Damascus, and from there toward the heart of the empire.

The subsequent collapse of the Ottoman Empire, along with the West's occupation of Iran, was, in the words of historian Bernard Lewis, "the culmination of the retreat of Islam before the advancing west."[9] Under the new mandate system established by the League of Nations, Britain and France took the lion's share of the Ottoman Empire's former Arab lands, such as Syria and Iraq, as well as establishing a home for Jews in Palestine, while an independent country emerged in Saudi Arabia. The strains of World War II led to the end of direct European control of these regions, but the area has remained one of the world's principal trouble spots. The degree of stability maintained by the Ottomans has never been reestablished.

THE DECLINE OF EMPIRE

The war was a transforming force that weakened Europe's ability to maintain its Asian and African empires, and it pointed toward a new relationship between the developed and underdeveloped portions of the globe. The participation of large numbers of Indian troops in the British war effort was matched by the role that troops and laborers from French North Africa, sub-Saharan Africa, and Indochina played in France's war effort. In India, the need for that crucial part of the British Empire to cooperate with the war effort had led to significant change. In August 1917, the British made what historian Judith M. Brown called "a critical departure" by announcing that they were committed to bringing Indians into every branch of the administration and gradually developing institutions of self-government. India was not, in the reformers' view, to become independent, but rather to become similar to white portions of the empire in governing itself under the supervision of the home country. In 1919 the promised reforms got under way. Thus began "a process of adaptation which finally broke the imperial bonds tying India to Britain."[10]

The transforming forces were also at work in Africa. As Robin Hallett has put it, "Wartime service was a powerful solvent in breaking down the isolation of many African communities, while the spectacle of white men trying to kill each other served to erode the mystique of unquestioned white superiority."[11] In Egypt, a major staging ground for the Gallipoli operations in 1915 and then for General Allenby's offensive against the Ottoman Empire, the stationing of hundreds of thousands of British troops heightened prewar opposition to the British presence and led to the founding of the important Wafd nationalist party that would bid for Egyptian independence.

In the aftermath of the war, Germany's African possessions were transferred to France, Britain, and Belgium as mandates under the authority of the League of Nations. This served to put the governing role of the European powers in question in regions such as British Tanganyika (formerly German East Africa) under some international scrutiny, and they were now bound to govern these territories with a view toward their eventual independence. To the combination of a diminished Europe and colonial peoples aware of their contribution to the war effort was added Woodrow Wilson's universalist rhetoric about the self-determination of peoples. The outward form and size of the colonial empires seemed intact, but the framework in which they existed had now begun to change in a way not visible before 1914. It would take the later impact of World War II—which weakened Europe even more severely and again required the British and French governments to rely on the populations of their empires—to bring the empires down by the 1960s.

CHANGING EUROPEAN DOMESTIC POLITICS

In the world of domestic politics, the war produced long-range changes that embittered the century. Prewar Europe, for all the differences among its various countries, followed basic political norms: constitutions, growing electorates, formally established civil rights, limits on monarchical absolutism. Military dictatorship was not impossible—Italy had one in the late 1890s—but it hardly seemed likely among the Great Powers. Dictators with radical ideologies for reshaping their country's government and even society were scarcely imaginable. Napoleon III had been a crowned dictator in the mid-nineteenth century, and General Georges Boulanger had been a threat in the late 1880s, but France, like the rest of Europe in 1914, seemed no candidate for such a sharp departure from the norms of the continent.

The failure of existing forms of government to fight the war successfully or to create a prosperous postwar order opened the road to radical change in several countries. In the decades following the war, embittered populations, first in Italy, then in Germany, turned to demagogues. Adolf Hitler could never have been a serious candidate for national power in the stable and hierarchical political system of imperial Germany. Even in the most unstable circumstances of Italian politics, Benito Mussolini had no discernible route to power. The burdens and shame Germans felt the settlement of the war had placed on their nation were the principal fuel for Hitler's engine. The disappointment and frustration of many Italians—over the cost of the war and the small rewards Italy got, as well as over the surge of political and social unrest after the Armistice—opened the way for Mussolini.

Beyond the emergence of dictators one can see the war as a force coarsening and brutalizing political and social life. Ernst Jünger, a combat veteran of the war, wrote with ominous eloquence in the 1920s about the gap between the "front fighters" and those who had remained at home. Every European society now contained large numbers of men who had killed or tried to kill the enemy, and many of them, as Mussolini and Hitler knew, were willing to bring violence into domestic politics. On a larger scale, individual leaders had sent tens and even hundreds of thousands of men to their deaths in military operations during the course of the war. Mass slaughter was now a recent memory for many Europeans. The ethnic massacres of World War II such as the Jewish Holocaust—which had their model in the Turkish slaughter of

Armenians in the earlier war—seem inconceivable without this preliminary massacre of Europe's young men in uniform.

The circumstances of economic life resulting from the war heightened the opportunities for radical political leaders. In contrast to the increasingly prosperous Europe of pre-1914, the postwar world was a place of stagnating living standards and diminished hopes in most countries. The international trading system never recovered from the disaster of the war. Currencies were inflated to the point of becoming worthless—quickly in Germany after the war, more slowly but just as effectively in France. A potent image of Europe's postwar economic distress was the German worker bringing a wheelbarrow to work in order to carry away his daily pay. In the fall of 1923, at the peak of the inflation in Germany, a university student who left home with funds to cover a year's living expenses might well find, the next day, that all he could buy with this money was a beer or a postage stamp.

FADING LONG-RANGE EFFECTS

Of course, the passage of time has made some of the conflict's effects diminish—and even reverse themselves. The economic trauma of the war was renewed and intensified in World War II, but Europe's postwar economic recovery has brought back more than mere pre-1914 prosperity. In the end, however, the limits placed upon Germany did not prevail. Of course, a resurgent Germany again dominated Europe under Adolf Hitler after 1933. Its division after World War II turned out to be temporary, and since Germany's reunification in 1990, Europe again finds itself facing a German state, albeit one free of military aggressiveness, dominant through its population of 80 million and its economic skills. Thus, World War I served as one of two checks—but only temporary ones—to Germany's ascendance during the century. In Russia, too, as seen from the late twentieth century, the shaping force of World War I seems to be giving way to larger realities. The collapse of the Soviet Union and the end of Russian communism in 1991 have created a new Russia whose future remains uncertain. Russia seems on its way to rejoining the European community, at least to the degree it had belonged before 1914. Its historic economic backwardness and ethnic divisions—as well as its role as a magnet for foreign capital and entrepreneurs—seem to be reasserting themselves.

The force of nationalism—reminiscent of the pre-1914 era—has brought an end to two nations that were products of World War I. The peaceful dissolution of Czechoslovakia into separate Czech and Slovak republics is one example. The bloody and traumatic collapse of Yugoslavia is another, returning this part of Europe to the pattern of fragmentation that dominated the Balkans before 1914.

In the non-Western world, the preeminence of the industrialized countries of the Atlantic Rim remains, if not completely, then generally intact as the century moves toward its conclusion. The bulk of the African continent remains economically dependent to a degree that impinges on its political autonomy. Political freedom for India has likewise not been matched by enough economic success to shatter the pattern that existed before 1914. The great economic success story in the non-Western world, with attendant political ramifications, has been the ascendancy of Japan. That development harkens back to the start of the twentieth century.

In the end, the dictatorships did not prevail, although it took World War II to block them effectively. Seen from the century's close, most of Europe is once again on the same path—with the same basic norms of democratic politics and free market economies in the regions north of former Yugoslavia and west of Russia.

THE WORLD OF IDEAS AND THE ARTS

Changes in the world of the intellect are harder to measure. The sense of doom, of being wounded, of living in a diminished, irrational, and dangerous world penetrated the circles of Europe's artists and writers. As Raymond Sontag put it, "Among intellectuals and artists in France and throughout western Europe, no less than in defeated Germany and in the fragments of the Austrian empire, there was recognition that the Europe of earlier centuries was broken, possibly beyond repair."[12] Artistic movements like the dadaists and surrealists pointed to the meaninglessness of the world around them and the need to flout old social conventions. Memoirs and novels such as Robert Graves's *Goodbye to All That* (1929) and Erich Maria Remarque's *All Quiet on the Western Front* (1929) pointed to the senseless horror of the war and the equally senseless sacrifices the young men of Europe had made. The American writer Ernest Hemingway presented his recollections of the war on the Italian front with equal bitterness in *A Farewell to Arms*, also published in 1929. Numerous European and American artists and writers echoed those themes.

But the lasting impact of the war on the world of intellectuals and artists is elusive. Figures like Hemingway and the French writer-adventurer André Malraux, for example, committed themselves to the new political challenge of fighting fascism, first in the Spanish Civil War, then in World War II. Sometimes, as in the case of Malraux, communism for a time provided a political compass for renewed and meaningful activity. The participation of writers like J. B. Priestley—for many Britons the voice of their country along with Winston Churchill between 1940 and 1945—in the great effort of World War II shows the lessened alienation as the distance from 1918 grew.

In the visual arts, the war had a traumatic and lasting effect on German artists like Käthe Kollwitz and Otto Dix. Already a critic of social injustice in her work before 1914, Kollwitz became a committed pacifist in response to the carnage that cost the life of her younger son Peter in Belgium in 1914. She expressed her ongoing grief in a sculptured memorial entitled *The Parents*, placed at the cemetery in Roggevelde, Belgium, in 1932. Dix, who served for four years on both the eastern and western fronts, made the war and its human cost a central motif of his painting for decades after the Armistice. The burden the war placed on him, visible in *Self Portrait as Mars* (1915) and *Star Shells* (1917), was still in evidence in paintings like *Trench Warfare* in 1932.

But the revolutionary developments in modern art—such as expressionism and cubism—had appeared before the war, and giants of the art world such as Pablo Picasso and Henri Matisse had already done their most imaginative work. Thus, historians of art such as Hugh Honour and John Fleming see the war as an event "cutting short a great outburst of creative genius in the late nineteenth and early twentieth centuries." Matisse abandoned the forceful painting of his prewar work for a more refined style, while Picasso threw his talents into a variety of different styles. The war had been a cultural calamity, and "western civilization has never recovered from it."[13] Thus, the war may have stifled the great artistic innovations in prospect; certainly, it redirected artistic energy and vision.

THE WAR AND SCIENCE

The war brought together the power of science and industry and the power of government as never before. The personification of this union was Fritz Haber, the German chemist.[14] By synthesizing nitrogen before the war, Haber made it possible for Germany to produce munitions even when the Allied blockade cut it off from the outside world. His seminal act, however, was to convince the German government and military of the uses of poison gas, then to supervise its application on the western front.

In all, between 1914 and 1918, governments called on their scientists and inventors for new discoveries and on their industrialists for new feats of production. The war was the seed ground for the weapons of the future. Great Britain, for example, put the world's first aircraft carrier into the water in time for the Battle of Jutland in 1916. In several countries, including Germany and the United States, the airplane went from the primitive, barely armed models of 1914 to sophisticated, long-range types available in time for the final years of combat. The growing use of tanks by the Americans, British, and French in the final offensive of 1918 likewise began to open a new era in armed conflict. Soon after the war's end, devices first invented or first widely used in wartime found vast application in the civilian world. Radio became first a basic tool for warring armies, then, after 1918, a common conveyor of news and entertainment in middle-class homes. In June 1919, Captain John Brown of Britain's Royal Air Force (RAF) and a fellow officer made the first successful flight across the Atlantic. Their trip from Newfoundland to Ireland opened the way for long-range commercial aviation. The scientist in government employ or under government contract, active in the development of weaponry, remains a living legacy of the war.

At the close of the century, the immense destructive capacity of modern weapons, which first became fully evident in World War I, remains a factor in international life. Nonetheless, the ultimate destructive tool of war, nuclear weapons (which came out of the World War II experience), has not been employed for the past five decades, though Iraq's use of chemical weapons in the Iran-Iraq war in the 1980s and the threat of biological and chemical weapons use during the Persian Gulf War in 1990 and after recalls the extremes, and horrors, of World War I. The World War I era's readiness to resort to whatever weaponry existed or could be conjured up has not continued to its logical conclusion. The horror and the irrationality of launching nuclear salvos has so far restrained the international powers that have such weapons at hand. As in other areas, the trajectory of events set in motion by the war has gone forward in a twisted and unpredictable fashion.

NOTES

1. George Kennan, *At a Century's Ending: Reflections, 1982–1995* (New York: W. W. Norton, 1996), pp. 17–22, 141–42.

2. Patrick O'Brian, "The Economic Effects of the Great War," *History Today* 44 (December 1994): 29.

3. John Steele Gordon, "What We Lost in the Great War," *American Heritage*, July–August 1992, 82.

4. Arthur Marwick, *War and Social Change in the Twentieth Century: A Comparative Study of Britain, France, Germany, Russia and the United States* (New York: St. Martin's Press, 1974), p. 2.

5. Ibid.

6. Trevor Wilson, *The Myriad Faces of War: Britain and the Great War, 1914–1918* (Cambridge: Polity Press, 1986), pp. 752, 758–59.

7. Gordon Wright, *France in Modern Times: From the Enlightenment to the Present*, 3rd ed. (New York: W. W. Norton, 1981), pp. 322–23.

8. On *A Broken World*, see William Langer's book of the same title, *A Broken World, 1919–1939* (New York: Harper and Row, 1971), p. xv.

9. Bernard Lewis, *The Middle East: A Brief Survey of the Last 2,000 Years* (New York: Scribner, 1995), p. 341.

10. Judith Brown, "War and the Colonial Relationship: Britain, India and the War of 1914–1918" in M.R.D. Foot, ed., *War and Society: History Essays in Honor and Memory of J. R. Western, 1928–1971* (New York: Harper and Row, 1973), pp. 85, 106.

11. Robin Hallett, *Africa since 1875: A Modern History* (Ann Arbor: University of Michigan Press, 1974), p. 58.

12. Sontag, *Broken World*, p. 223.

13. Hugh Honour and John Fleming, *The Visual Arts: A History*, 4th ed. (New York: Harry N. Abrams, 1995), p. 745.

14. On Haber's immense role in the war, see M. F. Perutz, "The Cabinet of Dr. Haber," *New York Review of Books*, June 20, 1996, pp. 31–36.

Biographies: The Personalities Behind the War

Theobald von Bethmann Hollweg (1856–1921)

Theobald von Bethmann Hollweg was the prime minister of Germany from 1909 to the middle of 1917. He was the major civilian official empowered to deal with German foreign policy and the conduct of the war. His freedom of action was restricted, however, by the predominant role Emperor Wilhelm II played in the German political system. Similarly, the leaders of the military establishment had extraordinary influence. Bethmann's responsibility for the start of World War I has been a highly controversial question. Of course, other powerful figures such as the country's military commanders stood at the top of the system. If Bethmann, the civilian leader, deliberately helped to bring on the war, the taint of waging aggressive war can scarcely be placed on the military alone. Historians once saw Bethmann as a German moderate with good intentions tragically carried along by the fanaticism of military leaders and the kaiser. A newer trend in scholarship sees him as a prime mover in bringing Germany into the war.

Bethmann was born November 29, 1856, at Hohenfinow. He was the son of a Prussian landowner who also held local political office. Educated as a lawyer, the future prime minister served with distinction in the Prussian government until 1907. At that point, he took a leading role in the German imperial government as well, becoming minister of the interior and deputy prime minister. In 1909 he took over as prime minister.

Bethmann's bland personality and his mixture of policies have made him difficult to characterize. He tried in vain to halt the naval competition between Germany and Great Britain, but he also expressed concern about the danger posed by Serb nationalism to Austria-Hungary, Germany's chief ally. Similarly, he was bedeviled by the apparent increase in Russian military power on the eve of World War I.

In the July crisis of 1914, Bethmann quickly followed the lead of Emperor Wilhelm II in backing Austrian plans to punish Serbia for the assassination of Archduke Franz Ferdinand. Most historians now reject the view that the kaiser and the military leaders took an aggressive stance and thus dragged an unwilling prime minister along a path that led to war. Instead, Bethmann himself encouraged Austria to act vigorously against Serbia; otherwise, he feared, Austria might feel forced to turn away from its alliance with Germany. Thus, he used German influence to promote a war in the Balkans, and he accepted the possibility of a much larger conflict involving all the Great Powers. Bethmann's most vocal critics have claimed that he intended from early July onward to go much further in exploiting the crisis brought on by the assassination. In this view, his intentions included crushing Serbia, humiliating Russia, and establishing German domination in Europe.

Once the conflict had broken out, Bethmann more clearly followed a policy of moderation. He sought to limit the wilder plans of nationalist groups that advocated annexation of huge chunks of territory after Germany had won the war with a decisive military victory. He preferred a reorganized Europe in which Germany would quietly dominate a group of political and economic satellite states like Belgium and Poland. The prime minister also opposed the policy of unlimited submarine warfare against merchant shipping. In his eyes, such aggressive actions were certain to pull the United States into the war.

Bethmann was less perceptive when it came to choosing among military leaders. He was appalled by the failure of General Erich von Falkenhayn, the army chief of staff, to win a decisive victory at Verdun, and he promoted the idea of bringing in Paul von Hindenburg and Erich Ludendorff, the successful generals from the eastern front, to take over the high command. He hoped that their prestige would facilitate the search for a compromise peace. Instead, the arrival of the eastern generals in Berlin in fall 1916 quickly eroded Bethmann's position.

Facing Hindenburg and Ludendorff, the prime minister found it impossible to take advantage of American efforts to get a compromise peace in late 1916. The military leaders blocked such possibilities by insisting on keeping Belgium in any peace settlement. And Bethmann had to give way to the military's demands for the unrestricted use of submarines starting in early 1917. Nonetheless, Germany's highest military leaders became increasingly uncomfortable with a prime minister they could not control completely. Under pressure from the military chieftains, he fell from office in mid-1917.

Bethmann spent the remainder of his life at Hohenfinow writing his memoirs. He died at his ancestral home on January 1, 1921.

Alexis Brusilov (1853–1926)

General Alexis Brusilov was the outstanding military commander in the Russian army during World War I. Brusilov's successful offensive against the Austrians in spring and summer 1916 showed that effectively trained and well-led Russian forces could win important victories. By the time Brusilov became commander-in-chief of the army, in June 1917, his undeniable talents were no longer able to affect the course of events.

Alexis Brusilov was born on August 31, 1853, in Tiflis. He followed in the footsteps of his father, a Russian general of aristocratic lineage, by entering the army in 1872. His career centered in the cavalry, and he rose steadily. Brusilov fought with distinction in the Russo-Turkish War in 1877–1878 and subsequently commanded the Officers Cavalry School. He became a major general in 1902. In the years before the outbreak of the war, he rose to command a succession of army corps in the strategically crucial Polish portion of the Russian Empire.

The talented and aggressive officer conducted a fighting retreat at the head of the Eighth Army as German forces pushed the Russians from Poland in the summer of 1915. The following spring he took charge of the Russian army's southwestern front. This placed him in command of a group of four armies containing 600,000 men.

For the bulk of the war, however, the overall command of the army was in the unimaginative hands of Mikhail Alekseev. Alekseev was a competent military manager who rebuilt the army after its disastrous retreat from Poland in 1915. Nonetheless, his most notable policy was to allow Russian offensive operations to conform to the needs of his country's allies. Alekseev had agreed to an Allied plan for Russian participation in a general and coordinated offensive on the eastern and western fronts in 1916. Brusilov threw himself into preparing for the part his armies would play. Pondering the problem of breaking the enemy's defenses, he developed plans for surprise assaults at widely separate points on his front. But events in the spring altered the overall plan. The Austrian assault in the Trentino on the Italian front created an emergency in the Allied camp. Russia's partners in the war asked for quick action on the eastern front. Only Brusilov's forces were ready to advance so early in the year.

The armies of the southwestern front achieved a rare success for Russian troops; Brusilov's preparation and leadership made the difference. He carefully concealed the troops with which he prepared to attack. Widely separated but well-coordinated assaults broke the Austrian lines at several points in early June. Russian infantry and artillery now cooperated in an effective fashion unseen so far in the war. As Russian forces advanced over the course of the summer, Brusilov's successes diminished German pressure at Verdun and the Somme and hindered the Austrian effort in Italy. The influence of a sweeping Russian advance in eastern Europe propelled neutral Rumania into the war on the Allied side.

But Brusilov failed to get a full-scale Russian effort including other fronts that might have produced more extensive advances. Alekseev, ineffectual as usual, proved unable to get generals commanding fronts near Brusilov's neighbors to launch supporting offensives. Equally important, the Germans came to the rescue of their less skilled Austrian allies. The Russian offensive ended in September. Nonetheless, Brusilov's reputation was assured.

Following the Revolution of March 1917, Brusilov, like the other ranking leaders of the army, abandoned his loyalty to the monarchy and accepted the authority of the Provisional Government. Brusilov took over as commander-in-chief from Alekseev in June, but had only a brief time in office. Largely due to the overall disintegration of the army, the July offensive ordered by Minister of War Alexander Kerensky could not repeat the success of the previous year. Brusilov went into retirement. The aging cavalryman had a final moment of prominence. The civil war following the Bolshevik Revolution of November 1917 opened the way for a Polish invasion in spring 1920. Brusilov, a product of the prerevolutionary army, nevertheless offered his services to the Communists. He saw no combat, but his gesture was an important symbol showing how some traditional military leaders were willing to make their peace with the Russia of V. I. Lenin and Leon Trotsky.

Brusilov died in Moscow on March 17, 1926.

Georges Clemenceau (1841–1929)

Georges Clemenceau was the premier (prime minister) in the French government during the final twelve months of World War I. He stands as his country's most significant political leader during the hostilities, and he played an important role at the ensuing Versailles peace conference. In the first three years of the war, Clemenceau seized the opportunity to become the most vocal critic of France's leadership, both political and military. Once in office, he energized the war effort and committed his country to remaining in the conflict until victory. At the peace negotiations, he promoted the insertion of provisions into the Treaty of Versailles designed to prevent the revival of a powerful Germany.

Clemenceau was born on September 28, 1841, in Mouilleron-en-Pared, a small village in the Vendée region. He was the son of a prosperous landowner and physician. Educated as a physician himself, he entered politics during the Franco-Prussian War. His career in the French parliament began in 1876. Thereafter, Clemenceau was a prominent figure in French public life during the four decades prior to World War I. He rose to cabinet rank (as minister of the interior) in 1906, and he then served as premier from 1906 to 1909. A ferocious debater and an influential writer, Clemenceau was also a feared duelist. "The Tiger," as he was commonly known, promoted building up French military strength in the prewar period, advancing his views both as a member of the Senate and also as editor of his own newspaper, *L'Homme libre*.

The aged political leader (he was nearly seventy-three when hostilities began) rejected a minor post in René Viviani's wartime government. He openly declared that he would serve only as premier or as France's minister of war. He used his position as a member of the Senate to castigate both the military high command and France's succession of weak governments from 1914 to late 1917. Secret sessions of the parliament devoted to the conduct of the war gave him a prominent stage from which to launch his views.

Clemenceau began his criticism of the war effort by attacking the inadequacy of the military's medical services. He had been appalled to see wounded men from the war's first battles left untreated on a railroad train. He went on to deplore the terrible cost of General Joseph Joffre's offensives in Artois and Champagne, as well as the shift of troops from the western front to Salonika in 1915. He was equally vocal in attacking Joffre's high command for conducting the war without accepting effective government supervision. The military often refused, for example, to permit parliamentarians even to visit the front. Withal, Clemenceau did not offer any substantial alternatives to the general way in which the war was being managed.

Clemenceau's rise to power came in the grim circumstances of 1917. Russia's withdrawal from the war following the March Revolution threatened to end the entire conflict on the eastern front. Thus, by the winter of 1917–1918, Germany was gathering its forces for a climactic offensive in the west. The radical turn in Russian politics pushed French Socialists to end their support for their country's wartime government. Added to these woes was General Robert Nivelle's calamitous spring offensive, which sparked a mutiny throughout much of the French army. Meanwhile, Minister of the Interior Louis Malvy and other figures in the government were promoting a defeatist stand toward the war effort.

Clemenceau, who led the government starting on November 6, 1917, took firm control over this perilous scene. He immediately declared his policy in simple and direct terms: "I wage war." And he set out to keep France fighting, regardless of the cost, until the enemy finally collapsed. Clemenceau appointed a cabinet of talented and energetic technicians such as Louis Loucheur, the minister of munitions. The post of minister of war he kept for himself. As the dominant figure in the government, Clemenceau ended squabbling in the cabinet, brought the military high command under firm control, and kept labor unrest at manageable levels.

Clemenceau understood that the French population, which had suffered immensely since 1914, was willing to fight on. Thus, his indictment of figures like Malvy, his suppression of pacifist propaganda, and his support for fighting generals like Ferdinand Foch won popular approval. The Socialist party, which had now abandoned the wartime coalition, failed decisively when it tried to overthrow Clemenceau. He won votes of confidence from the Chamber of Deputies by overwhelming margins.

The fiery French leader backed the appointment of General Ferdinand Foch as supreme Allied commander when the German spring offensive threatened to drive a wedge between the French and British armies. In June, as the final thrust in Ludendorff's series of offensives brought the Germans perilously close to Paris, Clemenceau continued to support Foch. He found his judgment confirmed by the successful Allied counterattack against the Marne salient in July. Thereafter, Clemenceau left the military conduct of the war to the generals until the Armistice was signed. Although seriously ill, he visited the front regularly; often he placed himself close to the fighting.

Among the national leaders at the peace conference, Clemenceau emerged as the foremost advocate of imposing a harsh settlement on Germany. He rejected the extreme demands set forth by Foch, such as severing the entire Rhineland from Germany. But the French premier won important concessions from President Woodrow Wilson and Prime Minister David Lloyd George designed to maintain German weakness. These included placing a huge reparations burden on the defeated enemy, limiting the size of Germany's armed forces, and establishing a long-term Allied occupation of the Rhineland.

Clemenceau did not live to see Germany shake off the restrictions he had placed on his country's historic enemy. He retired from public life in 1920 and died in Paris on November 24, 1929.

Franz Conrad von Hotzendörf (1852–1925)

Conrad was chief of the Austrian general staff from 1906 to the spring of 1917 and the most important military leader on the Austro-Hungarian side during World War I. He occupies a notable place in the history of the conflict for three principal reasons. First, he was the only supreme military leader to occupy such a position for almost a decade before the war, then to lead his country's armed forces for most of the wartime period.

Second, Conrad stands as the epitome of the bellicose military leader, pressing for a preventive war before 1914 (and exercising a major influence in the summer crisis that led to the outbreak of hostilities). Third, Conrad's paradoxical position during the war, formally independent as the Austrian military commander but in fact a subordinate under Germany's leaders, illustrates how Austria-Hungary itself came under the sway of its powerful coalition partner. Some historians add a final note of distinction for Conrad. They praise him as the most skilled and imaginative strategist on either side. But his actual record during World War I lends little support for such praise.

Conrad was the scion of a military family, his father having been a colonel in the Austrian army. He was born on November 11, 1852, in the Austrian town of Penzing, outside Vienna. He became an army lieutenant in 1871, distinguished himself as a staff officer, then taught with notable success at the War Academy, reaching the rank of brigadier general in 1899. A personal tie with Archduke Franz Ferdinand combined with his sterling reputation in the army to elevate him to chief of the general staff in 1906.

As the leader of the Dual Empire's army, Conrad became a modernizer, albeit one hindered by the scant resources the governments of Austria and, especially, Hungary would give to the national force. He also made a name for himself as a military hothead. Since the Dual Empire faced three dangerous enemies in Russia, Serbia, and Italy, Conrad saw the salvation of the Habsburg state depending upon preventive wars. His call for waging such a war against Italy in 1911, when the Italians were bogged down in hostilities against Ottoman Turkey, led to dismissal from his post. He was restored to his position of supreme commander in late 1912. The First Balkan War had led to an expansion of the kingdom of Serbia; with Russia mobilizing to support the Serbs, Emperor Franz Joseph needed his most renowned general as chief of staff.

Conrad remained obsessed by the mortal danger Serbia posed for the Dual Monarchy. Throughout the last year and a half of peace, he urged preventive war against this enemy along his country's southern border. Thus, the Austrian firebrand saw Franz Ferdinand's assassination as an opportunity to settle things with Serbia. He helped stoke the fires of the July crisis of 1914 by urging immediate mobilization and an attack on the Dual Empire's dangerous Balkan neighbor. If Austria-Hungary failed to act quickly and decisively, Conrad expected its prestige in southeastern Europe, as well as its status as one of the continent's Great Powers, to collapse.

Once war had begun, Conrad failed to coordinate the fighting on Austria's two battlefronts, shifting his twelve-division reserve first toward Serbia, then reversing course and ordering it to meet the Russians. In the end, most of these troops played no role in the first weeks' fighting. The weak Austro-Hungarian force facing Serbia under General Oscar Potiorek was defeated when it took the offensive southward. Meanwhile, the armies under Conrad's direct command faced the Russians and also tried an offensive. Their failure permitted a Russian attack to reach the Carpathian Mountains, thereby threatening an advance into the Hungarian plain in the spring of 1915.

Conrad claimed credit for the Austro-German attack at Gorlice-Tarnow in May 1915 that forestalled the danger to Hungary. Nonetheless, other generals such as Germany's Erich von Falkenhayn had an equally good claim to be the father of the concept. In the full flood of success, the offensive then drove the Russians from the entire western portion of their empire by September. In the months following, Austro-German forces, linked to an offensive by the Bulgarians, drove the Serbian army from its home territory and permitted the Central Powers to dominate the Balkans. In both cases, despite a paper arrangement that gave Conrad the role of overall commander, the Austrian general found himself under the effective command of German leaders. It was their forces that provided the offensive striking power that brought victory, and their generals, such as August von Mackensen and Hans von Seeckt, his brilliant chief of staff, who actually directed operations.

Conrad's status and Austria-Hungary's role took a climactic fall in the summer of 1916. The Austrian commander launched an attack on the Trentino front against the Italians. Fighting without German units to add hitting power to his forces, he found he could not break through the enemy's defenses even after a month's effort. Meanwhile, a Russian offensive under General Alexis Brusilov struck Austro-Hungarian positions on the eastern front. It succeeded for several weeks, aided by the fact that Conrad had pulled a large number of troops away for use in Italy. Once again, German forces had to play the role of firemen to save Austria's house. The humiliation was compounded at summer's end. Rumania entered the war on August 27 and launched an assault across the border of the Dual Empire into Transylvania. This new enemy was brought under control, as usual, by the efforts of German field armies.

The death of Emperor Franz Joseph in November 1916 led to the end of Conrad's long run as chief of staff. Emperor Charles removed him from his post on March 1, 1917. Conrad managed to obtain command of an army group on the Italian front, but his major offensive there in the spring and summer of 1918 failed. Charles now dismissed him from high command for good in mid-July. The Austrian leader died in Germany on August 25, 1925.

Erich von Falkenhayn (1861–1922)

Erich von Falkenhayn was the commander of the German army from September 1914 through August 1916. His role in World War I involved constant friction with his ostensible subordinates on the eastern front, Paul von Hindenburg and Erich Ludendorff. Falkenhayn's most fateful measure was his 1916 attack at Verdun. There he tried to compel the French to fight a battle so costly and prolonged that it would destroy France's ability to continue the war. Falkenhayn's failure led to the rise of the eastern generals, of whom Ludendorff was the dominant figure, to replace him.

The future German commander was born on September 11, 1861, near Thorn. He was the son of an impoverished Junker (i.e., noble) family with long-standing ties to the military. He became an officer in 1880, served on the General Staff, and commanded some of the European troops who put down the Boxer Rebellion in China in 1900. He rose to the rank of major general in 1912 at the age of fifty-one. A favorite of Kaiser Wilhelm II, he took the post of minister of war in the Prussian government in 1913. Helmuth von Moltke's emotional disintegration in August and September 1914 during the failed German offensive against France opened the way for Falkenhayn. Despite the doubts of many colleagues about Falkenhayn's grit and determination, the kaiser chose him to take over from Moltke. He also remained minister of war until early in 1915.

Falkenhayn was one of the few military leaders to accept early on in the conflict that no quick victory was possible. One of his first decisions indicated some optimism, however. He launched a series of bloody attacks at Ypres, hoping to capture the enemy's strategic ports along the English Channel. Success here might have put Germany in an unbeatable position vis-à-vis the French and British. But the resulting failure sharpened his basic pessimism, and he came to believe that the best Germany could do was to obtain a favorable, negotiated peace settlement.

But Falkenhayn shared one view held by many leaders on both sides: the western front was the crucial area of fighting. Thus, he clashed with the eastern generals as they called for heavy reinforcements and promised a decisive victory against Russia. Falkenhayn preferred limited offensives in the east while searching for a separate peace with Russia. When Russia had left the war, he expected German victories on the western front to compel Britain and France into accepting a negotiated settlement tolerable for Germany.

In 1915 Falkenhayn won a trio of successes. Using his reserves sparingly, he oversaw grand stategy and saw German forces sweep the Russians out of their Polish possessions, then overrun Serbia, all the time holding fast on the western front against attacks in Artois and Champagne. Nonetheless, nothing Falkenhayn did in 1915 brought decisive victory, and a successful end of the war still seemed distant. He now turned to Verdun and struck there in February 1916.

The goal at Verdun was not to take the famous French fortress. Rather, Falkenhayn wished the French to fight a prolonged battle in the awkward bulge that Verdun made in the front. In such an encounter, he hoped to inflict intolerable losses on the French, to force them to leave the war, and thus to bring about the collapse of the anti-German coalition. But the French, led by General Philippe Pétain, mustered the skill and fortitude to fight a successful defensive battle at Verdun. German losses approached those of the enemy, and the singleminded emphasis on Verdun left the Central Powers vulnerable elsewhere. General Alexis Brusilov led a spectacular three-month-long advance on the eastern front in the summer of 1916. This helped draw Rumania into the war on the side of Germany's enemies. Meanwhile, German resources were stretched to the limit by the British offensive at the Somme. Bombarded by criticism of Falkenhayn from the eastern generals, the kaiser removed him in late August 1916.

Falkenhayn held a variety of high-level commands during the remainder of the war. His greatest success came in leading a field army in the German assault on Rumania shortly after he lost his position as commander-in-chief. The invasion of Rumania was a textbook example of successful offensive action, similar to the campaigns of World War II but rare in World War I. Falkenhayn proved himself a first-rate field commander. Thereafter he served with German troops supporting the Turks in Palestine, and in the spring of 1918 took command of a field army in Lithuania.

Falkenhayn retired from the army in 1919. He died on April 8, 1922.

Ferdinand Foch (1851–1929)

General Ferdinand Foch was the supreme Allied commander on the western front during 1918. He was elevated to this position in April to meet the dire threat of Ludendorff's climactic spring offensive. Foch coordinated the effective defensive moves by the British and French armies, then, with American troops joining the fray, moved to the offensive in the summer and fall. He proved capable of discarding his prewar attraction for bold offensive operations in favor of the systematic advances that brought victory in 1918. His calm, optimism, and aggressiveness made him the central figure in bringing the final Allied victory. In the aftermath of the fighting, however, Foch was less successful in trying to impose his version of a harsh peace on Germany.

The future military leader was born on October 2, 1851, in Tarbes, near the Pyrenees. His father was a French civil servant. Foch entered the army as a private during the Franco-Prussian War and received his commission after graduating from the École polytechnique in 1873. He reached the rank of brigadier general in 1907 and, as a major general on the eve of World War I, took command of the important XX Corps. It defended the French frontier at Lorraine against German attack. By then, Foch had distinguished himself in several areas: as a staff officer, as a field commander, and as a teacher at, then director of, the War College. Significantly, his prewar writings and War College lectures had emphasized the desirability of conducting war by means of decisive offensive operations.

Foch rose to prominence during the first two years of the war. As the favorite subordinate of French commander-in-chief Joseph Joffre, he fought with distinction in charge of the Ninth Army at the Battle of the Marne in early September 1914. There his aggressive leadership helped to hold the center of the embattled French position east of Paris. Starting the following month, he commanded a far larger force, the French Northern Army Group in Flanders. He held this command, with its forty divisions, through the summer of 1916, participating in the Artois offensive of 1915 and in the attack on the Somme in 1916.

Joffre's fall from power at the close of 1916 combined with the heavy losses Foch himself had incurred at Artois and the Somme to cast a shadow over Foch's prospects. During 1917, his career revived as he became chief of the French general staff. In October, in an important preview of his crucial role the following year, Foch coordinated the shift of six French and five British divisions to Italy. There they helped restore the Italian defenses following the successful German attack at Caporetto. He also found a new patron in Georges Clemenceau, who took office as France's premier in November.

The supreme crisis on the western front came in early 1918, and Foch received the task of resolving it. Brilliantly conducted German offensives smashed the British sector of the front near Amiens, and the French commander, General Pétain, fell into a state of panic. British government and military leaders pressed for the appointment of a Frenchman as supreme commander to coordinate Allied operations and also to keep Pétain under control. Foch insisted, with success, on getting the title "commander-in-chief" rather than the weaker "coordinator" of operations.

In theory Foch was the commander of the 6 million men on the western front. In practice, the French military leader had only two tools at his disposal; both depended on his powers of persuasion and inspiration. First, he could, with the consent of each nation's army chief, distribute reserves to the sectors facing the greatest danger. Concerning French reserves, this meant he could overrule Pétain and send these forces where they were most needed. But he had to convince commanders such as Field Marshal Douglas Haig and General John Pershing to send their troops where he thought they should go.

Second, Foch could map out the overall strategy for the multinational collection of armies holding the line in France and Belgium. Thus, starting in July, Foch put Allied forces on the offensive. A series of operations conducted consecutively along different portions of the front wore down Germany's resources. Foch avoided the trap into which Ludendorff had fallen in his offensives: there were no improvised operations or sudden changes in direction designed to exploit momentary successes. Instead, Allied offensives proceeded methodically until they reached their predetermined objectives.

Starting in late September, under the urging of Haig, Foch launched a general offensive along the entire western front. German armies, located in a large and increasingly vulnerable salient, found themselves pressed by the British in the west and by the Americans in the south. Meanwhile, French forces pushed forward in several sectors. Foch's strategy both drained the Germans' strength and pushed them steadily eastward. The German government and high command agreed to end hostilities starting on November 11. Ironically, Foch defeated the enemy without achieving the great strategic breakthrough toward which his prewar writings had pointed.

Foch drew up the military provisions of the Armistice, thereby crippling Germany's ability to renew the fighting. He demanded both the surrender of huge quantities of weapons and the establishment of Allied bridgeheads along the Rhine. At the subsequent peace negotiations he urged terms that included surrendering all German territory west of the Rhine to France. Even political leaders like Georges Clemenceau rejected Foch's plans as too harsh.

Foch spent much of the remainder of his life completing his memoirs. He died in Paris on March 20, 1929, and the supreme commander's highly regarded account of his wartime career appeared posthumously in 1931.

Douglas Haig (1861–1928)

Douglas Haig commanded the British army on the western front from the winter of 1915-1916 to the close of the war. He is the most controversial of the prominent military commanders of World War I, and the debate over his leadership continues to rage. Haig first became the target of vigorous criticism for his leadership of the failed offensive on the Somme in July 1916. Critics have leveled equally negative judgments about the way Haig conducted the campaign in Flanders the following year. That 1917 offensive, known for its most bloody and futile encounter with the enemy at Passchendaele, was marked by hideous casualties and impossible fighting conditions in the fall rains and mud.

Nonetheless, in the different conditions of 1918, a different Haig emerged. Or, better said, Haig's talents and attitudes appeared to better advantage. He kept his head and maintained the cohesion of his army in the face of the German offensives, then directed the British army in the final set of offensives that brought the war to a close. He played a key role in getting the Allied commander-in-chief, Ferdinand Foch, to make an all-out effort to win the war in 1918.

Douglas Haig was born in Edinburgh on June 19, 1861. The son of a family that had prospered in the distillery business, he entered the army as a cadet at the Royal Military College at Sandhurst in 1884. He received his commission the following year. His early career, in which he was marked by superiors for his unusual energy and professional zeal, took place within the ranks of the cavalry. Shortly after he graduated from the Staff College in 1898, his professional life took a crucial turn: he became chief staff officer to General John French, commander of the British cavalry force in the Boer War. Haig made a name for himself as both a staff officer and a field commander in South Africa. He became a major general in 1904 and reached his initial wartime rank of lieutenant general in 1911. His rise to eminence in the army had come partly through his connections to Britain's royal family, and he remained a confidant of King George V during the years of fighting in France.

With the outbreak of World War I, Haig led the I Corps of the British Expeditionary Force to France. He distinguished himself initially at the First Battle of Ypres in October and November, holding the crucial portion of the Allied front adjacent to the English Channel against ferocious German attacks. As a reward, he got command of one of the two British field armies forming in France at the start of 1915. He conducted offensives at Neuve Chapelle in March, then at Loos in September. Mismanagement of the

Battle of Loos by General French led to his removal as commander of the British Expeditionary Force. In mid-December, Haig took over.

During 1916, Haig's lasting reputation as an unimaginative, callous commander took shape. It contains several elements: his willingness to accept immense casualties; his conviction that the enemy was close to the limit of its resources; and his expectation of a breakthrough into open country that would end the war by destroying the German army.

Haig's divisions, composed entirely of volunteers, started the British role in the 1916 campaign with an attack on the Somme on July 1. His defenders are quick to point out that the British general bowed to his French colleague, General Joseph Joffre, attacking earlier than Haig wished, and in a sector Joffre had selected. Moreover, they note, Allied public opinion would not have tolerated a passive strategy for the western front despite the strength of the German defenses.

Nonetheless, the first day was a disaster without precedent in military history: Haig lost 60,000 men, one-third of them fatalities. The British bombardment had failed to cripple German defenses, and enemy machine gunners mowed down the inexperienced soldiers General Sir Henry Rawlinson, Haig's subordinate, sent out in close formation. Haig continued the fruitless offensive into the autumn, losing perhaps 400,000 men in all. But Haig's defenders note that the Germans also suffered from this bloody attrition.

In 1917 Haig once again took the offensive, this time in Flanders, on a sector of his choosing. Overcoming the opposition of Prime Minister David Lloyd George, who feared another pointless bloodletting, Haig conducted the Third Battle of Ypres over a period of four months. It is better known as the Passchendaele campaign, named after the small village around which much of the fighting centered.

As the attack began, the French armies were crippled by mutiny, and the Allies needed to distract German attention from the French sectors of the front. Moreover, Haig had high hopes; continued pressure on the Germans might even bring about their total collapse. But the British advance across water-soaked terrain saw Haig's men bogged down in the mud much of the time. Once again, Haig barely pushed forward, while young Britons died by the hundreds of thousands. Thus, Haig met the German onslaught in March 1918 in the shadow of Lloyd George's distrust. If the British prime minister had felt more politically secure, he would likely have replaced Haig by then. Some historians believe he deliberately avoided sending reinforcements to Haig in order to restrain the British commander from further offensives.

In contrast to the panicky French commander-in-chief, Philippe Pétain, Haig kept his composure during the dangerous German offensives Ludendorff launched from late March to mid-July. He accepted the need for an Allied supreme commander to control Pétain. And he held tenaciously even after Ludendorff had begun to break through British defenses in the crucial sector around Amiens. Then, in August 1918, he directed an offensive at Amiens that precipitated the long German retreat that ended with the Armistice. Later that month, he helped persuade Foch that the war was winnable in 1918 if the Germans had to face a series of coordinated offensives all over the western front.

Haig retired from the army in 1921, spending the remainder of his life as the commander of the British Legion, the nation's veterans' organization. He died on January 30, 1928, in London.

John Jellicoe (1859–1935)

Admiral Sir John Jellicoe stood at the center of the British naval effort in World War I. As commander of the Grand Fleet, which contained the bulk of Britain's naval strength, he directed the most important operations of the British navy from the start of the war until the close of 1916. At that point, he became First Sea Lord and took control of all aspects of the war at sea. Jellicoe proved a decisive commander in the period 1914–1916. In dealing with the crucial threat posed by the German submarine offensive in 1917, the admiral proved less steady, and he was forced from office in December 1917.

John Jellicoe was born on December 5, 1859. A member of a family with a long naval tradition, he entered the Royal Navy as a cadet in 1872. He rose rapidly, obtaining a glowing reputation as a gunnery officer. Jellicoe's career was enhanced by a stint of combat service in the Boxer Rebellion in 1900. Even more important, he early on became a protégé of Admiral Sir John Fisher, who, as First Sea Lord from 1904 to 1910, became the architect of the modern British navy. Fisher's favorite became an admiral in 1907 at the early age of forty-eight. In the years immediately before the outbreak of war, Jellicoe received assignments intended to groom him for larger responsibilities, becoming commander of the Atlantic Fleet and then serving as Second Sea Lord.

On the first day of the war, First Lord of the Admiralty Winston Churchill ordered Jellicoe, then deputy commander of the Grand Fleet, to relieve his superior, Admiral Sir George Callahan. Churchill considered Callahan too old to lead Britain's most important naval force. Jellicoe reluctantly complied, protesting the impropriety of moving into the shoes of his immediate superior in such a peremptory fashion.

Jellicoe now had the awesome responsibility of commanding the most important weapon in the Allied arsenal. The Grand Fleet controlled the crucial sea lanes of the North Sea. If it suffered a major defeat, the German navy could cut the British army on the continent off from its home base; just as fatally, it would cut Britain's essential supplies of food from the outside world. To add to his burdens, Jellicoe realized that his force of battleships, battle cruisers, and smaller ships operated in a new combat environment. The danger from submarines and mines made aggressive operations like those conducted by such legendary predecessors as Lord Horatio Nelson impossible. Jellicoe had to retain control of the sea while preserving his margin of strength.

The British naval leader conducted operations between 1914 and 1916 in that spirit of caution. Efforts to trap units and destroy significant parts of the German High Seas Fleet in the open waters of the North Sea failed repeatedly, and the British commander was embarrassed when German warships were able to shell coastal cities in eastern England.

The grand encounter between the battleships of the two powers came at the Battle of Jutland, off the coast of Denmark, on May 31, 1916. Jellicoe's leadership during the battle reflected his fear of seeing the British fleet hit by heavy losses. In the two hours of fading daylight in which the main action took place, Jellicoe twice saw the line of enemy battleships turn away from his fleet. His critics have charged him with excessive caution in failing to pursue the Germans with vigor, permitting the enemy's High Seas Fleet to return safely to port. Moreover, British ship losses were substantially greater than those inflicted on the Germans. Nonetheless, most students of Jutland have endorsed Jellicoe's decisions. In his moment of supreme responsibility, the British leader had chased the enemy from the open waters of the North Sea, and the Royal Navy retained its superiority in battleships and battle cruisers. Germany remained under blockade, and Allied sea traffic was safe from the enemy's surface fleet.

Jellicoe's next test came from beneath the sea. By the closing months of 1916, Germany's naval efforts centered on submarine attack against Allied merchant shipping. In late November, the government promoted Jellicoe to First Sea Lord, the officer in charge of the entire Royal Navy. His chief task was to combat the submarine menace.

At first, Jellicoe remained tied to the failing policy of patrolling the sea lanes and seeking out the underwater enemy. As commander of the Grand Fleet, he had vehemently opposed proposals to shift destroyers from their principal task of protecting his battleships to duty escorting merchant ships. Like most senior naval commanders, he had numerous objections against having Allied merchant ships travel in convoys. Convoying seemed to mean abandoning an offensive posture by the navy, creating large targets for enemy submarines, and relying on the dubious skills of merchant captains in coordinated maneuvering.

With losses climbing to frightening proportions in early 1917, Jellicoe plunged into despair. In a conversation with Admiral William Sims of the United States in April, he supposedly stated that German submarines were winning the naval war; Britain had nothing to counter the deadly threat.

In the end Jellicoe accepted the necessity for convoys. But the initiative came from his subordinates, from Prime Minister David Lloyd George, and possibly from Sims as well. The First Sea Lord implemented a convoy system deliberately rather than energetically. Perhaps due to his own reservations, perhaps due to his declining health and the strain of overwork, a full-fledged convoy system was in place only at the close of 1917. Lloyd George and his energetic new First Lord of the Admiralty, Sir Eric Geddes, both found Jellicoe lacking in drive and imagination. Geddes became especially concerned about the navy's failure to stop German submarines from passing through the English Channel. In late December, Geddes forced Jellicoe from his post, replacing him with the more vigorous and imaginative Rosslyn Wemyss.

Jellicoe had no major military responsibilities for the rest of the war. In the postwar period, he served as governor-general of New Zealand from 1920 to 1924. He died in London on November 20, 1935.

Joseph Joffre (1852–1931)

General Joseph Joffre was the commander-in-chief of the French army during the first two years of the war. His great achievement during this period was the successful defense of France against the German onslaught in 1914. But he played an equally decisive role in establishing the tragic pattern of subsequent fighting on the western front: offensive operations regardless of cost. To Joffre is attributed the revealing remark that each of his generals needed to lose 15,000 men before he could become a proficient commander! In 1916 his reputation suffered a fatal blow when the German assault surprised him at Verdun and Allied attacks failed at the Somme.

The future French leader was born on January 12, 1852, in Rivesaltes, a village near the Spanish border. His father was a prosperous barrel maker. He graduated from the École polytechnique in 1871, and then made his reputation in the army as an engineer. Much of his career took place in France's colonial army in such remote places as Indochina and Madagascar. In West Africa, he added a reputation as a gallant commander to his name by leading a dangerous expedition to take Timbuktu in 1894.

Joffre became a major general in 1905, and in 1911 the army's chief of staff, the designated commander in case of war. He presided over the formulation of Plan XVII, the war plan France was to use in 1914. The plan accepted the possibility of a limited German thrust through Belgium, but discounted its dangers. It looked to the decisive success of a French offensive eastward into Lorraine.

When the conflict began, Joffre sent his armies eastward according to plan. They were repelled with heavy losses. Meanwhile, as the Schlieffen plan became reality, German forces threatened to sweep around Paris and trap the French army. Joffre, a heavy-set man with an unflappable demeanor, was a center of calm and confidence as France's forces fell backward. He held the Allied armies together even as the British commander, Sir John French, approached panic. Dozens of French generals lost their commands when he found them insufficiently steady or inadequately aggressive. In early September, after building a new army near Paris that could strike the Germans on their western flank, he ended the retreat, then fought and won the Battle of the Marne.

In a long-standing dispute, some historians give General Joseph Galliéni, the commander of the Paris garrison, credit for the idea of a counteroffensive at this time and place. More award the major share of the laurels to Joffre, and all praise Joffre's steadiness during the long retreat southward prior to the first week of September. So long as the French commander remained resolute in those momentous days, Germany's hopes for the success of the Schlieffen plan faded, then died.

Even before the close of 1914, however, Joffre's well-deserved reputation for success at the Marne began to diminish. He now sent French forces forward in grim, futile offensives against the Germans entrenched in north-eastern France. In 1915, hoping to break through, he renewed the carnage. Meanwhile, more cautious generals like Philippe Pétain pointed out the slim chances for success. Since the French held most of the front, and Joffre informally played the part of the overall Allied commander in 1915, his efforts shaped British strategy as well.

But his decisive imprint could be seen not only in France and Britain's offensive posture. He also helped to establish the western front as the center of all Allied efforts for the remainder of the war. Moreover, he initiated a pattern of planning for coordinated offensives on both the eastern and the western fronts that was followed in 1915 and 1916.

By the close of 1915, Joffre was excusing his failure to strike a decisive blow by claiming he was "nibbling" away at enemy strength. But it was clear to his critics in the French government that France was suffering intolerable losses, and losses that were less than those the Germans experienced. France's political leaders, notably Georges Clemenceau, were outraged by Joffre's insistence that civilians should not interfere in the conduct of the war. Joffre gave this practical force by virtually barring government leaders from visiting the front. Still, he stood as the hero of the Marne; he could not be ousted.

In 1916 Joffre's star fell decisively. He was criticized for leaving Verdun without an adequate number of guns. The French commander had shifted its artillery elsewhere to help his 1915 offensives. But he showed the same calm in the face of German attacks that he had in 1914 in moving to hold Verdun. He considered it a symbol of French military power and resolve.

The heavy losses at Verdun made Joffre's position precarious when combined with the failure of the joint Anglo-French summer offensive, which also produced a grim casualty list. The government turned to General Robert Nivelle, a hero of the successful offensive operations in the closing phases of the Verdun campaign. Nivelle promised the decisive victory that had eluded Joffre, and the older general was removed from his command in December.

The government softened the blow for Joffre by awarding him the highest rank available in the French army, that of field marshal. But Joffre held no further command during the remainder of the war. He died in Paris on January 3, 1931.

V. I. Lenin (1870–1924)

Vladimir Ilyich Lenin, a Marxist revolutionary, took power in Russia in November 1917. By this stage in World War I, most of Europe's governments and societies were shaken by the trauma inflicted by the conflict. Lenin was the most successful radical leader to use this rare opportunity, raising himself from obscurity to national leadership.

Lenin was born Vladimir Ilyich Ulyanov on April 22, 1869, in Simbirsk in western Siberia. He was the son of a school administrator who died when Lenin was sixteen. Vladimir's youth was harshly disrupted in 1887 when his elder brother, Alexander, was executed for plotting to kill Tsar Alexander III. Lenin entered the Marxist political movement in Russia in the early 1890s. By the outbreak of World War I, he had become the leader of a small faction of Marxists known as the Bolsheviks. He also had acquired a sharply defined reputation as an independent, willful, and unorthodox follower of Marxist doctrine. He differed from most Russian Marxists in a number of areas.

Lenin called for an elite party based on educated, full-time revolutionaries. It would operate underground while the tsar's government did not permit open political activity, and would consist principally of middle-class intellectuals who would lead the cause of the factory workers. Moreover, he wanted to bring the peasantry to play a supporting role in a future revolution, aiding the factory workers whom all Marxists saw as the driving force in revolutionary change.

At the outbreak of the war, Lenin adopted still another controversial position. Many Marxists throughout Europe refused any support to their governments, a position Lenin found too weak. He saw the war as an opportunity for Marxist revolutionaries to take power. Thus, Lenin called for turning the international war into a series of civil wars as the proletariat struck at their middle-class rulers. Specifically, and to the shock of even his fellow Marxists, he hoped for Russian military defeats to make the revolutionary's task easier. Finally, the Bolshevik leader came to reject the idea that an initial revolution overthrowing the tsar had to be followed by an interval of years or decades of economic development before a workers' revolution could follow. Radical even when compared to his fellow Marxists, Lenin claimed that the war would end for Russia only if its capitalist leaders were also overthrown. This articulate, stubborn man in his mid-forties seemed to more moderate revolutionaries someone in a hurry to take power, even at the cost of bending Marxist ideology.

Wartime conferences in Switzerland in 1915 and 1916 brought together Marxists from both sides of the fighting line. Lenin found he could not win over a majority to back his position of turning the war into civil wars. But he was unwavering. In 1916, in a book entitled *Imperialism*, he argued that the conflict had arisen out of the economic competition of the imperialist Great Powers. It could end only when the workers in Europe's belligerent countries overthrew those governments. In March 1917, while living in Zurich, Switzerland, Lenin received word of the spontaneous revolution that had broken out in Russia's capital. He returned to his country in April, soon after the new Provisional Government had announced it would stay in the war. He got vital help from German authorities to reach Russia from Switzerland. They hoped he would help to push Russia out of the war.

Upon his arrival at Petrograd's Finland Station, Lenin denounced the Provisional Government. He offered a radical agenda: land to the peasants, control of factories to the workers, and Russia's immediate withdrawal from the war. The program proved attractive, notably in the urban centers of the country. There, Russia's long string of military defeats and the harsh living conditions brought on by the war had pushed many Russians, such as factory workers and their families, to desperation.

An initial effort to take power failed in July, and Lenin was forced into hiding. But in November 1917, Lenin and his Bolshevik faction (soon renamed the Communists) took control of Russia's main cities: the capital, Petrograd, and the old capital, Moscow. They lacked the power to dominate the countryside, but the Communists formed the only effective center of government inside Russia.

Within a matter of days, Lenin as leader of the new government and Leon Trotsky as the director of foreign affairs began negotiations for an armistice. They found that Russia's wartime allies would not join them in this effort. An isolated Russia had to negotiate on its own. The armistice between Russia and the Central Powers was signed on December 15, 1917, and was followed by peace negotiations at Brest-Litovsk.

Lenin dominated the process of peacemaking. The Germans demanded that Russia surrender large stretches of territory along its western border and make economic concessions. Some Communists like Nikolai Bukharin wanted to continue the war in order to promote revolution in enemy countries like Germany. Trotsky, chief negotiator at Brest-Litovsk, wanted to end the fighting without making any formal agreement with the Germans. Lenin rejected their views. Using his prestige as the Communist party's leader, Lenin got the other principal figures of the party to agree to the harsh German terms. He made it clear that he did not expect the settlement imposed by the Treaty of Brest-Litovsk in early March 1918 to be a permanent one. Nonetheless, it gave German leaders like General Erich Ludendorff the hope of removing forces from Russia to strike on the western front in the spring of 1918.

In the waning months of World War I, Lenin faced the start of armed intervention by Russia's former allies such as the United States, Britain, and France. By then, a diverse coalition of anti-Bolshevik Russian forces known as "the Whites" controlled large portions of Russian territory. The ensuing civil war lasted until the closing months of 1920.

Although disabled by a series of strokes starting in the spring of 1922, Lenin remained the head of the government of Soviet Russia (renamed the Soviet Union in 1922). During these last years, he initiated the New Economic Policy (NEP). A temporary departure from revolutionary ideals, NEP let the battered country recover from its long ordeal. The Communist party now permitted a partial revival of free enterprise and relaxed political controls on the Russian population. This final major decision in his political life again showed Lenin's immense tactical skills. He died in Moscow on January 21, 1924.

independent Ireland and the conflict between Greece and the new Turkey of Kemal Attaturk. The Chanak crisis of 1922, resulting from the Greco-Turkish hostilities, led to his resignation. He never held high office again.

In the postwar period, the former prime minister criticized the harsh treatment Germany had received at the peace conference. He also openly admired Adolf Hitler as an energetic national leader. During 1939 and 1940, the great World War I leader, now in his late seventies, emerged as an advocate of a negotiated peace with Hitler. Rumors flew among his colleagues in Parliament that he saw himself as the future prime minister working out such a deal. He died at his farm in the Welsh countryside outside Criccieth on March 26, 1945.

Erich Ludendorff (1865–1937)

Eric Ludendorff, although nominally a subordinate of Field Marshal Paul von Hindenburg, was the most significant German leader of the war. He directed the German military effort on the eastern front during the first two years of the conflict, and controlled the entire land war from the close of 1916 until the eve of the Armistice. In the guise of assistant to Hindenburg, Ludendorff not only exercised supreme military power, he came to overshadow the political authority of Germany's prime ministers and the emperor, Wilhelm II. Ludendorff, more than any military commander in the war, became virtual dictator over the affairs of his country.

The future World War I leader was the son of a small landowner with an estate near Posen. Ludendorff was born there on April 9, 1865. He became an army officer in 1883, received training at the General Staff Academy, then rotated between positions as a unit commander and staff officer. In 1904 he returned to Berlin as a member of the prestigious General Staff itself. Marked as a particularly promising officer with uncompromising views, he ignored the strength of the political opposition in the Reichstag by insisting on a large expansion in the size of the army in 1913.

Exiled from the General Staff, Ludendorff greeted the war as commander of an undistinguished infantry brigade at Strasbourg. Upon the start of mobilization, he became deputy chief of staff to the Second Army, one of the key units designated to invade Belgium. He emerged as the hero of the hour in helping to capture an important stronghold defending the city of Liège, the key to the German advance through Belgium.

The deteriorating situation in East Prussia gave Ludendorff the opportunity to leap to higher command. Facing a Russian advance into this region from the east and the south, a distraught General Max von Prittwitz called for a withdrawal back to the Vistula. When Prittwitz was thereupon relieved,

Ludendorff received orders to restore the situation as chief of staff of the Eighth Army. The new army commander, under whom Ludendorff was to serve, was Paul von Hindenburg.

The ensuing campaign brought Germany's greatest wartime victory; it established the pattern for the relationship between Ludendorff and Hindenburg; and it began Hindenburg's rise to supreme command. The German Eighth Army turned southward to annihilate the forces of General Alexander Samsonov in the Battle of Tannenberg. Meanwhile, a weak German screening force held Russian forces invading from the east. This daring plan originated with figures on Prittwitz's staff and came to fruition under Ludendorff. During the dangerous operations involved in ignoring one enemy force in order to concentrate against another, Hindenburg played the secondary but valuable role of steadying the nerves of his mercurial assistant.

Over the next two years, the team of Hindenburg and Ludendorff, with the latter playing the dominant part, came to control all German operations, as well as much of the Austrian effort, on the eastern front. Ludendorff clashed regularly with General Erich von Falkenhayn, the German commander-in-chief. Falkenhayn saw the western front as the war's center of gravity. He refused to provide the eastern front with the forces that Ludendorff believed would bring total victory against Russia.

In August 1916, Hindenburg and Ludendorff returned to Berlin to take Falkenhayn's place. Hindenburg became chief of the General Staff, that is, supreme commander. Ludendorff, still the dominant member of the pair, took the title of first quartermaster general.

Ludendorff pushed commanders in the west to develop more effective offensive tactics and to shorten the front. He seized control of the debate over the use of unrestricted submarine warfare. He accompanied this initial plunge into the political arena with "the Hindenburg program." This was a plan to put the entire adult male population from ages seventeen to sixty at the disposal of the war effort. Although milder in application than in theory, it represented an important milestone on the road to total war.

In January 1917, Ludendorff got Kaiser Wilhelm II to agree to the navy's call for unlimited submarine warfare. In another political decision with momentous consequences, Ludendorff arranged for V. I. Lenin to return to Russia from his isolated place of exile in Switzerland. The Russian revolutionary was expected to help pull Germany's eastern enemy from the war. Another political move came in July: by threatening to resign, he compelled the kaiser to oust Theobald von Bethmann Hollweg. The obscure Prussian bureaucrat Georg Michaelis took the now weakened post of prime minister. The issue at stake was the possibility of a negotiated peace, and Ludendorff's success kept Germany on the disastrous path leading either to total victory or total defeat.

The year 1918 brought Ludendorff's final effort to win the war. The submarine campaign of 1917 had failed; the United States had responded to unlimited submarine warfare by entering the conflict; American troops were now reaching Europe in large numbers. The general overrode the objections of the foreign office and obtained the punitive Treaty of Brest-Litovsk with Russia. Ludendorff dismissed the fact that Britain and France were certain to use such a settlement to motivate their own populations into a fight to the finish. Still, the end of combat on the eastern front released large numbers of German troops for shipment to France.

Ludendorff's 1918 offensive on the western front was a desperate gamble employing the last substantial resources of the German army. Successful German attacks broke enemy defenses with a skillful combination of artillery fire and highly trained infantrymen. But Germany lacked the men to split the British from the French. In a momentous, much criticized decision, Ludendorff shifted the direction of the main German advance several times to exploit momentary successes. The Allies held on, their morale bolstered by the arrival of a growing American army. The enemy counteroffensive began in August. Convinced that the gamble had failed, Ludendorff went to the brink of nervous collapse before resigning his post at the close of October.

The man who had been virtual dictator of Germany fled to Scandinavia for several months after the Armistice. In the political turmoil of the postwar period, Ludendorff returned home and turned to the extreme right. He was one of several leaders of the Kapp putsch in Berlin in 1920, which sought and failed to overthrow the Weimar Republic. He then became an ally of Adolf Hitler, marching at the Nazi leader's side when Hitler tried unsuccessfully to seize power in Munich in November 1923. Thereafter, he faded into the political background. With his mental health in apparent decline, he busied himself with the publication of anti-Catholic pamphlets. Ludendorff died in the Bavarian town of Tutzing, near Munich, on December 20, 1937.

Thomas G. Masaryk (1850–1937)

Thomas Masaryk was the most significant leader of the World War I era movement to break up the Austro-Hungarian (or Habsburg) Empire. He aimed at establishing an independent Czechoslovak state out of several components of the empire. In this cause, Masaryk benefitted from the work of talented collaborators like Eduard Benes. Eloquent as he was in speaking out for Czech independence, Masaryk had to wait for the course of hostilities to make his aims practical. By the closing months of the war, however, Allied hostility toward Austria-Hungary and the instability of the empire made Masaryk's cause a winning one.

Prior to the outbreak of World War I, Masaryk had stood as an advocate of lesser change, notably a federal system that would give the peoples of the Austro-Hungarian Empire more autonomy while preserving the historic Habsburg state. In these same years, however, he emerged as a vocal critic of the empire's domestic and foreign policies. The circumstances of the war pushed Masaryk to a more extreme position, or, at the least, encouraged him to take a public stand that had not seemed feasible before 1914.

During the first sixty-four years of his life, Masaryk raised himself from humble origins to a position of academic renown and political influence. Born the son of a coachman in the small Moravian town of Hodonín on March 7, 1850, he had both Slovak blood (from his father's side of the family) and Czech ancestry (from his mother's family). A gifted linguist and scholar, he rose through the academic world, obtaining a doctorate in philosophy, holding a professorship at the University of Prague, and writing extensively on topics ranging from philosophy and religion to history and literature. He married an American woman, Charlotte Garrigue, whom he met while studying at the University of Leipzig.

The future statesman entered politics in 1891 as a deputy in the Austrian parliament. He served both there and in the Czech Diet. His pronouncements on the future of the Habsburg Empire prior to 1914 were guarded and sometimes contradictory. But two consistent elements emerged. First, he believed that the system, which seemed unlikely to collapse entirely, needed to be transformed into a federal state. Second, as 1914 approached, he became increasingly pessimistic that such a transformation would take place. Masaryk lagged behind some Czech leaders who called for outright independence, but he was sharp—some even called him traitorous—in criticizing the empire's diplomatic ties to Germany and its hostile policies toward Balkan countries like Serbia.

Following the outbreak of war in the summer of 1914, Masaryk became an advocate of an independent state that would contain the ethnically related Czechs and Slovaks of the old empire. At first, he expected it would be a monarchy with a king from a small country like Belgium or Denmark. In deference to Czech leaders who looked for help in Russia, he also mentioned the possibility of a Russian ruler for postwar Czechoslovakia.

In December 1914, he left the Habsburg Empire to organize a movement abroad. While he traveled in Italy and Switzerland, his family was placed under police surveillance in Prague. Masaryk used the financial support of

Czechs and Slovaks living in the United States to promote the cause of independence. His major tool was publicity in magazines he put out in the Allied countries. In private conversations with western European leaders like Prime Minister Aristide Briand of France, he called for a Europe rebuilt on the principle of nationality, acknowledging that the Austro-Hungarian Empire had no place in this new political world. In November 1915, he made these views public in a manifesto published by his Czech Committee Abroad.

Masaryk spent most of the early wartime years in London. He mixed his political efforts with teaching stints at the University of London's King's College. The first promising results of his efforts surfaced at the start of 1917. Then, the governments of Britain and France suggested as one of their war aims the dissolution of the Habsburg Empire and the creation of a number of successor states, Czechoslovakia among them.

In May 1917, following the revolution in Russia that had toppled the old monarchy, Masaryk traveled to Petrograd. He had long advocated the formation of an army consisting of Czech and Slovak prisoners of war in Russia. It would be a potent tool in promoting the idea of an independent Czechoslovakian state. The effort to form such a force and to transport it to France kept him in Russia until early 1918.

Masaryk made his way to the United States via Tokyo starting in March 1918. The United States had declared war on Austria-Hungary in December 1917, and he saw the government in Washington as a crucial center of power in the struggle for a Czechoslovakian state. He toured the large Czech and Slovak communities in the United States, and met with President Woodrow Wilson. In late May, Secretary of State Robert Lansing announced American backing for an independent Czechoslovakia. In the next months, the initiative of Eduard Benes, Masaryk's energetic colleague in western Europe, won over first the French, then the British government to the same goal.

With the Central Powers collapsing, the pace of events quickened. On October 18, Masaryk rejected an offer from the young Emperor Charles of Austria-Hungary to transform the empire into a federal state. Czech leaders in Prague declared the establishment of a Czechoslovak state on October 28. Slovak leaders issued a similar declaration on October 31. In early November, Masaryk, still in the United States, received word that he had been named the president of the new republic. The former professor served as his nation's leader for the next two decades. Despite the difficulties in governing a multinational state that included a large German minority, Masaryk maintained a democratic form of government. Historians consider him the most successful government leader in the newly independent states of eastern Europe. Masaryk retired from office in 1935 and died at his country home outside Prague on September 14, 1937.

Nicholas II (1868–1918)

Nicholas II was the tsar (emperor) of the Russian Empire from 1894 until he was forced to abdicate in 1917. A personally charming individual, he lacked the intelligence and force of character to influence events effectively. Given the immense power that rested in the tsar's hands, Nicholas's personality flaws, inactivity, and irresponsible decisions contributed first to military, then political catastrophe. In Germany, the comparable inadequacies of the monarch put power into the hands of military leaders. In Russia, where there were no candidates for the role of a General Erich Ludendorff, Nicholas's failings contributed to a more chaotic scene. At best, only the Empress Alexandra and her personal favorite, Rasputin, ruled, giving misdirection to the engines of national policy.

Nicholas was born at the imperial palace of Tsarskoe Selo, outside St. Petersburg, May 18, 1868. He was the grandson of the reigning tsar, Alexander II, and the son of Alexander III, who ruled from 1881 to 1894. Educated by private tutors, he then served happily as an officer in the Imperial Guards. The inexperienced young man took the throne suddenly in 1894 when his father, then only fifty, died after a brief illness.

The first twenty years of the new tsar's reign were tumultuous. Russia went through the first throes of industrialization and urbanization, and the country fought a disastrous war with Japan in 1904–1905. In the wake of the Revolution of 1905, which stemmed partly from wartime defeats, Nicholas allowed the political form of his age-old monarchy to be modified. A Duma (parliament) with limited power was established. Under the political surface, however, a variety of revolutionary groups worked to overthrow the existing system. Nicholas remained a deep-dyed conservative determined to preserve Russia's social and political order, uncomfortable with any reforms. Even the changes of 1905 he hoped to reverse at some future date.

Nicholas played the role of privileged bystander during the summer crisis of 1914. Stronger personalities like Foreign Minister Sergei Sazonov and Minister of War Vladimir Sukhomlinov determined the Russian government's responses as war neared. The tsar signed the mobilization orders that his ministers demanded, appointed his uncle, Grand Duke Nicholas, to direct military operations, then faded from the scene.

When he reemerged, in the summer of 1915, it was to make a fatal decision. The tsar relieved his uncle, who had presided over the disastrous spring and summer retreat as a German offensive conquered Russia's western provinces, and took over the high command himself. But the country's social and economic fabric was already straining, and opposition in the Duma to the conduct of the war was becoming more vocal.

Ironically, Nicholas presided over no further military disasters. He left the actual decision making to his diligent chief of staff, Mikhail Alekseev. And the campaign of 1916 featured the successful offensive led by General Alexis Brusilov. Only in the area of military appointments, where the tsar had promoted the careers of incompetent court favorites since 1914, did Nicholas cause immediate harm. Nonetheless, Nicholas's absence from the capital at St. Petersburg (renamed Petrograd at the war's start) added to the woes of the monarchy and the general instability of the nation and its government.

With the tsar gone—he took up residence at military headquarters in Mogilev, over four hundred miles from the capital—only Empress Alexandra stood at the center of national decision making. Her liaison with Rasputin, the disreputable holy man, tainted the reputation of the monarchy. But equally harmful were the bootlicking ministers whom Rasputin put into office, often in place of men immeasurably more competent. Thus, the energetic Alexis Polivanov, the most effective Russian war minister during the conflict, found himself pushed from office in March 1916.

Nicholas was at Mogilev in March 1917 as Russia's armed forces prepared for the new year's campaign. When a women's demonstration in the capital escalated, first into bread riots, then into military mutiny, he could barely follow the situation. His efforts to return to Petrograd to regain control of the country's affairs failed. Striking railroad workers blocked his route, and he was forced to detour to the headquarters of the northern front, where the armies defending Petrograd were located. There, a coterie of his generals convinced him to abdicate.

The former tsar and his family were confined, first at their palace near Petrograd, then in the remote city of Ekaterinburg in the Urals. Sadly for them, the tsar and his family were still a political factor elsewhere in Europe in this troubled era. The British government, for example, might have assured their safety by demanding their safe passage from Russia. But for Prime Minister David Lloyd George to do so would have endangered London's ties with the postrevolutionary government. For Britain's King George V, efforts in behalf of his Russian relatives might endanger his own throne. In consequence, concern for the lives of Nicholas and his family was pushed aside.

With the Revolution of November 1917, the Bolsheviks took power. Russia's population polarized and drifted toward civil war. When White forces, the opponents of the Communists, neared the place of confinement for the former reigning family, Nicholas, his wife, and their five children were executed during the night of July 16/17, 1918. Their remains were only recently discovered and identified.

Vittorio Orlando (1860–1952)

Vittorio Orlando served as Italy's prime minister during the final year of the war, then represented his country at the Paris Peace Conference. As a wartime leader, he firmed up the Italian war effort and kept his country fighting following the military disaster at Caporetto in October 1917. At the ensuing peace conference, however, Orlando played a less successful role. He found himself overshadowed by his determined foreign minister, Sidney Sonnino, and Orlando's moderate stance toward obtaining territorial acquisitions for his country collided with Italian popular opinion as well. The Italian desire for sweeping territorial gains on the eastern shore of the Adriatic clashed with the determined views of President Woodrow Wilson. Wilson's desire to award territory claimed by Italy to the new state of Yugoslavia illustrated the intractable problems faced by postwar leaders in trying to redraw the map of eastern and southern Europe. Orlando's failure embittered postwar Italian political life as fervent nationalists pointed to Italy's "mutilated victory."

Orlando was a Sicilian, born in Palermo on May 19, 1860. Trained as a lawyer, he served in the Chamber of Deputies from 1897 into the years of World War I. Orlando made a name for himself as a versatile government minister, holding the posts of minister of education and minister of justice before 1914. Shortly after the outbreak of the war, he became minister of justice once again; then, in June 1916, he took over the powerful position of minister of the interior. He had been a supporter of Italy's entrance into the war in May 1915, and, with the interior portfolio and its responsibility for domestic security, he now stood as a pillar of the country's wartime government. Nonetheless, the presence of a large number of deputies opposed to the war helped persuade Orlando to crack down only in a measured way on antiwar demonstrations and other forms of domestic dissent. So too did his own conviction that civil liberties should be respected even in wartime.

In October 1917, Orlando's moment came. With newly arrived German troops taking the lead, the armies of the Central Powers crashed through the apparently immovable battlefront along the Isonzo River and penetrated northeastern Italy. Their speedy advance threatened to capture Venice and, beyond that, to knock Italy from the war. In these perilous circumstances, Orlando took over as prime minister on October 30, 1917.

Orlando bolstered the fragile situation in a number of ways. His voice helped persuade King Victor Emmanuel II to replace General Luigi Cadorna, the army's commander and the military figure most responsible for the fiasco at Caporetto. Cadorna also had long resisted effective control of the military by civilian authority. The new Italian commander, Armando Diaz, was younger, more optimistic, and more inclined to work with Italy's political leaders. Orlando also got Georges Clemenceau and David Lloyd George to provide six French and five British divisions to help the Italians hold on. Despite his earlier reservations, Orlando also struck sharply at domestic opponents of the war, imprisoning, for example, a number of leading Socialists.

But Orlando found Diaz a trying subordinate. Only with extreme difficulty did the Italian prime minister get his leading general to take the offensive in the closing weeks of the war. The need for Italy to attack was pressing: its failure at Caporetto had undercut Rome's diplomatic position at any future peace conference. Refusing to follow the call of Field Marshal Ferdinand Foch, the supreme Allied military commander, to join in the final offensive against the Central Powers threatened to make the damage irreparable. Orlando, perhaps fearing the political effects of a bloody and ineffective offensive, vacillated. But he finally pushed Diaz forward. The only victorious Italian offensive action of the war, the Battle of Vittorio Veneto, came in late October and early November 1918.

At Versailles, Orlando found himself at loggerheads with the American president when he pressed Italy's claims to territory along the northeastern shore of the Adriatic. In fact, Orlando was inclined toward compromise on territorial issues. But Sonnino, the director of foreign policy throughout the war, remained wedded to gains promised Italy in the Treaty of London in April 1915. And vocal Italian nationalists demanded even more, notably the port city of Fiume. In contrast, Wilson favored claims of the new state of Yugoslavia; its chief ethnic group, the Serbs, had fought with far greater success and effectiveness than Italy.

In a dramatic gesture, Orlando and Sonnino left the peace negotiations in late April 1919. But within ten days they were compelled to return: the other victorious powers ignored Italy's gesture of defiance and simply went on with the conference. In the end, Orlando's efforts to win a glorious settlement for Italy failed. The prime minister was the first to pay the price: his government fell on June 19, 1919.

The bitterness resulting from Italy's treatment at the peace conference paved the way for the rise of Benito Mussolini and his Fascist party. Orlando himself was a quiet ally of Mussolini until the nationalist demagogue established a full-fledged dictatorship after 1924. Orlando then went into political retirement, reappearing briefly after World War II to lead Italy's constituent assembly. He died in Rome on December 1, 1952.

John J. Pershing (1860–1948)

John J. Pershing was the commander of the American Expeditionary Forces (AEF) in Europe during World War I and the most important American military leader in the conflict. Two of his strongly held beliefs shaped his country's participation in the war: building an American army to fight in an American sector of the front under American leaders; and pursuing offensive operations without regard to the cost in lives.

The future general was born on September 13, 1860, in Laclede, Missouri, the son of a farmer and storekeeper. He graduated from West Point in 1882, served in the last stages of the Indian wars from 1886 to 1891, and saw combat as a first lieutenant in Cuba during the Spanish-American War. A turning point in his career came in 1906 when President Theodore Roosevelt promoted Pershing, then a captain, over the heads of many of his fellow officers to the rank of brigadier general. In his newly elevated rank, Pershing went on to important commands in the Philippines and the United States. In a second critical point in his career, Pershing commanded the cavalry force that pursued Pancho Villa into Mexico in 1916. Thus, within the tiny officer corps of the United States Army, Pershing had an unmatched record of command in the field.

Shortly after the country entered World War I in April 1917, President Woodrow Wilson named Pershing commander of the American Expeditionary Forces. Wilson's only specific instructions to the general required Pershing to build and lead an independent fighting force. It was a guideline Pershing followed zealously.

With a small staff, Pershing arrived in France in June. Despite the bitter experience of the British and French earlier in the war, Pershing was enthusiastic about taking the offensive. He hoped to transform the fighting into a conflict marked by what he called "open warfare." He rejected the idea of placing his troops under British and French commanders. And he organized his troops into divisions twice the size of those of Britain and France. He hoped thereby to absorb heavy casualties without being forced to withdraw the units from combat. Large divisions also offered a way to overcome the shortage of experienced American commanders and staff officers.

Pershing bent his principles in the summer of 1918 as Allied forces faced the storm of the final German offensives. He despatched some Americans to critical sectors under British or French leadership. Nonetheless, he remained committed to having a large and independent American force fighting in its own sector of the western front. In a famous confrontation with Allied military and government leaders at Versailles in early June, Pershing told them he was willing to risk seeing the Allies retreat to the Loire rather than abandon his basic stance. Meanwhile, American troops in substantial numbers had their first encounters with the German army. Pershing showed his enthusiasm for offensives in the form of mass frontal assaults at Belleau Wood and Chateau-Thierry. These showed how costly the American leader's style of fighting would be.

In early September 1918, Pershing achieved his long-standing ambition. Attacking the St. Mihiel salient near Verdun, an independent American field army fought on its own portion of the front. Encouragingly, it won an easy victory. The Germans paved the way for American success by withdrawing from the salient without heavy resistance. Later that month, commanding a force of over a million men, Pershing launched his Meuse-Argonne offensive. It continued to the close of the war, and historians view it as the event by which to judge Pershing as a fighting general.

In this climactic effort, Pershing bowed to Foch's wishes. He turned away from the St. Mihiel region and his hopes of advancing on Metz. Instead, in accordance with the overall Allied offensive effort Foch promoted, Pershing attacked along a narrow front between the Meuse River and the Argonne Forest. Under its aggressive commander, a massive American force, eventually composed of two field armies and numbering 1 million men, moved forward on September 26.

Pershing's advance bogged down almost immediately. German resistance, featuring skilled machine gun crews, was stubborn. The mass attacks by American troops, often across open terrain, led to heavy casualties. Meanwhile, German artillery fired on Pershing's forces from the Argonne Forest to the west and the heights of the Meuse to the east. An equally heavy burden on the Americans was the breakdown of the army's staff. Pershing had concentrated a huge number of forces on this narrow section of the front, and inexperienced staff officers could not maintain a system of supply and communication. Liaison among Pershing's units, especially the crucial links between artillery and infantry units, also broke down.

With casualties mounting, confusion rampant, and the rear filled with deserters, Pershing paused to reorganize, then pressed forward. Only in the last days of the war, starting on November 1, did the forces in the Meuse-

Argonne achieve a breakthrough. Pershing later defended his leadership and his troops' performance by noting how the German high command was forced to divert numerous forces to block the American advance.

The American contribution to victory in 1918 rested in the additional pressure Pershing's AEF put on the German front. At the least, it released more experienced French and British units to conduct successful advances elsewhere. Historian David Trask has suggested that Pershing should have been more flexible in permitting greater temporary amalgamation of AEF units with British and French forces. This would have created more experienced American troops as well as American commanders and staff officers able to lead a complex offense such as the Meuse-Argonne operation. In his view, Pershing was losing the confidence of President Wilson as the war drew to a close and might well have been replaced if the war had gone on into 1919.

Pershing stepped awkwardly into the political arena in the last days of the war when he argued against an Armistice. He desired the war to continue until the Germans surrendered unconditionally. Nonetheless, he returned to the United States in triumph. He received the unusual and highly prestigious rank of general of the armies, and he took over as the army's chief of staff in 1921. He retired in 1924 and lived long enough to offer his services, at the age of eighty-one, to President Franklin Roosevelt at the start of World War II. Pershing died in Washington, D.C., on July 15, 1948.

Philippe Pétain (1856–1951)

General Philippe Pétain was the commander of the French army in the Battle of Verdun in 1916. In the spring of 1917, after his country's forces had been crippled by mutinies, Pétain became the army's commander-in-chief. His skill in holding out at Verdun was matched by his ability to restore stability, then to build the fighting spirit in France's battered military units on the western front. In 1918, however, his reaction to the German spring offensive bordered on panic. The Allies established a unified command in April largely to place Pétain under effective control. Nonetheless, he ended the war with a glowing reputation. This paved the way for him to become a political figure, notably during World War II.

Pétain was born on April 24, 1856, in northern France in a village near Arras. He was the son of a peasant family. Thus, even in a French officer corps open to men from all social levels, his background was a modest one. He was commissioned in 1878, then rose slowly. He became an expert on infantry tactics, but his views were unpopular ones. In particular, he opposed the emphasis on the offensive that dominated French military thinking at the time. Some of his ideas penetrated the infantry regulations before 1914, but he was a mere colonel, and close to retirement, when war broke out.

Pétain rose quickly, leading first a brigade, then a division with great skill during the campaign that ended with the Battle of the Marne. In 1915 he commanded a corps in the spring offensive in Artois, then a field army in the September assault in Champagne. Even in the bloody failure in Artois, Pétain distinguished himself by his adept use of artillery to open the gate for his infantry. He soon had a rare reputation among the army's rank and file for being stingy with the lives of his men.

Verdun elevated Pétain to the upper level of the French army. Brought in by General Joseph Joffre during the first week of fighting, he led the tenacious defense. Much of the battle took the form of massive artillery duels, and Pétain alleviated the resulting strain on his forces by rotating entire divisions into the battle line for short stays, then removing them for a period of recovery. This sterling performance failed, however, to raise Pétain to the level of commander-in-chief of the army. Instead, that post went to his offensive-minded subordinate, General Robert Nivelle.

Nivelle's offensive in Champagne failed catastrophically in spring 1917, and Pétain's moment arrived. Much of the army had sunk into mutiny by the time Pétain took over in May. The new commander-in-chief restored the situation by improving food and leaves, and by making personal, inspirational visits to ninety divisions. Representatives from units as small as infantry companies had a chance to tell Pétain personally of their grievances. He also used rougher measures: leading mutineers were executed or imprisoned, although the number that received such treatment remains uncertain.

Pétain's most potent tool was a pledge that the army would end costly and ill-prepared offensives. "I am waiting for the Americans and the tanks," he stated. As the army returned to health, Pétain gave it new confidence by carrying out successful, well-planned offensives. Typical was the French attack at Verdun in late August. Conducted on a narrow front, it combined an effective artillery bombardment, overwhelming strength for the attacking infantry, and a limited set of objectives. As the year went on, Pétain increasingly relied on artillery, tanks, and aircraft to bear the weight of his attacks. At the start of 1918, he urged the French government to accept a defensive strategy for the entire coming year.

Pétain did not bear up well when the crisis of 1918 struck. With Ludendorff's March offensive threatening to rupture the Allied line, he lost his composure. The French commander prepared to pull much of the French army back to defend Paris, thereby exposing the flank of the British forces under

Haig. The appointment of General Ferdinand Foch as Allied commander-in-chief took place in large measure to limit Pétain's freedom of action.

Pétain's excessive caution was on display again in mid-July. Foch prepared to launch his first counterattack against Ludendorff's extended lines. With French and American troops under General Charles Mangin poised to hit the western flank of the bulge in the German line between the Marne and the Aisne, Pétain called for the attack to be canceled. He feared that the Germans would continue to move southward. Foch overruled Pétain, and the attack achieved a striking success.

For the remainder of the war, Pétain pushed his armies steadily forward without further friction with his superiors. He received his reward for his entire wartime service in December 1918, when he was promoted to the rank of field marshal. He remained on active duty until 1931.

Pétain was the only military commander from World War I to play a significant role in World War II. Tragically, it besmirched his reputation. Following the fall of France in 1940, the old general, now eighty-four, became the head of the Vichy government. Tainted as a collaborator with the Nazis, he found himself tried by his countrymen after the war. He ended his life imprisoned on the Isle d'Yeu off the coast of western France on July 23, 1951.

Gavrilo Princip (1894–1918)

Gavrilo Princip was the teenage assassin who murdered Austrian Archduke Franz Ferdinand, thereby precipitating the diplomatic crisis that led to the outbreak of World War I. Princip was a Serb living in Bosnia-Herzegovina, and he was steeped in the national hatreds that dominated life in the Balkans. The young man and his friends despised the fact of Habsburg rule over their homeland; they belonged to a group of radical schoolboys who longed to see Bosnia-Herzegovina united with the kingdom of Serbia. Enthusiastic but barely competent amateur killers, they were willing to take up the tools of the assassin to shake the power of Austria-Hungary over its Serb population. They expected great results of some sort by murdering the heir to the Austro-Hungarian throne. Princip ignited a diplomatic crisis that soon plunged most of the continent into hostilities.

The future political murderer was born on July 13, 1894, in the Krajina region of northwestern Bosnia. He was the son of a poor peasant who supported his family by farming and carrying the mail. A small, quiet child as well as a diligent student, Gavrilo grew up in a rural environment filled with nationalist propaganda calling for the creation of a Greater Serbia. Such a prize could come only by uniting the kingdom of Serbia with

Serb-inhabited territories like Bosnia-Herzegovina, under Austrian control, and Macedonia, under the rule of the Ottoman Empire.

In 1907 the thirteen-year-old finished his studies at his village school and moved to Sarajevo, where he continued his education at a local commercial school. There he had his first contact with one of the secret nationalist groups that thrived among schoolboys in the Serb communities of Bosnia-Herzegovina. For Serb nationalists of any age, the annexation of Bosnia-Herzegovina by Habsburg authorities in 1908 raised their passions to fever pitch. The move seemed a new and intolerable barrier to the united Serb state of their dreams.

In 1911 Princip joined a secret student group. He now had the example of a recent attempt at political assassination: in June 1910, a young Serb had tried unsuccessfully to murder the governor of Sarajevo. Meanwhile, in May of the same year, more competent Serb nationalists, many of them military and political figures of consequence in the kingdom of Serbia, had formed a group known as the Black Hand. It pledged to pursue "with all means" its goal—"the union of all Serbs."

In 1912 Princip took a crucial step toward his fateful encounter with Archduke Franz Ferdinand. Expelled from school after participating in a political demonstration, he crossed the border into the kingdom of Serbia; there he joined the horde of impoverished young Bosnian exiles who gathered in cheap cafés and dreamed of heroic actions. Serbia's victorious war against Turkey in the winter of 1912–1913 offered some of the exiles the chance for action. Princip, still undersized and apparently sickly, found himself rejected for service with Serbia's fighting forces. Embittered and frustrated, he spent the next months wandering between Sarajevo and Belgrade, the Serbian capital.

In early 1914, while Princip was still only nineteen, he joined a group of like-minded young Bosnian exiles. All were fervent Serb patriots; when Princip, in March, read of the archduke's planned visit to Sarajevo, all agreed with his call to murder the Austrian leader. At this point, Princip's group and the Black Hand made firm contact.

Some historians believe that the Black Hand decided to murder Franz Ferdinand; they feared that his plans for reforming the Austro-Hungarian Empire would cool the discontent of Serbs within the empire. In this view, Princip and his fellow teenagers were the triggermen for a group of politically sophisticated Serb leaders. More plausibly, Princip and his crew were the initiators of the plot, with no clear goal other than to strike at an Austrian leader who was making himself available as a target. The Black Hand merely provided weapons—pistols and bombs—for the youngsters, without knowing what they were up to or expecting much in the way of results. Black Hand leaders, such as the head of military intelligence in the Serbian army, were not likely to choose amateurs like Princip—who barely knew how to fire his pistol—as agents to carry out a carefully structured plot.

Starting in late May, Princip and two companions made their way to Sarajevo with their hoard of weapons. They brought a number of other amateur plotters into their circle, and on July 28 they struck. Most of the crew got cold feet or botched their chance at success. A mistake by the driver leading the archduke's entourage, however, placed Franz Ferdinand and his wife only a few feet from Princip. The young Bosnian fired twice—without aiming. Each shot found its mark, killing the archduke and his wife.

At the subsequent trial, Princip stood out from his fellow conspirators by refusing to plead guilty to any crime. Too young to receive the death penalty under Austrian law, all the convicted conspirators were sentenced to long prison terms. Princip died of tuberculosis in the military prison at Theresienstadt on April 28, 1918.

William S. Sims (1858–1936)

Admiral William S. Sims was the commander of American naval forces in Europe following the American entry into World War I. He eventually led a force of 75,000 officers and men and 370 ships, with forty-five bases scattered from Murmansk in northern Russia to Corfu in the eastern Mediterranean. Sims differed sharply from his army counterpart, General John Pershing, in his commitment to meet the needs of America's allies and his willingness to put American forces under British command. Deeply concerned by such immediate tasks as defeating the threat posed by German submarine warfare, he promoted the use of the convoy and the deployment of American destroyers in order to make this device work. His willingness to view British needs and leadership sympathetically exposed him to charges that he was excessively pro-British.

Sims was born in Canada on October 15, 1858. His father, an American engineer, had married a young Canadian woman from Ontario and then settled there for over a decade. The Sims family returned permanently to the United States when William was thirteen. The future admiral graduated from the United States Naval Academy in 1880, completed a subsequent two-year cruise, and received his commission in 1882.

Sims distinguished himself both as a gunnery expert and as an outspoken mid-level officer. His concern about the low standards of armament and marksmanship on U.S. naval vessels led him to write directly to President Theodore Roosevelt in 1901 to point out the failings of the American fleet.

assassination of Archduke Franz Ferdinand, he urged Austria to take harsh action against Serbia and offered unqualified German support. Thus, Wilhelm pointed Europe toward a Balkan war and, potentially, hostilities among the Great Powers. But the flighty German monarch's role in the crisis then diminished. On the eve of hostilities, for example, he welcomed both Serbia's conciliatory response to the Austrian ultimatum and hints that Britain would remain neutral in case of a European war. In the end, his political and military officials had no difficulty in getting him to sign the declaration of war.

In the wartime years, Wilhelm played a limited role. He had the prerogative of appointing and removing the top military leaders: in early September 1914, for example, he replaced the mentally exhausted army commander Helmuth von Moltke with an imperial favorite, Erich von Falkenhayn. He also made his views felt in naval affairs. There, he forbade the use of the High Seas Fleet in any action against the British navy that threatened the loss of Germany's battleships. He was initially effective in barring a wide use of the submarine that would bring the United States into the war.

When it came to the conduct of the land war, however, he was reduced to the role of bystander. Even in 1914, he complained to his companions at the imperial court that the high command no longer consulted him. Moreover, the strain of the war quickly fell on Wilhelm's unstable personality. He had fits of depression, alternating with unrealistic surges of optimism. Meanwhile, his main activity was restless traveling from one military headquarters to another.

In 1916 Wilhelm's wartime role shrank further. Even naval leaders neglected to consult him, and he was not involved in the decisions leading to the Battle of Jutland, in which his prized battleships were put at risk. As Falkenhayn's disastrous losses at Verdun combined with the entry of Rumania into the war, Prime Minister Bethmann Hollweg persuaded the emperor to bring in the eastern generals, Ludendorff and his nominal superior von Hindenburg, to direct the war effort. They quickly went to work with little regard for Germany's monarch.

By the close of 1916, pressure from the military leaders made the emperor drop his earlier opposition to unlimited use of the submarine. In the summer of 1917, the military leaders, led by Ludendorff, pushed Wilhelm to dismiss Bethmann Hollweg from the position of prime minister. They threatened resignation if their voices were not heard. Given Wilhelm's inability to hold them back, the military chieftains now stood as the country's real rulers.

By the final stages of the war, Wilhelm was less an actor than an observer who was downright dangerous to the interests of his country. A brutally effective Allied propaganda campaign used him as a symbol for Germany's misdeeds. In the United States, for example, "Kaiser Bill" became the chief villain on the enemy side. By his stubbornness, Wilhelm impeded the armistice negotiations that President Woodrow Wilson directed in the fall of 1918. His refusal to abdicate, for example, meant that Germany's enemies insisted on continuing the fighting. In the end, revolution swept Germany in the first weeks of November. Without waiting for the emperor's consent, Prince Max of Baden, the prime minister, announced Wilhelm's departure from the throne on November 9.

Germany's former ruler went into exile in Holland the following day. He lived there quietly for more than two decades, dying at his home at Doorn on June 4, 1941, while the country in which he had found refuge was under occupation by Adolf Hitler's Nazi armies.

Woodrow Wilson (1856–1924)

Woodrow Wilson was the president of the United States from 1913 to 1921 and the political leader of his country during the years of World War I. Wilson charted a course of neutrality for the United States during the first years of the war, but his policies in defense of what he considered American rights involved his country in confrontations with the belligerent powers. He wanted to avoid American military intervention, but, at the same time, he wanted to play a political role, especially as mediator and peacemaker, in the unfolding events.

In the end, Wilson led the United States into the war in early 1917, directed the mobilization of America's resources, and determined the policy of his government toward America's allies and opponents. He emerged as a leading figure in both the Armistice negotiations that ended the fighting and in the peace negotiations that established the postwar order in Europe. Thus, Wilson stands as the first American president to take the role of global leader.

Woodrow Wilson was born in Staunton, Virginia, on December 28, 1856, the son of a Presbyterian minister. Educated at Princeton and Johns Hopkins as both a lawyer and a historian, he made his mark in the academic world as a college professor and as Princeton's president before entering politics. He won the governorship of New Jersey in 1910, and he was elected president two years later. The Democratic Wilson pushed his own brand of Progressivism, calling for renewed governmental efforts to restore economic competition and protection for the small producer and consumer. During the years before World War I, Wilson conducted a program of domestic reform called "the New Freedom" that, in theory, tried to limit reliance on executive regulatory agencies and to establish a more coordinated legislative program between Congress and the presidency. His foreign policy focused on issues close to home such as the crisis in Mexico following that country's revolution of 1910, where Wilson practiced his "missionary diplomacy," a policy that encouraged democracy and progressive reform in the Western Hemisphere. Wilson's internationalism, like his domestic policy, looked to strong leadership, but it also caused him, his critics said, to meddle too much in others' affairs and to try to control events.

When war broke out in July 1914, Wilson called upon his countrymen to remain neutral in thought as well as deed. Given his respect for the British system of government and institutions, Wilson favored the Allied side against the Central Powers, and the course of the war led him into sharp conflict with the German government. Although the British infringed on American rights on the high seas, the German submarine campaign against merchant shipping brought harsher condemnation from Wilson. The British threatened property, but the Germans took lives. When a German submarine sank the British passenger liner *Lusitania* in May 1915, killing over a thousand civilians, including 128 Americans, Wilson pressured Berlin to halt unrestricted use of the submarine. He made it clear that otherwise the United States was now sufficiently interested in the course of the conflict to enter the war against Germany.

Wilson tried to act as mediator between the two sides, possibly with the hope of augmenting American global influence as well as bringing the carnage to an end. He was reelected, in a tight contest, in 1916 as the candidate who had kept America out of war. And as late as 1916, he placed limits on the buildup of American land and naval forces in order to promote the position of the United States as a neutral.

With the resumption of unlimited submarine warfare by Germany in early 1917, Wilson led the United States into World War I. The submarine issue was the immediate cause, but biographers of Wilson see a larger motive: with the failure of mediation, Wilson thought that only entering the war would allow the United States an important place in shaping the peace settlement.

Wilson appointed strong military leaders in the persons of General John Pershing and Admiral William Sims to wage the war in Europe. He gave both of them, but especially Pershing, wide latitude in conducting the American role in the fighting. When the course of domestic economic mobilization broke down, Wilson put Bernard Baruch in a position to direct much of the U.S. economy and turned increasingly to powerful boards and commissions to coordinate American policy and promote the war.

The American president became the spokesman in the eyes of the world for the Allied side in January 1918, when he set down the outlines of a generous peace settlement in his Fourteen Points. It was a program for a new world order that many on both sides of the fighting lines found hopeful and inspiring. He took on a dominant role in the diplomacy of World War I in the closing weeks of the fighting. German leaders approached Wilson in order to negotiate an armistice. Wilson's distrust of Germany's governing elites led him to insist that Germany adopt a parliamentary form of government similar to that of Britain before the shooting could come to a stop. His call for an end to "monarchical autocrats" was a clear demand that Kaiser Wilhelm II give up the throne.

Wilson left the United States for Europe in late 1918 in order to participate directly in the peace negotiations. There he found Allied leaders committed to a harsh peace. Both their own views and the pressure from their electorates led France's Georges Clemenceau and Britain's David Lloyd George away from a peace of reconciliation with Germany.

In the end, Wilson gave in to many of the demands of the countries alongside which the United States had fought. But he put his imprint on the settlement in his successful calls for national self-determination and for treaty arrangements to protect national minorities. But primarily Wilson hoped that the League of Nations, a postwar association of the leading powers of the world, would serve to create a just and stable peacetime system.

America's refusal to enter the League stands as the greatest disappointment Wilson saw contained in the peace settlement. Historians criticize Wilson himself, however, for his failure to lay the groundwork for American acceptance of membership. They note that the Democratic president neglected to bring leading Republican senators with him to Europe to take part in the peace negotiations. Moreover, a rigid personality that had always characterized Wilson's dealing with his political opponents made difficult any compromise with major American figures such as Senator Henry Cabot Lodge of Massachusetts. Wilson also failed to cultivate public opinion sufficiently to accept his brand of internationalism.

Blocked by his opponents at home, Wilson tried to rally the American people. He had long been burdened by fragile health, and his railroad tour of the United States led, in October 1919, to a stroke and complete physical collapse. The United States Senate rejected the Treaty of Versailles with Germany and thus refused to enter the League of Nations. Wilson's hopes that the war would lead to a world organization that included the United States were not realized.

Woodrow Wilson remained an invalid for the final year and a half of his term of office, and he died in Washington, D.C., on February 3, 1924.

Primary Documents of the War

GERMANY GOES TO WAR

By August 4, 1914, Germany was already at war with Russia and France. That afternoon, the German prime minister, Theobald von Bethmann Hollweg, addressed the Reichstag to ask its members to vote for war credits, the financial means by which Germany would carry on the conflict. The German leader painted a picture of a peaceful Germany threatened by aggressive and envious neighbors. Others had forced war on his newly united and prosperous country.

But Bethmann had to speak publicly about the reality of German aggression against its small neighbor, Belgium. In his address before the Reichstag, Bethmann stumbled verbally in trying to justify Germany's actions. By admitting that what Germany had done was "a breach of international law" and justifying it by claiming that "necessity knows no law," Bethmann blackened Germany's image permanently. The claim that harm to Belgium would be made good "as soon as our military aims have been attained" merely reminded enemy and neutral alike of German hopes for a quick victory. That same evening he met to say good-bye to British ambassador Sir Edward Goschen—Britain was scheduled to join Germany's opponents at midnight—and the German leader provided the Allies with a further potent propaganda theme when he referred to the treaty protecting Belgium's neutrality as "a scrap of paper."

Document 1
SPEECH OF THE IMPERIAL CHANCELLOR BEFORE THE GERMAN REICHSTAG, ON AUGUST 4TH, 1914

A stupendous fate is breaking over Europe. For forty-four years, since the time we fought for and won the German Empire and our position in the world, we have lived in peace and have protected the peace of Europe. In the works of peace we have become strong and powerful, and have thus aroused the envy of others. With patience we have faced the fact that, under the pretense that Germany was desirous of war, enmity has been awakened against us in the East and the West, and chains have been fashioned for us. The wind then sown has brought forth the whirlwind which has now broken loose. We wished to continue our work of peace, and, like a silent vow, the feeling that animated everyone from the Emperor down to the youngest soldier was this: Only in defence of a just cause shall our sword fly from its scabbard.

The day has now come when we must draw it, against our will, and in spite of our sincere endeavours. Russia has set fire to the building. We are at war with Russia and France—a war that has been forced upon us. . . .

Gentlemen, we are now in a state of necessity (*Notwehr*), and necessity (*Not*) knows no law. Our troops have occupied Luxembourg and perhaps have already entered Belgian territory.

Gentlemen, that is a breach of international law. It is true that the French Government declared at Brussels that France would respect Belgian neutrality as long as her adversary respected it. We knew, however, that France stood ready for an invasion. France could wait, we could not. A French attack on our flank on the lower Rhine might have been disastrous. Thus we were forced to ignore the rightful protests of the Governments of Luxembourg and Belgium. The wrong—I speak openly—the wrong we thereby commit we will try to make good as soon as our military aims have been attained.

He who is menaced as we are and is fighting for his highest possessions can only consider how he is to hack his way through (*durchhauen*). . . .

Gentlemen, so much for the facts. I repeat the words of the Emperor: "With a clear conscience we enter the lists." We are fighting for the fruits of our works of peace, for the inheritance of a great past and for our future. The fifty years are not yet past during which Count Moltke said we should have to remain armed to defend the inheritance that we won in 1870. Now the great hour of trial has struck for our people. But with clear confidence we go forward to meet it. Our army is in the field, our navy is ready for battle—behind them stands the entire German nation—the entire German nation united to the last man.

Gentlemen, you know your duty and all that it means. The proposed laws need no further explanation. I ask you to pass them quickly.

Source: Great Britain Foreign Office. *Collected Documents Relating to the Outbreak of the War* (London: His Majesty's Stationery Office, 1915), pp. 436, 438–439.

BRITAIN ENTERS THE WAR

On September 19, 1914, David Lloyd George, Britain's Chancellor of the Exchequer, spoke at a mass meeting in London. This was the first public address by a ranking member of the government after the bloody early battles of the war had failed to bring decisive success to either side.

Lloyd George spoke in part to encourage enlistments in the British army. Great Britain did not yet have compulsory military service. Between August 4 and September 12, almost 480,000 Britons had already offered themselves as volunteers; still more were needed. But Lloyd George had a larger purpose as well. With the war likely to continue for some time, it was crucial to rally public support for Britain's war effort. Thus, he offered the entire nation a call for unity and an explanation why Britain was at war.

The fiery Welsh orator, the most renowned British speaker of his time, presented several reasons to justify a vast and costly national effort. Britain was bound by treaty and honor to defend tiny Belgium against Germany, its gigantic and aggressive neighbor. And, while he expressed sympathy for the German people, Lloyd George harped on the iniquity and arrogance of their leaders. He ignored Germany's bland prime minister and used the flamboyant Kaiser Wilhelm II himself as the symbol of German evil. To his listeners, Lloyd George offered two emotionally satisfying rewards for their coming contribution to victory: first, the gratification of sacrifice in a good cause; second, the hope of a better country, even a better world, emerging from the battlefields.

The speech was a resounding success, although Lloyd George, nervous before he spoke and depressed afterward, did not realize it at the time. Hailed by members of his own Liberal party and by leaders of the rival Conservatives as well, it was widely read in the country's newspapers, translated into more than a dozen languages, and reprinted several times in pamphlet form. The words Lloyd George uttered that Saturday afternoon set down many of the themes that dominated the British government's appeal to the population for wartime sacrifice. No less important, it put Lloyd George himself, along with Minister of War Lord Kitchener, before the public as the symbol of Britain's war effort. Along with his future service as minister of munitions, the Queen's Hall address opened the way for Lloyd George to become prime minister at the height of the conflict.

Lloyd George referred only obliquely—"Wrest the trident out of her hands"—to the war as one in which Germany threatened British power and security. Most historians and biographers of the Welsh leader see the desire to meet that threat as his prime motive for helping to bring Britain into the costly conflict. But it was scarcely the theme he chose to emphasize in this emotional appeal to the nation as a whole.

Document 2
"HONOUR AND DISHONOUR"

Why is our honour as a country involved in this war? Because, in the first place, we are bound in an honourable obligation to defend the independence, the liberty, the integrity of a small neighbor that has lived peaceably, but she could not have compelled us, because she was weak. The man who declines to discharge his debt because his creditor is too poor to enforce it is a blackguard. We entered into this treaty, a solemn treaty, a full treaty to defend Belgium and her integrity. Our signatures are attached to the document. Our signatures do not stand alone there. . . .

It is now the interest of Prussia to break the treaty, and she has done it. Well, why? She avowed it with cynical contempt for every principle of justice. She says treaties only bind you when it is to your interest to keep them. "What is a treaty?" says the German Chancellor. "A scrap of paper." . . .

We are fighting against barbarism. But there is only one way of putting it right. If there are nations that say they will only respect treaties when it is to their interest to do so, we must make it to their interest to do so for the future. What is their defence? Just look at the interview which took place between our Ambassador and great German officials when their attention was called to this treaty to which they were partners. They said: "We cannot help that." Rapidity of action was the great German asset. There is a greater asset for a nation than rapidity of action, and that is—honest dealing. . . .

Belgium has been treated brutally, how brutally we shall not yet know. . . . She was one of the most unoffending little countries in Europe. . . . Hundreds of thousands of her people have had their quiet, comfortable little homes burned to the dust, and are wandering homeless in their own land. What is their crime? Their crime was that they trusted to the word of a Prussian King. . . .

I would not say a word about the German people to disparage them. They are a great people; they have great qualities of head, of hand, and of heart. I believe, in spite of recent events, there is as great a store of kindness in the German peasant as in any peasant in the world. But he has been drilled into a false idea of civilisation, efficiency, capability. It is a hard civilisation: it is a selfish civilisation: it is a material civilisation. . . . God made man in his own image—high of purpose, in the region of the spirit. German civilisation would re-create him in the image of a Diesler machine—precise, accurate, powerful, with no room for the soul to operate. That is the "higher" civilisation. . . .

. . . Treaties? They tangled the feet of Germany in her advance. Cut them with the sword. Little nations? They hinder the advance of Germany. Trample them in the mire under the German heel. The Russian Slav? He challenges the supremacy of Germany and Europe. Hurl your legions at him and massacre him. Britain? She is a constant menace to the predominancy of Germany in the world. Wrest the trident out of her hands. Ah! more than that. The new philosophy of Germany is to destroy Christianity. Sickly sentimentalism about sacrifice for others—poor pap for German digestion. We will have a new diet. We will force it on the world. It will be made in Germany. A diet of blood and iron. . . .

That is what we are fighting, that claim to predominancy of a civilisation, a material one, a hard one, a civilisation which if once it rules and sways the world, liberty goes, democracy vanishes, and unless Britain comes to the rescue, and her sons, it will be a dark day for humanity. We are not fighting the German people. The German people are just as much under the heel of this Prussian military caste, and more so, thank God, than any other nation in Europe. It will be a day of rejoicing for the German peasant and artisan and trader when the military caste is broken. . . .

I envy you young people your youth. They have put up the age limit for the army, but I march, I am sorry to say, a good many years even beyond that. But still our turn will come. It is a great opportunity. It only comes once in many centuries to the children of men. For most generations sacrifice comes in drab weariness of spirit to men. It has come to-day to you; it has come to-day to us all, in the form of the glow and thrill of a great movement for liberty, that impels millions throughout Europe to the same end. It is a great war for the emancipation of Europe from the thraldom of a military caste, which has cast its shadow upon two generations of men, and which has now plunged the world into a welter of bloodshed. . . .

. . . . Those who have fallen have consecrated deaths. They have taken their part in the making of a new Europe, a new world. I can see signs of its coming in the glare of the battlefield. The people will gain more by this struggle in all lands than they comprehend at the present moment. It is true they will be rid of the menace to their freedom. But that is not all. There is something infinitely greater and more enduring which is emerging already out of this great conflict; a new patriotism, richer, nobler, more exalted than the old. I see a new recognition amongst all classes, high and low shedding themselves of selfishness; a new recognition that the honour of a country does not depend merely on the maintenance of its glory in the stricken field, but in protecting its homes from distress as well. It is a new patriotism, it is bringing a new outlook for all classes. A great flood of luxury and of sloth which had submerged the land is receding, and a new Britain is appearing. We can see for the first time the fundamental things that matter in life and that have been obscured from our vision by the tropical growth of prosperity.

Source: David Lloyd George. A Speech by the Rt. Hon. D. Lloyd George, at Queen's Hall, London, September 19, 1914. (London: Methuen and Co., [1914]).

A CIVILIAN GREETS THE WAR

Crowds in the capitals of Germany, France, Austria-Hungary, and Britain met the outbreak of war with heated enthusiasm. From the man in the street to intellectuals in their salons or coffeehouses, Europe's population threw itself emotionally into the conflict: glorifying the nation's armed forces, casting the enemy in devilish form, and hoping for immeasurable rewards following the inevitable victory.

In his memoirs Stefan Zweig (1881–1942), a leading Austrian author and a widely traveled member of Europe's intellectual elite, recorded his observations and personal reactions at the start of the conflict.

Document 3
MEMOIRS OF STEFAN ZWEIG:
THE WAR'S BEGINNING

The next morning I was in Austria. In every station placards had been put up announcing general mobilization. The trains were filled with fresh recruits, banners were flying, music sounded, and in Vienna I found the entire city in a tumult. The first shock at the news of war—the war that no one, people or government, had wanted—the war which had slipped, much against their will, out of the clumsy hands of the diplomats who had been bluffing and toying with it, had suddenly been transformed into enthusiasm. There were parades in the street, flags, ribbons, and music burst forth everywhere, young recruits were marching triumphantly, their faces lighting up at the cheering—they, the John Does and Richard Roes who usually go unnoticed and uncelebrated.

And to be truthful, I must acknowledge that there was a majestic, rapturous, and even seductive something in this first outbreak of the people from which one could escape only with difficulty. And in spite of all my hatred and aversion for war, I should not like to have missed the memory of those first days. As never before, thousands and hundreds of thousands felt what they should have felt in peace time, that they belonged together. . . . All differences of class, rank, and language were flooded over at that moment by the rushing feeling of fraternity. Strangers spoke to one another in the streets, people who had avoided each other for years shook hands, everywhere one saw excited faces. Each individual experienced an exaltation of his ego, he was no longer the isolated person of former times, he had been incorporated into the mass, he was part of the people, and his person, his hitherto unnoticed person, had been given meaning. The petty mail clerk, who ordinarily sorted letters early and late, who sorted constantly, who sorted from Monday until Saturday without interruption; the clerk, the cobbler, had suddenly achieved a romantic possibility in life: he could become a hero, and everyone who wore a uniform was already being cheered by the women, and greeted beforehand with this romantic appellation by those who had to remain behind. They acknowledged the unknown power which had lifted them out of their everyday existence. Even mothers with their grief, and women with their fears, were ashamed to manifest their quite natural emotions in the face of this first transformation. . . .

. . . Solemnly the poets swore never again to have any cultural association with a Frenchman or an Englishman, they went even further, they denied overnight that there had ever been any French or English culture. All that was insignificant and valueless in comparison with German character, German art, and German thought. But the savants were even worse. The sole wisdom of the philosophers was to declare the war a "bath of steel" which would beneficially preserve the strength of the people from enervation. The physicians fell into line and praised the prosthesis so extravagantly that one was almost tempted to have a leg amputated so that the healthy member might be replaced by an artificial one. The ministers of all creeds had no desire to be outdone and joined in the chorus, at times as if a horde of possessed were raving, and yet all these men were the very same whose reason, creative power and humane conduct one had admired only a week, a month, before.

The most shocking thing about this madness was that most of these persons were honest. For the most part, old or physically unfit for military service, they thought themselves in decency obligated to take part in every supporting effort. All that they had achieved they owed to the language and thus to the people. And so they desired to serve their people by means of the language and let them hear what they wished to hear: that justice was solely on their side in this struggle, and injustice on the other, that Germany would triumph and the enemy be ignominiously conquered—quite oblivious of the fact that in so doing they were betraying the true mission of the poet, the preserver and defender of the universal humanity of mankind. Of course many felt the bitter taste of disgust on their tongues at their own words as soon as the fumes of the initial enthusiasm had evaporated. But in the early months those who raved the loudest attracted most attention, and so they sang and yelled in a wild chorus here, there and everywhere. . . .

. . . The mental confusion increased in absurdity. The cook at her stove, who had never been outside the city and had never looked at an atlas since her schooldays, believed that Austria could not endure without Sanchschak (a small frontier hamlet somewhere in Bosnia). Cabdrivers argued on the streets about the reparations to be imposed on France, fifty billions or a hundred, without knowing how much a billion was. There was no city, no group that had not fallen prey to this dreadful hysteria of hatred. The ministers preached from their pulpits, the Social Democrats, who but a month before had branded militarism as the greatest crime, clamored perhaps louder than all the others so as not to be classed as "people without a fatherland" in the words of Emperor Wilhelm. . . .

It soon became impossible to converse reasonably with anybody in the first war weeks of 1914. The most peaceable and the most good-natured were intoxicated with the smell of blood. . . . Every conversation ended in some stupid phrase such as: "He who cannot hate cannot really love," or in coarse inculpations. Comrades with whom I had not quarreled for years accused me rudely of no longer being an Austrian; why did I not go over to France or Belgium? They even hinted cautiously that sentiments such as the war was a crime ought to be brought to the attention of the authorities, for "defeatists"—that nice word had just been invented in France—were the worst betrayers of the fatherland.

Nothing remained but to withdraw into one's self and to keep silent while the others ranted and raved. . . .

After a few weeks, determined to escape this dangerous mass psychosis, I moved to a rural suburb to commence my personal war in the midst of war, the struggle against the betrayal of Reason by the current mass passion.

Source: Stefan Zweig, *The World of Yesterday* (Lincoln: University of Nebraska Press, 1964), pp. 222–24, 230–31, 235–37.

A FRENCHMAN GOES TO WAR

In August 1914, millions of young European men were pulled from their peacetime lives, put into uniform, and hurled into the unfamiliar world of war. Standing armies numbering hundreds of thousands of men grew, with the influx of reservists, into mammoth forces within a matter of days. In France and Germany in particular, the mobilization went smoothly, eased by years of elaborate planning and the wave of patriotism that swept through most of the population. French military authorities had feared that more than 13 percent of their reservists would fail to answer the call to arms. In fact, only 1.5 percent did not report as ordered.

Each of the young men called to the colors must have had a variety of thoughts: upon hearing of the outbreak of war, upon going into the military, and upon experiencing combat for the first time. The young Frenchman André Cornet-Auquier, in peacetime a professor at the University of Glasgow, can serve as a spokesman for the millions of Englishmen, Germans, Austrians, Russians, and members of other nationalities who went through this brutal and unexpected turn in their lives.

A Protestant with relatives in England and the United States, Cornet-Auquier greeted the war with a combination of enthusiasm and resignation. As a French reservist, he joined his unit upon the outbreak of the conflict and marched immediately into combat. He served on the relatively quiet sector of the front where French troops penetrated the province of Alsace, taken from France by Germany in 1871. Nonetheless, within a few weeks the horrors of the carnage entered his life, and his attitude to the war came to include new elements: fear, disgust, and a growing, if complex, attachment to his religious beliefs. Cornet-Auquier served at the front for more than a year and a half. On March 2, 1916, he died of wounds received in combat.

Document 4
LETTERS OF CAPTAIN ANDRÉ CORNET-AUQUIER

Colwyn Bay, North Wales, August 3, 1914.

Dearest Parents: The latest news shows that we are in for war. I learned this yesterday afternoon. When we heard it in the house where I was staying, everybody grew pale. We thereupon had family prayers and sang, "Be with us, Lord." How beautiful are the words of that hymn. Our host prayed for me and for mama, expressing the hope that she might have God's support in her trial. "We recommend to Thee the mother of our brother," were his words; "Thou knowest what they are to one another." I was and am still calm. God is there; fear nothing. And you know I have a military soul. Tell the British uncles that I am proud to fight not only for France but also for England, that dear second native land of mine; and if I must die for those two countries, I shall do so happily, provided only that we are victorious. But I am a French soldier all the same. I shall reach Paris to-morrow, during the day.

Châlon-sur-Saône, August 5.

Tell the English uncles that I shall fight like a Frenchman and die like an Englishman. The order will be Nelson's famous one: "England expects that every man will do his duty!" So let us be of good courage. Hurrah for France and England!

Belley, August 6.

You cannot imagine the delirious enthusiasm of the troops. A British officer whom I met at the Ambérieu station can't get over his surprise at it. I am back again in the military spirit,—soldier to my fingers' tips. . . .

Alsace, August 25.

What a reception we have had! "You are our saviors," the people said to us this morning. . . . My German is very useful, but the people here are very proud to speak French. The morale is good. . . .

September 4.

I have been under fire for the first time! Oh, the horrors of war! The ravaged villages! How it all tries your nerves! God be with us! I feel that He is with me!

September 10.

I am writing you a few hundred yards from the enemy's lines. I have been lying only two hundred yards from the Germans and I can assure you I kept my eyes open. We are all beat out. It is ten days since I have had a wash, and I haven't had my shoes off for a week. I couldn't give you an idea of my complexion if I tried. It was the heavy artillery which gave me my first baptism of fire. For three hours we lay flat on the ground while the shells fell all around us. One of them burst scarcely more than five or six yards from me, making a great hole in the ground and covering me with earth and debris. But the worst thing about all this is the smell of the dead bodies. The other day my section was detailed to bury some thirty half-putrefied corpses. You cannot imagine what this work is. Oh what horrors I have witnessed,— terrible wounds and ruined villages. What brutes these Germans are to burn the farms. I am quite ready to give my life if I know that you will make the sacrifice of it for France. I feel that I am surrounded with prayers, and I often pray for you all. One of my best comrades here is a priest who is also a second lieutenant like myself. A thousand affectionate remembrances to all. God preserve us all as He has done so far. Your son and brother who sends warmest love. . . .

September 22–24 and 27.

I have been two weeks without taking off my shoes, washing or shaving. I am writing you under shell fire, and I eat and sleep in the same conditions. It is terrible the state of mind you get into on a battle field. I would never have believed that I could remain so indifferent in the presence of dead bodies. For us soldiers, human life seems to count for nothing. To think that one can laugh, like a crazy man, in the midst of it all. But as soon as you begin to reflect an extraordinary feeling takes possession of you,—an infinite gravity and melancholy. You live from day to day without thinking of the morrow, for you ask yourself, may there be a morrow? You never use the future tense without adding, If we get there. You form no projects for the time to come. Everything for the moment is at a standstill. What a strange life. You almost think you would prefer to know what is coming. And to think that God knows and that He had foreseen it all! A captain who is a friend of mine and who is a very pious Catholic, said to me the other day that before every battle he prays. Our major answered that it was not the moment for such things and that he would do better to attend to his military duties. The captain replied: "Major, that doesn't prevent me from command-ing, taking orders, and fighting. On the contrary, it braces me up." I said: "Captain, I do just as you do, and I too find that it does me good." My dear little mother writes me that she would so like to press my weary head to her heart. And I too; for sometimes I am all done up, especially since I have had this company to command. To-day is Sunday, ten A.M. You are going downstairs to prayers, and papa will pray for "our soldiers and sailors." Oh pray earnestly for them. How painful it is to hear the cannon roar on Sunday, instead of listening to songs of praise and prayers. I embrace you all most tenderly, my dear ones.

Source: André Cornet-Auquier, *A Soldier Unafraid: Letters from the Trenches on the Alsatian Front,* ed. and trans. Theodore Stanton (Boston: Little, Brown, 1918), pp. 1–2, 4–6, 7–9.

WARTIME LOSSES AND CIVILIAN BEREAVEMENT

Europeans soon discovered that the cost of the war in human life exceeded all their worst expectations. France in 1914 lost a total of 955,000 men killed, wounded, and captured. The following year, the bloodiest of the entire conflict for France, the losses were 50 percent greater: 1,430,000. Britain suffered in a lesser way in the first years of the conflict, although the casualty lists lengthened in grim fashion. By the close of 1914, that country's losses totalled 90,000, of whom 9,500 had been killed. A year later, the total was 512,000, almost half of whom were listed as killed or missing in action.

Families in all of the belligerent countries learned of the death of relatives and friends. For many women, this was their first and most direct contact with the reality of the fighting.

In her memoirs, Vera Brittain (1893–1970), a university student who served during the war as a nurse's aide, recorded her reactions as the war's cost struck her and her family.

Document 5
VERA BRITTAIN'S PERSONAL TRAGEDY

[September 1915] Early in September, we heard of the first casualty to happen in our family. A cousin from Ireland, we learnt, had died of wounds after the landing at Suvla Bay; the original bullet-wound behind the ear had not been serious, but he had lain untended for a week at Mudros, and was already suffering from cerebral sepsis when operated on, too late, by an overworked surgeon on the crowded *Aquitania. I* had hardly known my cousin, but it was a shock to learn that lives were being thrown away through the inadequacy of the medical services in the Mediterranean. Was it, I wondered, a repetition of Scutari, with no Florence Nightingale to save the situation? . . .

[December 1915] Directly after breakfast, sent on my way by exuberant good wishes from Betty and Marjorie and many of the others, I went down to Brighton. . . .

When, by ten o'clock at night, no news had come, I concluded that the complications of telegraph and telephone on a combined Sunday and Christmas Day had made communication impossible. So, unable to fight sleep any longer after a night and a day of wakefulness, I went to bed a little disappointed, but still unperturbed. . . .

The next morning I had just finished dressing, and was putting the final touches to the pastel-blue crêpe-de-Chine blouse, when the expected message came to say that I was wanted on the telephone. Believing that I was at last to hear the voice for which I had waited for twenty-four hours, I dashed joyously into the corridor. But the message was not from Roland but from Clare; it was not to say that he had arrived home that morning, but to tell me that he had died of wounds at a Casualty Clearing Station on December 23rd. . . .

WHENEVER I think of the weeks that followed the news of Roland's death, a series of pictures, disconnected but crystal clear, unroll themselves like a kaleidoscope through my mind.

A solitary cup of coffee stands before me on a hotel breakfast-table; I try to drink it, but fail ignominiously.

Outside, in front of the promenade, dismal grey waves tumble angrily over one another on the windy Brighton shore, and, like a slaughtered animal that still twists after life has been extinguished, I go on mechanically worrying because his channel-crossing must have been so rough.

In an omnibus, going to Keymer, I look fixedly at the sky; suddenly the pale light of a watery sun streams out between the dark, swollen clouds, and I think for one crazy moment that I have seen the heavens opened. . . .

At Keymer a fierce gale is blowing and I am out alone on the brown winter ploughlands, where I have been driven by a desperate desire to escape from the others. Shivering violently, and convinced that I am going to be sick, I take refuge behind a wet bank of grass from the icy sea-wind that rushes, screaming, across the sodden fields. . . .

I am buying some small accessories for my uniform in a big Victoria Street store, when I stop, petrified, before a vase of the tall pink roses that Roland gave me on the way to *David Copperfield;* in the warm room their melting sweetness brings back the memory of that New Year's Eve, and suddenly, to the perturbation of the shop-assistants, I burst into uncontrollable tears, and find myself, helpless and humiliated, unable to stop crying in the tram all the way back to the hospital.

It is Sunday, and I am out for a solitary walk through the dreary streets of Camberwell before going to bed after the night's work. In front of me on the frozen pavement a long red worm wriggles slimily. I remember that, after our death, worms destroy this body—however lovely, however beloved—and I run from the obscene thing in horror.

It is Wednesday, and I am walking up the Brixton Road on a mild, fresh morning of early spring. Half-consciously I am repeating a line from Rupert Brooke:

"The deep night, and birds singing, and clouds flying. . . . "

For a moment I have become conscious of the old joy in rainwashed skies and scuttling, fleecy clouds, when suddenly I remember—Roland is dead and I am not keeping faith with him; it is mean and cruel, even for a second, to feel glad to be alive. . . .

[June 1918] I had just announced to my father, as we sat over tea in the dining-room, that I must do up Edward's papers and take them to the post office before it closed for the week-end, when there came the sudden loud clattering at the front-door knocker that always meant a telegram.

For a moment I thought that my legs would not carry me, but they behaved quite normally as I got up and went to the door. I knew what was in the telegram—I had known for a week—but because the persistent hopefulness of the human heart refuses to allow intuitive certainty to persuade the reason of that which it knows, I opened and read it in a tearing anguish of suspense.

"Regret to inform you Captain E. H. Brittain M.C. killed in action Italy June 15th."

"No answer," I told the boy mechanically, and handed the telegram to my father, who had followed me into the hall. As we went back into the dining-room I saw, as though I had never seen them before, the bowl of blue delphiniums on the table; their intense colour, vivid, ethereal, seemed too radiant for earthly flowers. . . .

Long after the family had gone to bed and the world had grown silent, I crept into the dining-room to be alone with Edward's portrait. Carefully closing the door, I turned on the light and looked at the pale, pictured face, so dignified, so steadfast, so tragically mature. He had been through so much—far, far more than those beloved friends who had died at an earlier stage of the interminable War, leaving him alone to mourn their loss. Fate might have allowed him the little, sorry compensation of survival, the chance to make his lovely music in honour of their memory. It seemed indeed the last irony that he should have been killed by the countrymen of Fritz Kreisler, the violinist whom of all others he had most greatly admired.

And suddenly, as I remembered all the dear afternoons and evenings when I had followed him on the piano as he played his violin, the sad, searching eyes of the portrait were more than I could bear, and falling on my knees before it I began to cry "Edward! Oh, Edward!" in dazed repetition, as though my persistent crying and calling would somehow bring him back.

Source: Vera Brittain, *Testament of Youth: An Autobiographical Study of the Years 1900–1925* (New York: Penguin, 1989), pp. 195, 236, 239–41, 438–39.

AMERICA RESPONDS TO THE WAR, 1914–1915

American public opinion toward World War I, as reflected in the nation's press, shifted sharply between July 1914 and May 1915. Most New York newspapers, for example, led by the influential *New York Times*, took a generally pro-Allied, anti-German position in the first months of the conflict. Nonetheless, during the war's first days, they mixed uncertain thoughts about how the conflict would develop with strong views that the war ought not to involve the United States directly.

Thus, on July 28, as Austria-Hungary invaded Serbia, the leading editorial in the *Times* expressed the hope that Kaiser Wilhelm II would guide "the sober-minded statesmen of Europe" to show they "are not men of blood but of peace." With war among the Great Powers erupting on August 1, such hopes vanished, but the *Times* now assured its readers that Americans "need only keep our heads and go about our daily tasks with the determination to let war interfere with us as little as possible." Even this view was subject to second thoughts. And so, on August 5, the *Times* lamented how "a struggle we do not share and that we utterly condemn" would cause Americans economic harm: "losses, distress, discouragement, the check to enterprises, enforced idleness of multitudes dependent on work for daily bread."

Within a few months, the *Times* was more direct in expressing its concerns about Europe's tragedy. An editorial of December 15 castigated "the head-strong, misguided, and dangerous rulers of Germany." Nonetheless, for most citizens of the world's most important neutral power, the main feature of the war was its remoteness from the shores of the United States.

That sense of distance from the conflict faded as a handful of Americans died, starting in late March 1915, as Germany's submarine war struck merchant shipping in British waters. It vanished forever with the sinking of the giant British liner *Lusitania* on May 7, 1915, in what Patrick Devlin has described as "the supreme act of unrestricted warfare." On May 8, the *New York Times* expressed its outrage at the submarine attack that had killed 128 American civilians.

Document 6
NEW YORK TIMES EDITORIAL:
"WAR BY ASSASSINATION"

From our Department of State there must go to the Imperial Government at Berlin a demand that the Germans shall no longer make war like savages drunk with blood, that they shall cease to seek the attainment of their ends by the assassination of non-combatants and neutrals. In the history of wars there is no single deed comparable in its inhumanity and its horror to the destruction, without warning, by German torpedoes of the great steamship *Lusitania*, with more than 1800 souls on board and among them more than 100 Americans. Our demand must be made, and it will be heeded, unless Germany in her madness would have it understood that she is at war with the whole civilized world. For many hours yesterday the hope was cherished that the passengers and crew of the ship had been saved, but later it was made certain that there had been an appalling loss of life, and then there was here full realization of the extreme seriousness of this latest act of barbarity and of its effect upon our relations to the war. It will stir the American people as they have not been stirred since the destruction of the *Maine* in the harbor of Havana and Government and people will be united in the resolve that Germany must be called upon to bring her practices into conformity with the usages of civilized warfare.

Germany has wantonly and without provocation sent to their death a large, though as yet unknown, number of Americans. The American passengers aboard the *Lusitania* were going about their lawful concerns, they were entirely within their right, for no effective and lawfully established blockade annulled their privilege to take passage for England aboard a British ship. Had such a blockade been established, even, it would have been a monstrous crime for a German submarine to send the ship to the bottom without warning and without affording an opportunity to save the lives of the ship's company. The commander of the German submarine had a right to destroy the *Lusitania*, an enemy ship, since it is obvious that he could not with safety have attempted to take her as a prize to a German port, but it has always been the law of war at sea that the passengers and crew of a ship stopped or seized must be taken off before she is sunk. The loss of so great a number of the passengers and crew of the *Lusitania* shows that this humane rule was ruthlessly disregarded by the German Captain. It is an act, therefore, which falls clearly within the scope and intent of our solemn admonition to Germany. . . .

The evidence of deliberation, of an intent to destroy this particular ship, is too nearly conclusive to be ignored. Upon the very day the *Lusitania* sailed the Imperial German Embassy at Washington caused to be published in the newspapers of this country an advertisement warning travelers that ships flying the flag of Great Britain were liable to destruction in the waters about the British Isles and that passengers "sailing in the war zone" on ships of Great Britain or her "allies do so at their own risk." There were other warnings. They were not heeded by the passengers who sailed on the *Lusitania* simply because it was impossible for them to believe that a great civilized nation like Germany would wantonly destroy a merchant ship carrying only peaceable non-combatants. We have learned much about Germany since the war began, much that has shocked the world's sense of humanity, but this frightful deed was held to be within the domain of the incredible until it was perpetrated. . . .

. . . . We must demand that Germany shall not continue to make war on us. We may present the demand with reasonable confidence that Germany will pay heed to it. She has done herself irreparable harm by her procedures in the war, beginning with the devastation of Belgium, and it is harm in this latest dreadful instance without any compensating gain. The Germans cannot advance their cause by forcing the world to perceive and admit that they are a people apart, that they are bent upon making war by methods and practices which civilized nations have long since renounced and condemned and by exhibiting a degree of brutality which is commonly associated with madness. It is not to be believed that either the German Government or the German people are wholly mad, and the notice we are compelled to take of the destruction of the *Lusitania* will, we hope, serve to recall them to sense and reason.

They cannot fail to understand the effect this deed will have upon public sentiment in the United States. While there may have been some among us who, up to this moment, were inclined to hold a suspended judgment as to the justifications and procedures of Germany, now the American people will be of one mind. We are proverbially a people not easily aroused to passion, there will now be little of that. The American people will feel that it is their duty to be calm, because the occasion is too serious for indulgence in vain excitement. And happily there is at the head of the nation a man of proved strength and balance. President WILSON, because of his strength and the habitual soberness of his judgment, will resist all prompting to unreasonable or hasty action. But he knows the people who have put him at the head of the nation, he will instinctively know and understand the feeling that pervades the country today, and he will respond to it by taking the firm, wise course which justice, right, and honor demand.

Source: New York Times, editorial, May 8, 1915.

HUNGER IN CENTRAL EUROPE

During World War I, the fighting nations used food as a weapon against their enemies, and the inability to feed their populations adequately became a crucial weakness for the governments involved in the conflict. Britain's blockade of the Central Powers put immediate pressure on the food supply in Germany and Austria-Hungary. The need to feed huge armies—in which men needed more nourishment than in civilian life—combined with the loss of imported goods such as fertilizers and a reduced number of farm workers to limit the amount of food available. In 1917 German submarine warfare put comparable strain on the British food supply, most of which came over the sea lanes.

There were numerous things governments could do to ease the strain. As a first set of measures, they could urge or require farmers to increase food production, shift shipping patterns to facilitate the import of additional food, adulterate foods like bread, and limit the use of grains for making beer and other alcoholic drinks. But swollen government authority over civilian populations in wartime allowed for even vaster measures, including rationing many or most items of food. As a last resort, governments could set up food kitchens to feed segments of their populations directly.

In 1917 and 1918 the British government resorted to all of the possibilities in the first category and, eventually, to direct rationing. The Central Powers from the first months of the war moved more rapidly to impose rationing, and eventually set up food kitchens. Nonetheless, in Germany and Austria-Hungary, food shortages made life on the home front grim for all and desperate for many. Black markets thrived, and populations were divided into those with the wealth and connections to ease their hunger and those—a much larger number—who had no such possibility.

A witness to the food crisis faced by the Central Powers from 1914 to the start of 1917 was George Abel Schreiner (1875–1942). A naturalized American citizen who had been born in Germany, Schreiner served as a war correspondent in Central Europe for the Associated Press until the United States entered the war.

Document 7
GEORGE ABEL SCHREINER AND HUNGER
IN THE CENTRAL POWERS

A high tide in hoarding set in. Everybody filled garret and cellar with the things which the farm produces. Flour was stowed away in all possible and impossible places. Potatoes were accumulated. Butter and eggs were salted away, and so much fruit was preserved that sugar ceased to be obtainable in countries which had formerly exported much of it. . . .

The practice of hoarding was well enough for the well-to-do. But it left the poor entirely unprovided. The average wage-earner did not have the means to buy food at the fancy prices that governed the illicit food market, and the food that went to the hoarder cut short the general supply upon which the poor depended for their daily allowance. It was quite the regular thing for the wife of a poor man to stand in line three hours and then be turned away. The retailer would still have food in the cellar, but that was to go out by private delivery. The food cards held by the women were no warrant on the quantities they prescribed, but merely the authorization to draw so and so much if the things were to be had. The woman had to take the retailer's word for it. When that august person said, "Sold out," there was nothing to do but go home and pacify the hungry children with whatever else the depleted larder contained. . . .

The food situation in Central Europe became really desperate in the third year of the war. The year's wheat crop had been short in quantity and quality. Its nutritive value was about 55 per cent of normal. The rye crop was better, but not large enough to meet the shortage in breadstuffs caused by the poor wheat yield. Barley was fair under the circumstances. Oats were a success in many parts of Germany, but fell very low in Austria and Hungary. The potato crop was a failure. . . .

Up to this time the war-bread of the Central states had been rather palatable, though a steady loss in quality had been noticeable. Soon it came to pass that the ration of bread had to be reduced to about one-quarter of a pound per day. And the dough it was made of was no longer good.

The 55–25–20 war-bread was good to eat and very nutritious. The stuff now passing for bread was anything but that, so far as Austria was concerned. Its quality fluctuated from one week to another. I was unable to keep track of it. Indian corn was already used in the loaf, and before long ground clover hay was to form one of its constituents. Worst of all, the bread was not always to be had. At the beginning of November the three slices of bread into which the ration was divided, as a rule, fell to two, so that the daily allowance of bread was not quite four ounces. On one occasion Vienna had hardly any bread for four days. . . .

Germany, on the other hand, was better off than either Austria or Hungary. The rye crop had been fairly good, and food regulation was further advanced there. It was, in fact, close to the point of being perfect. But the quantity allotted the individual was inadequate, of course.

Throughout Central Europe the cry was heard: "Give us bread!"

So far the several populations had borne all hardships in patience and stoical indifference. The limit of endurance was reached, however. Colder weather called for a greater number of calories to heat the body. The vegetable season was over. The hoardings of the poorer classes had been eaten up. The cattle were no longer on pasture, and, fed with hay only, gave now less milk than ever.

It was a mournful season. . . .

Many hours were wasted by the women of the household in the course of a month by standing in line. The newspapers conducted campaigns against this seemingly heartless policy of the food authorities, but without result. The food-line was looked upon as essential in food conservation, as indeed it was. In the course of time it had been shown that people would call for food allotted them by their tickets, whether they needed it or not, and would then sell it again with a profit. To assure everybody of a supply in that manner would also lead to waste in consumption. Those who did not absolutely need all of their ration did not go to the trouble of standing in a food-line for hours in all sorts of weather. . . .

Sad in the extreme was the spectacle which the food-lines in the workman quarters of Berlin, Vienna, and Budapest presented. Upon the women of the households the war was being visited hardest. To see a pair of good shoes on a woman came to be a rare sight. Skirts were worn as long as the fabric would keep together, and little could be said of the shawls that draped pinched faces, sloping shoulders, and flat breasts. There were children in those food-lines. Thin feet stuck in the torn shoes, and mother's shawl served to supplement the hard-worn dress or patched suit. Everything had to go for food, and prices of apparel were so high that buying it was out of the question.

Once I set out for the purpose of finding in these food-lines a face that did not show the ravages of hunger. That was in Berlin. Four long lines were inspected with the closest scrutiny. But among the three hundred applicants for food there was not one who had had enough to eat in weeks. In the case of the younger women and the children the skin was drawn hard to the bones and bloodless. Eyes had fallen deeper into the sockets. From the lips all color was gone, and the tufts of hair that fell over parchmented foreheads seemed dull and famished—sign that the nervous vigor of the body was departing with the physical strength.

Source: George Abel Schreiner, *The Iron Ration: Three Years in Warring Central Europe* (New York: Harper and Brothers, 1918), pp. 101–3, 213–15, 255–58.

WAR AT THE HIGHEST LEVEL: A GENERAL PLANS THE BATTLE OF VERDUN

General Erich von Falkenhayn, like a handful of other supreme military leaders, directed the way in which his country tried to wage World War I. With more than 3 million men under his command, the chief of the German General Staff had immense resources to throw into battle. But he also had the heavy task of deciding how to use those armed men to bring the conflict to a favorable conclusion for Germany. That meant adding up the damage that Germany had already inflicted on its enemies, weighing the wishes and resources of its allies, and deciding what military operations could be carried out under the circumstances of the war. In the end, Falkenhayn—like his counterparts Douglas Haig and Joseph Joffre—had to decide whether to strike at the enemy, and if the answer was "yes," how, where, and when to do it.

Reviewing Germany's situation in the winter of 1915–1916, Falkenhayn concluded that time was working in favor of the other side. Germany had to attack its foes before the course of the war became even more difficult for it to control. Russia and Serbia he counted as secondary factors in the war. Earlier offensives on the western front had shown that Germany could not strike directly at England, its most dangerous opponent. Therefore, Falkenhayn turned to France—and its vulnerable fortress at Verdun. Supplied by a single road and located close to the German border, Verdun seemingly offered a prime target. Yet it was a historical stronghold that the French could not readily abandon without suffering a crushing blow to their morale. To destroy the French army through a great encounter at Verdun would also see "England's best sword knocked out of her hand." To spare his own troops, he intended to rely upon the power of German artillery to pound the French into submission.

But Falkenhayn was mistaken. As he assumed, the French met the German assault with a decision to stand and fight. But after that, Falkenhayn miscalculated. Like other high-ranking military commanders throughout the war, he could not make events conform to his plans. Under the leadership of General Philippe Pétain, Verdun received a steady flow of new troops. Scores of divisions served briefly in Verdun—enduring the horrors of Falkenhayn's barrages— then left for periods of rest behind the lines. The single road supplying Verdun from the rear was repaired constantly, and truck traffic was organized to permit huge quantities of supplies to get through.

The Battle of Verdun raged for ten months. In the grim figures that summarized what Verdun cost—probably 700,000 killed, wounded, and missing—Germany's share of losses was close to those suffered by the French. Falkenhayn bled both armies and gained no decisive result.

The plan for the indecisive carnage first took shape in a memorandum Falkenhayn wrote for Kaiser Wilhelm II in December 1915. Discarding the possibility of attacking Belfort, Falkenhayn chose Verdun.

Document 8
GENERAL ERICH VON FALKENHAYN DECIDES TO ATTACK VERDUN

France has been weakened almost to the limits of endurance, both in a military and economic sense—the latter by the permanent loss of the coalfields in the northeast of the country. The Russian armies have not been completely overthrown, but their offensive powers have been so shattered that she can never revive in anything like her old strength. The army of Serbia can be considered as destroyed. Italy has no doubt realized that she cannot reckon on the realization of her brigand's ambitions within measurable time and would therefore probably be only too glad to be able to liquidate her adventure in any way that would save her face. . . .

England, a country in which men are accustomed to weigh up the chances dispassionately, can scarcely hope to overthrow us by purely military means. She is obviously staking everything on a war of exhaustion. We have not been able to shatter her belief that it will bring Germany to her knees, and that belief gives the enemy the strength to fight on and keep on whipping their team together.

What we have to do is to dispel that illusion.

With that end in view, it will not, in the long run, be enough for us merely to stand on the defensive, a course in itself quite worthy of consideration. Our enemies, thanks to their superiority in men and material, are increasing their resources much more than we are. If that process continues a moment must come when the balance of numbers itself will deprive Germany of all remaining hope. . . . We must show England patently that her venture has no prospects. . . .

In Flanders, north of the Lorette ridge, the state of the ground prevents any far-reaching operations [against England] until the middle of the Spring. South of that point the local commanders consider that about 30 divisions would be required. The offensive in the northern sector would need the same number. Yet it is impossible for us to concentrate those forces on one part of our front. Even if, as was planned, we collected a few more divisions from the German sectors in Macedonia and Galicia . . . the total reserve in France would still amount to little more than 25 or 26 divisions. When all these are concentrated for the one operation all other fronts will have been drained of reserves to the last man. . . . Attempts at a mass break-through, even with an extreme accumulation of men and material, cannot be regarded as holding out prospects of success against a well armed enemy, whose morale is sound and who is not seriously inferior in numbers. The defender has usually succeeded in closing the gaps. This is easy enough for him if he decides to withdraw voluntarily, and it is hardly possible to stop him doing so. The salients thus made, enormously exposed to the effects of flanking fire, threaten to become a mere slaughterhouse. The technical difficulties of directing and supplying the masses bottled up in them are so great as to seem practically insurmountable. . . .

If we put [the armies of England's allies] out of the war, England is left to face us alone, and it is difficult to believe that in such circumstances her lust for our destruction would not fail her. It is true there would be no certainty that she would give up, but there is a strong probability. More than that can seldom be asked in war. . . .

When we come to the question how we are to proceed against England's tools on the Continent, Austria-Hungary is pressing for an immediate settlement of accounts with Italy. We cannot agree with that proposal. . . . The military achievements of Italy are so small, and she is, in any case, so firmly in England's grip, that it would be very remarkable if we let ourselves be deceived on that score. . . .

The same applies to Russia. . . . A thrust at Petersburg, with its million inhabitants—whom we should have to feed from our own short stocks if the operations were successful—does not promise a decision. An advance on Moscow takes us nowhere. We have not the forces available for any of these undertakings. For all these reasons Russia, as an object of our offensive, must be considered as excluded. There remains only France.

Fortunately these views, based more on negative grounds, are supported by the corresponding positive grounds.

As I have already insisted, the strain on France has almost reached the breaking-point—though it is certainly borne with the most remarkable devotion. If we succeeded in opening the eyes of her people to the fact that in a military sense they have nothing more to hope for, that breaking-point would be reached and England's best sword knocked out of her hand. To achieve that object the uncertain method of a mass break-through, in any case beyond our means, is unnecessary. We can probably do enough for our purposes with limited resources. Within our reach behind the French sector of the Western front there are objectives for the retention of which the French General Staff would be compelled to throw in every man they have. If they do so the forces of France will bleed to death—as there can be no question of a voluntary withdrawal—whether we reach our goal or not. If they do not do so, and we reach our objectives, the moral effect on France will be enormous. For an operation limited to a narrow front, Germany will not be compelled to spend herself so completely that all other fronts are practically drained. She can face with confidence the relief attacks to be expected on those fronts, and indeed hope to have sufficient troops in hand to reply to them with counter-attacks. For she is perfectly free to accelerate or draw out her offensive, to intensify it or break it off from time to time, as suits her purpose.

The objectives of which I am speaking now are Belfort and Verdun.

Source: General [Erich] von Falkenhayn, *The German General Staff and Its Decisions, 1914–1916* (New York: Dodd, Mead, 1920), pp. 239–45, 247–49.

CIVILIANS: RAVAGED HOMES AND REFUGEES

In the fall of 1915, the full force of the war struck the population of Serbia. Austria's first efforts to invade Serbia early in the war had failed against fierce Serb resistance. But the course of the war endangered the small kingdom's defenses. German forces under Field Marshal August von Mackensen shifted to southeastern Europe after participating in a spectacularly successful advance into Russia in the spring and summer. Meanwhile, the diplomats of the Central Powers scored a major victory in bringing Bulgaria into the war as the ally of Germany and Austria. On October 7, German and Austrian forces struck southward across the Save and Danube Rivers; four days later, Bulgarian forces joined in the assault, hitting Serbia from the east. The Serbian army found itself outnumbered and outflanked. Its position became perilous when the Bulgarians, by late October, cut the railroad from Belgrade to Salonika at several key points, blocking the Serbs from retreating southward to safety.

The harsh Balkan winter now approached. Accompanied by large numbers of civilians, Serb forces found their only escape route to be westward over the mountains of Montenegro and neutral Albania to the Adriatic Sea. Out of a force of 170,000 soldiers, only 140,000 survived to be picked up by the French navy. Fortier Jones, an American serving as a relief worker in Serbia, recorded the horrors of Serb communities under enemy attack and the desperate flight of their civilian populations.

In the first excerpt, he draws on his acquaintance with a Serb family in Belgrade to recount their experience when the city first came under full-scale enemy attack. In the second, he presents his own observations of the grim retreat by civilian refugees accompanying the remnants of the Serbian army across the mountains to the Adriatic. The final paragraphs come from Jones's diary.

Document 9
FORTIER JONES AND THE COLLAPSE OF SERBIA

. . . . As you romp with the children, you hear distantly a dull clap of thunder, just as if a summer shower were brewing. A second, a third clap, and you walk out to the entrance to scan the sky. It is deep blue and cloudless, but away over the northern part of the city, while you look, as if by magic, beautiful, shiny white cloudlets appear far up in the crystal sky, tiny, soft, fluffy things that look like a baby's powder-puff, and every time one appears a dull bit of thunder comes to you. For twelve months off and on you have seen this sight. You think of it as a periodic reminder that your nation and the one across the way are at war. You know that heretofore those powder-puffs have been directed at your own guns on the hills behind the city and at the intrenchments down by the river. But there are many things you do not know. . . . You do not know that from a busy group of men in Berlin an order has gone out to take your city and your nation at any cost, and if you knew these things, it would now be too late. For as you look, in a few brief moments, the thunder-storm rolls up and covers the city, such a thunder-storm as nature, with all her vaunted strength, has never dared to manufacture. . . . With increasing rapidity the rain falls now, five to the minute, ten, fifteen, twenty, twenty-five, every sixty seconds, and every drop is from fifty pounds to a quarter of a ton of whirling steel, and in the hollow heart of each are new and strange explosives that, when they strike, shake the windows out of your house. Looking toward Semlin, you see the aeroplanes rising in fleets. Some are already over the city, directing the fire of the guns across the river, and others are dropping explosive bombs, incendiary bombs, and darts. In a dozen places already the city is blazing terribly. . . .

Now you are in the outskirts of the city. No word can be spoken because of the constant roar of your own and the enemy's guns—a roar unfaltering and massive, such as in forty-eight hours sixty thousand huge projectiles alone could spread over the little city. On the road you pass frequently those irregular splotches of murder characteristic of bomb-dropping. Here only one man was blown to pieces by a precious bomb, yonder two women and a child, farther along eight people, men, women, and children, lie heaped.

* * *

. . . Few people had sufficient transportation to carry even the barest necessities, so they waded along in the river of dirty water. Dozens of peasant women I saw leading small children by each hand and carrying Indian fashion on their backs an infant not yet able to take one step. Old men, bent almost double, splashed about with huge packs on their shoulders, and many young girls, equally loaded, pushed forward with the wonderful free step the peasant women of Serbia have, while children of all ages filled in the interstices of the crowd, getting under the oxen and horses, hanging on the automobiles, some whimpering, some laughing, some yelling. Every one was wet, every one was a mass of mud, every one was hungry, but summer was still with us, and no one was freezing. Affairs were rapidly approaching the limit of human endurance for many in that snake-like, writhing procession, but as yet none had succumbed. Then it began to snow. . . .

In less than an hour our soaked clothes were frozen stiff. From the long hair of the oxen slim, keen icicles hung in hundreds, giving them a glittering, strange appearance, and many of them despite the hard work were trembling terribly with the cold. For a short time the freezing wind accelerated the pace of the refugees on foot. The old men shouted to the women, and the women dragged along their children. But soon this energy was spent. The hopelessness of their situation was too obvious even for Serbian optimism to ignore. . . .

The plight of these refugees seemed so hopeless, it brought us the ever-recurring question, Why did all these people leave their homes? Surely nothing the invader could or would do could justify them in a thing like this. But all the peasants had heard stories of the fate of Belgium, and many had seen what the Bulgarians were capable of doing. So here they were. It seemed foolish to me, but for them it was obedience to an instinct. . . .

We now began to overtake many of the peasant families who earlier in the day had gone ahead of us, walking being about twice as fast as ox-cart speed. They were losing strength fast. The children, hundreds of them, were all crying. Mothers with infants on their backs staggered, fell, rose, and fell again. . . .

For some time I had noticed an old peasant couple who moved along just at our speed, staying within view. They were very aged even for Serbs, and carried no provisions of any sort that I could see. The old woman was following the old man. I saw them visibly grow weaker and weaker until their progress became a series of stumbling falls. We came to a place where low clumps of bushes grew by the roadside. The snow had drifted around and behind them so as to form a sort of cave, a niche between them. This was sheltered from the gale to some extent. By unspoken consent they made for it, and sank down side by side to rest. Their expression spoke nothing but thankfulness for this haven. Of course they never got up from it. This was quite the happiest thing I saw all that day, for such episodes were repeated with innumerable tragic variations scores of times. The terrible arithmetic of the storm multiplied them until by the end of the day we had ceased to think or feel.

Source: Fortier Jones, *With Serbia into Exile: An American's Adventures with the Army that Cannot Die* (New York: Grosset and Dunlap, 1916), pp. 32–34, 36–37, 194–97, 199, 201.

AMERICA GOES TO WAR

In the winter of 1916–1917, the German government made the momentous decision to begin unlimited warfare against vessels headed for the ports of Great Britain and its allies. Germany had been constrained since the spring of 1915 by President Woodrow Wilson's threat to break off diplomatic relations between the United States and Germany. That threat carried the underlying warning that the United States was considering armed intervention in the war, prompting the authorities in Berlin to sharply curtail the use of submarines against civilian shipping in the waters around Great Britain. When the Germans torpedoed the British channel steamer *Sussex* in March 1916, causing more American casualties, President Wilson warned even more strongly that further action of this sort would bring a break in relations.

In the first months of 1917, the American people and their government faced a direct German challenge. Forces in the German government led by Prime Minister Theobald von Bethmann Hollweg that had opposed a confrontation with the United States found themselves overshadowed by the advocates of unlimited use of the submarine. Germany's military leaders, most notably General Erich Ludendorff, gambled that the submarine offensive would force Britain from the war before American intervention could make itself felt.

The editorials of the *New York Times* reflected the dominant trend in American politics—and probably in American public opinion—in the wake of the German moves. Following the German declaration that limits on the submarine would end on February 1, the *Times* declared its outrage at Germany's high-handed threats to American commerce and lives.

In the next week, President Wilson, with the strong support of Congress, broke off relations with Germany. He received equally fervid backing in Congress in early March when he sought authority to arm American merchant ships, although a filibuster by antiwar senators blocked formal passage. The Zimmermann telegram, in which the German government offered to help Mexico recover Texas, New Mexico, and Arizona in return for aid in a future German war against the United States, was an additional blow to opponents of the war. So too was the growing list of American ships and lives lost in March to submarine assaults.

President Wilson's request for a declaration of war got the firm support of the *Times*. Following the theme set down by the president in his speech of April 2, the leading American newspaper made entry into the war more than merely a defense of American rights to travel the high seas. This would be, in Wilson's words, a war "for democracy"; it would "bring peace and safety to all nations and make the world itself at last free."

Viewing the war from that lofty perspective, the *Times* castigated antiwar senators like Robert La Follette for "quibbles over the respective methods of England and Germany in conducting war." And it hailed the fact that America was joining the war like a "mighty wheel which their puny arms could not obstruct."

Document 10
NEW YORK TIMES EDITORIAL:
"GERMANY WARS AGAINST THE WORLD"

The inhibitions which Germany puts upon the world's trade with the British Islands, France, and Italy are such as no nation has ever submitted to if it had the power to resist. They are beyond the law, they are not to be tolerated. Within the limits of the designated zones which Germany announces her purpose to make dangerous by mines and apparently, also, by the use of submarines, we are warned that neutral ships will venture at their own risk, we are urgently "advised" to warn our ships to take other routes. By permission of Germany one American passenger steamer per week may ply each way between our ports and Falmouth, England, provided the steamer follow the course laid down in German orders, display the signals and distinguishing marks prescribed by Germany, and sail under the guarantee of our Government that no contraband is carried. And Germany, "sincerely trusting" that our people and our government will understand the motives of this proclamation, expresses the hope that in considering the action of the Imperial Government in declaring war upon all neutral commerce we may "view the new situation from the lofty heights of impartiality" and assist "to prevent further misery and unavoidable sacrifice of human life." . . .

Will the Government and the people of the United States put up with this German order forbidding to them the open pathways of the sea? They will not, they cannot. It aims to destroy billions of our trade, by far the greater part of our commerce, it commands us to obey rules and regulations which no sovereign nation can permit another to impose. . . .

When the earlier war zone proclamation was issued the Government of the United States, sincerely desiring that no misunderstanding should cloud the intercourse of the two Governments, expressed "the confident hope and expectation that the Imperial German Government can and will give assurance that American citizens and their vessels will not be molested by the naval forces of Germany otherwise than by visit and search, though their vessels may be traversing the sea area delimited in the proclamation of the German Admiralty." That hope we may again express. It will be equivalent to calling upon Germany to abandon her announced purpose of lawless and murderous sea warfare. . . . Designing to deprive England of food, she deprives herself of whatever friends she may have left. She sets all the world against her, for this is a declaration of war upon the trade, the rights, the sovereignty of all neutral nations, and if ever a nation needed friends, Germany will need them during the negotiations for peace and after its conclusion.

The German Government says it is the only way, that it must continue to fight for existence, and that it has resolved to fight in this abhorrent manner "in order to serve the welfare of mankind in a higher sense and not to wrong its own people." Mankind will know how to safeguard its welfare, and it is by prolonging the war by these means, or by any means, that the Imperial Government puts the greatest imaginable wrong upon its own people. Germany's defeat is certain, it cannot be long deferred, the interests of mankind and of the German people would be best served by facing the truth now. The new war zone order is a counsel of desperation and in itself may be considered an indication that the end of the war is not very far distant.

Source: New York Times, editorial, February 1, 1917.

Document 11
NEW YORK TIMES EDITORIAL:
"THE NATION SPEAKS"

Nothing in its life will more become the Sixty-fifth Congress than the beginning of it—the high plane on which the discussion of yesterday and Wednesday was conducted, the dignity and gravity of its manner, and the sober simplicity, without truculence or bombast, of its speech, as it made its forty-eight hours way to the momentous decision. The American people have cause to feel pride in it; it made a picture for all the world to see of democracy rising to an occasion. It kept the note struck by the President. Its foreordained and inevitable task was performed without cheap violence or strutting defiance; the tone it held throughout was that of a pacific nation taking up, without fear or boasting, the sword that was forced upon it.

Nor did it fail to set the issue clearly forth, to show that we are going to war, not merely to avenge injuries nor even to prevent future ones, but to answer the question, Shall the world become democratic or autocratic? The progress of two years and a half of war has shown that, in LINCOLN'S phrase, "It must become all one or all the other." Either democracy must be worldwide or democracy must perish, and in that contest, the greatest ever forced upon the world, and forced upon it, not by democracy, but by autocracy, the first of the democracies is now called upon to bear her part. "The world must be made safe for democracy," said President WILSON on Monday night and on Wednesday Senator Lodge answered:

We enter this war to unite with those who are fighting the common foe in order to preserve human freedom, democracy, and modern civilization. They are all in grievous peril. . . .

. . . Too long democracy and autocracy have tried to exist side by side in the world, and one or the other must go, though the issue would not have been made by democracy, which was called to arms to defend itself against an assault which began with Serbia and Belgium, and would never have stopped short of the dominion of the world.

Source: New York Times, editorial, April 6, 1917.

WARTIME MORALITY

George Abel Schreiner, war correspondent for the Associated Press, had a close-up view of the changing moral climate in the Central Powers between 1914 and the start of 1917.

Document 12
GEORGE ABEL SCHREINER AND THE CHANGE IN SEXUAL BEHAVIOR

In the first place, many of the slender social threads that restrain sex impulse in the modern state snapped under the strain of the war. . . .

War takes from his home and family the man. Though the governments made some provision for those left behind, the allowance given them was never large enough to keep them as well as they had been kept by the labor of the head of the family. . . . From the family had also been taken much of the restraint which makes for social orderliness. The man was away from home; the young wife had seen better times. Other men came into her path, and nature is not in all cases as loyal to the marriage vows as we would believe. In many cases the mother now unassisted by the authority of the father was unable to keep her daughters and sons in check. . . .

. . . Rendered irresponsible by sexual desire and the monotony of a poverty-stricken existence, many of the younger women whose husbands were in the army started liaisons, *Verhältnisse*, as they are called in German, with such men as were available. It speaks well for the openness of mind of some husbands that they did not resent this. I happen to know of a case in which a man at the front charged a friend to visit his wife. . . .

Shortly afterward I learned of the case of a woman who had sold herself in order to provide food and fuel for her two children. She was the widow of a reserve officer who had fallen in Galicia. Her own pension amounted to one hundred and ten crowns a month, and for the support of the children she was allowed another one hundred crowns, I believe. . . . At that time life in Vienna was as costly as it is normally in the United States. While her husband had been alive the woman had led a very comfortable life. She had kept a servant and lived in a good apartment in the Third Municipal District. The thing that struck me in her case was that she had not taken the step before. It is extremely difficult to be virtuous on twenty-seven dollars a month when one has not known need before. . . .

In the "Hall" of the Hotel Excelsior of Trieste were sitting at café tables some sixty Austro-Hungarian officers from the Isonzo front. . . .

. . . [They] were poor devils who had been sitting in the Carso trenches for months and had now come to Trieste to have a good time, even if that meant that next morning the pay of several months would be in the pocket of the hotel manager and in the hands of some good-looking Italo-Croat woman. . . .

. . . Each day might be the last, and why not enjoy life to-day when to-morrow there might be a burial without coffin, without anything except the regrets of comrades? . . . One of the women was able to take a very intelligent survey of the situation. She was capable of sensing real sympathy for these men. I learned that she had lost her husband in the war. It was the same old story. She had found the small pension for herself and the allowance for her boy entirely insufficient, was not minded to do poorly paid hard work, and had concluded that it was easy for the well-to-do to be decent. The poor had to do the best they could in these days of high prices. . . .

. . . Men and women drank to one another's good health, the former oblivious, for the time being, that this might be the last good time they would ever enjoy.

It strikes me that not much fault can be found with this, so long as we are human enough to allow those whom we are about to execute for the commission of some crime to choose their last breakfast—or is it supper? To be detailed into the advanced trenches was generally no better than to be sentenced to death.

Only those who have been constantly threatened by the dangers of war can realize what state of mind these men were in. Nothing mattered any more, and, nothing being really important, the pleasures of the flesh were everything. . . . At the same time, I am not ignorant of the fact that sleek communities living in peace and plenty cannot be expected to understand the moral disintegration which the dangers of war had wrought in this instance.

I made the acquaintance of similar conditions in Berlin and other cities of the Central states. Being a matter-of-fact individual, I cannot say that they shocked me. The relations of cause and effect cannot be explained away, much as we may wish to do it. With some fourteen million men taken away from their families, whose sole support they were in the vast majority of cases, nothing else was to be expected. It speaks well for mankind in general that the resulting conditions were not worse. The responsibility involved falls rather upon those who brought on the war than upon the men and women who transgressed. . . .

More than fifty thousand Russian prisoners-of-war petitioned the Austrian government to be admitted to citizenship in the country that held them captive. Many of these men had been sent into the rural districts to assist the farmers. Others were busy around the cities. They had come to be reconciled with their lot, had acquired a fair working knowledge of the language, and association with the women had led to the usual results. The crop of "war" babies increased.

The Russians were willing to marry these women, but under the law could not do so. Hence the petition for admission to the usual civil rights. The Austrian government recognized the situation, but in the absence of the necessary legislative authority could do nothing to admit the Russian to Austrian *Staatsangehörigkeit* [nationality]. Yet it was eager to do that. The new blood was needed. . . .

A state which was losing men at a frightful rate every day could not be expected to view this increase in population with alarm.

Source: George Abel Schreiner, *The Iron Ration: Three Years in Warring Central Europe* (New York: Harper and Brothers, 1918), pp. 326–28, 332, 335–36, 339–42, 346–47.

A SHATTERED EUROPE AT WAR'S END

At the close of the war, Europeans in many parts of the continent found themselves living in a world of frightening novelties. In the defeated countries, old political systems had been overthrown, and crowned heads fled into exile. Meanwhile, the collapse of economic life meant hunger and poverty for tens of millions. With old currencies made worthless by inflation, middle-class Europeans who had lived according to the old rules of saving and conservative investment found themselves destitute.

Austrian writer Stefan Zweig was a witness to these changes. The long-term prospects of his new and economically vulnerable country were poor. But its immediate condition was pitiable. Roaring inflation had destroyed the value of Austria's currency, making the krone virtually worthless and encouraging foreigners to snatch up property for a song. Meanwhile, hunger and cold were the common experiences of the Austrian population.

Document 13
STEFAN ZWEIG, "HOMECOMING TO AUSTRIA"

From the standpoint of reason the most foolish thing I could do after the collapse of the German and Austrian arms was to go back to Austria, that Austria which showed faintly on the map of Europe as the vague, gray and inert shadow of the former Imperial monarchy. The Czechs, Poles, Italians, and Slovenes had snatched away their countries; what remained was a mutilated trunk that bled from every vein. . . . Boundary lines were still unsettled, the Peace Conference having scarcely begun; reparations had not been fixed, there was no flour, bread, or oil; there appeared to be no solution other than a revolution or some other catastrophe. . . .

At that time a visit to Austria called for preparation[s] similar to those for an Arctic expedition. Warm clothes and woolen underwear were needed because it was known that across the border there was no coal with winter at the door. . . .

Slowly, almost majestically, it seemed, the train rolled near, a special sort of train, not the customary, shabby, weather-beaten kind, but with spacious black cars, a train de luxe. The locomotive stopped. There was a perceptible stir among the lines of those waiting but I was still in the dark. Then I recognized behind the plate glass window of the car Emperor Karl, the last emperor of Austria standing with his black-clad wife, Empress Zita. I was startled; the last emperor of Austria, heir of the Habsburg dynasty which had ruled for seven hundred years, was forsaking his realm! . . ."The Kaiser!" From earliest childhood we had learned to pronounce those words reverently for they embodied all of power and wealth and symbolized Austria's imperishability. And now I saw his heir, the last emperor, banished from his country. From century to century the glorious line of Habsburg had passed the Imperial globe and crown from hand to hand, and this was the minute of its end. All of those who stood about sensed history, world history, in this tragic sight. . . . I knew it was a different Austria, a different world, to which I was returning. . . .

Hardly was the train out of sight when we were obliged to change from the spruce, clean Swiss cars into the Austrian. One had but to enter them to become aware beforehand of what had happened to the country. The guards who showed us our seats were haggard, starved and tatterdemalion; they crawled about with torn and shabby uniforms hanging loosely over their stooped shoulders. . . . Through the broken windows the late fall wind blew the soot and cinders of the miserable lignite with which the locomotives were fueled. It smudged the floor and walls, but its odor at least tempered the smell of iodoform, a reminder of the sick and wounded who had been transported in these skeleton cars during the war. . . . Distances which used to take an hour now required four or five, and when dusk set in we remained in darkness. The electric bulbs had either been smashed or stolen so that whoever searched for anything had to feel his way with matches; and if we did not freeze it was only because we had been crowded together throughout, with six or eight people in each compartment. . . . From the midst of peace I was riding back into the horror of war which I had thought to be over. . . .

Every descent into the town at that period was a moving experience; it was my first sight of the yellow and dangerous eyes of famine. The bread crumbled into black particles and tasted like pitch and glue, coffee was a brew of roasted barley, beer like yellow water, chocolate like colored sand and the potatoes were frozen. Most people raised rabbits, in order not wholly to forget the taste of meat; a young lad shot squirrels in our garden for his Sunday dinner and well nourished dogs or cats returned only seldom from lengthy prowls. . . . Every step through the street, where show-windows had a plundered look, where decaying houses shed crumbling mortar like scurf, where visibly undernourished people painfully dragged themselves to their work, served to trouble one's soul. Out in the country the food situation was better; no peasant-farmer allowed himself to be influenced by the general breakdown of morale to sell his butter, eggs, or milk at the legally prescribed "maximum prices." He concealed his goods wherever he could and waited at home for the highest bidder. . . . There were those who had to take their wedding ring from their finger or the leather belt from around their body merely to keep that body alive. . . .

. . . An economist who knew how to describe graphically all the phases of the inflation which spread from Austria to Germany, would find it unsurpassed material for an exciting novel, for the chaos took on ever more fantastic forms. Soon nobody knew what any article was worth. Prices jumped arbitrarily; a thrifty merchant would raise the price of a box of matches to twenty times the amount charged by his upright competitor who was innocently holding to yesterday's quotation; the reward for his honesty was the sale of his stock within an hour, because the news got around quickly and everybody rushed to buy whatever was for sale whether it was something they needed or not. Even a goldfish or an old telescope was "goods" and what people wanted was goods instead of paper. . . . In consequence of this mad disorder the situation became more paradoxical and unmoral from week to week. A man who had been saving for forty years and who, furthermore, had patriotically invested his all in war bonds, became a beggar. A man who had debts became free of them. A man who respected the food rationing system starved; only one who disregarded it brazenly could eat his fill. . . .

. . . Because Austrian money melted like snow in one's hand everyone wanted Swiss francs or American dollars and foreigners in substantial numbers availed themselves of the chance to fatten on the quivering cadaver of the Austrian krone. Austria was "discovered" and suffered a calamitous "tourist season." Every hotel in Vienna was filled with these vultures; they bought everything from toothbrushes to landed estates, they mopped up private collections and antique shop stocks before their owners, in their distress, woke to how they had been plundered.

Source: Stefan Zweig, *The World of Yesterday* (Lincoln: University of Nebraska Press, 1964), pp. 281–86, 289–92.

THE PEACE SETTLEMENT: A GERMAN URGES ACCEPTANCE

Germany's government reluctantly accepted the Treaty of Versailles. The most effective advocate of this course, even though it was admittedly bitter medicine for the German people, was Matthias Erzberger (1875–1921). A leader of Germany's Catholic Center party, Erzberger had begun the war as a fervent believer in a victor's peace for Germany that would bring his country massive territorial acquisitions. During the war, as Germany's military prospects diminished, he shifted to become a leading advocate of a negotiated peace settlement. Erzberger entered the cabinet of Prince Max of Baden in October 1918, and he served as a member of the delegation that signed the Armistice agreement with the United States and the Entente.

Erzberger saw his country standing in deadly peril if German leaders disregarded reality and permitted their emotional responses to the treaty to govern their decisions. The clock would turn back as Germany, its unity won only in 1871, dissolved into a horde of weak, independent states. Communist insurrections, which only recently had been put down by Germany's postwar government, would start up again, this time moving on to success.

Erzberger had a dual success. As minister of finance and deputy prime minister, he first persuaded the German government to accept the Allied demands; next, he helped get a majority of the National Assembly to ratify the treaty. Erzberger soon had proof that his life was in danger: shots were fired through his window at the finance ministry within days after the vote for ratification. His enemies did not rest until they hunted him down. He was murdered by right-wing assassins on August 26, 1921.

In preparation for Prime Minister Scheidemann's cabinet ministers to consider the treaty on June 3 and 4, 1918, Erzberger wrote the following memorandum setting down his position.

Document 14
MEMO FROM MATTHIAS ERZBERGER
TO THE GERMAN CABINET

I. *If the Treaty is signed.*

. . . .

1. *Foreign policy consequences:* The state of war and the blockade will be terminated. The borders will be opened, food and raw materials will enter Germany, and our merchants will again secure private credit. Exports will revive. The prisoners of war will return. Poland will be forced to terminate its aggressive designs. The unity of Germany will be preserved.

2. *Domestic policy consequences:* The tax burden will be crushing, but this will be compensated for business by the fact that imports will revive and internal order will be restored. Employment will rise, with output for both export and the domestic markets returning to normal. Bolshevism will lose its attraction. Working morale and working efficiency will be restored. Increased coal production will end the transportation bottleneck. . . . The present government will presumably remain in power, though the Right and a part of even the Liberal bourgeoisie will oppose it vehemently. It is even possible that there may be a military putsch [against a pro-ratification government] organized in eastern Germany. One must reckon on the east opposing the implementation of the treaty by force of arms, and starting a general agitation to this effect. But this movement will probably collapse quickly on account of the deep yearning for peace among the vast majority of the people and the visible improvement in the general situation once the treaty has been accepted.

II. *If the Treaty is Rejected*

1. *Foreign policy consequences:* Active warfare will be resumed three days after the Allied denunciation of the armistice. The Allied armies, the Americans included, will advance at least up to Kassel in a line parallel to

the Rhine. The entire Ruhr area will be occupied. There are also reports that the Allies will create a corridor from Frankfurt to Prague to separate north from south Germany. The blockade will be sharpened, the borders will be sealed hermetically. . . . The Poles will advance from the east.

2. *Domestic consequences:* A general shortage of food and raw materials throughout Germany. The border population will flee before the advancing armies and will concentrate in the interior of Germany, leading to a catastrophic famine. The loss of the Ruhr will mean an end to Germany's coal supplies, meaning a collapse of transport and consequent paralysis in all big cities. The hour of Bolshevism will come. Plunder and murder will be the order of the day. The communications system will cease to function in the general anarchy. Hence the atomization of Germany. The civil service will be paralyzed in the absence of instructions from higher authority. The shortage of goods will lead to a crazy inflation and complete worthlessness of the currency. Russian conditions will come to Germany. Numerous bourgeois elements will be driven by sheer terror into the arms of the extreme Left. The rest will go to the extreme Right. The result will be civil war, especially in Berlin and the other big cities.

The unity of the German nation will be destroyed. The individual states will not be able to withstand Allied pressure to sign separate treaties of peace. Separatist tendencies have already shown themselves in Bavaria, the Rhineland, and the east. These tendencies will be much strengthened following the total disintegration of the German state. A Rhenish Republic would be proclaimed within a few days. The Allies will attach the individual states to themselves by bonds so firm that a German national state will cease to exist. Several smaller German areas would also seek independence to secure the favor of the Allies. The map of Germany would again become a crazy patchwork quilt, thereby realizing the dream that has long guided French ambitions. The unoccupied part of Germany would soon be forced to seek terms from the Allies as an exhausted and ruined country. Even if the consequences of an Allied advance were less catastrophic than here assumed, the Rhineland would in any case be lost and German unity destroyed. A still worse peace than the present one would be imposed upon the German people within a short period. The hope that the Allies would be willing to assume the administration of an utterly ruined Germany is probably mistaken. A powerful current in France and England wishes the total impotence of Germany. The Allies would partition the country and leave each part to stew in its own juice.

The results of the failure to sign the treaty and the consequent military advance of the Allies can be summarized briefly:

1. The dissolution of national unity and the establishment of several German states. The hatred of the various states against Prussia, which is widely blamed for the present catastrophic situation, would make the separation a permanent one.

2. Peace would have to be signed after a brief interval, but it would be signed by the several different states separately. They would be obligated, under imposed terms, to pledge themselves not to enter into any future German national state. Such a peace would be still worse than that now proposed.

3. Overthrow of the government and its replacement by Independent Socialists and Communists, dissolution of the army, and anarchy throughout the entire country.

Source: Klaus Epstein, *Matthias Erzberger and the Dilemma of German Democracy* (Princeton: Princeton University Press, 1959), pp. 315–17.

THE RUSSIAN REVOLUTION

In 1917 Russia experienced two revolutions. A spontaneous and undirected wave of unrest in early March toppled the monarchy, placing a weak Provisional Government in power. Its leaders determined to remain in the war and to defer implementing drastic domestic reforms until the conflict had ended. A carefully planned and effectively led coup in the first week of November ousted the Provisional Government and placed the Bolshevik party (which soon renamed itself the Communist party), led by V. I. Lenin, in power.

These events in Russia soon had a widening impact. First, the old Russian state and empire crumbled away, and the world now faced a radical Marxist government determined to spread the cause of proletarian revolution. Second, and more immediately, the Germans had the fruits of victory on World War I's eastern front. The Russian war effort ground to a halt, then ended completely as the Communists published the war's secret treaties made among the Allies, negotiated an armistice, then started peace negotiations. These earthshaking developments aroused a combination of fascination and alarm in Count Louis de Robien (1888–1958), then a young French diplomat stationed in Petrograd.

Document 15
DIARY OF COUNT LOUIS DE ROBIEN: THE
COLLAPSE OF OLD RUSSIA

Tuesday 13th March 1917

. . . In the afternoon the rifle fire began again with such intensity that at first I took it to mean the arrival of troops to restore order. But it is only the soldiers who, believing the police (who are now called "pharaohs") to be hidden on the roofs of churches and houses, are possessed by real terror. Lorries are stationed at every street corner, their machine-guns aimed in the air and emptying round upon round of ammunition. The bullets fall back on the assailants or on soldiers of other units, making them believe that their fire is being returned. But people are shooting in all directions. . . .

Meanwhile the populace, realizing that the revolutionaries are now masters, take advantage of the situation to give free vent to their hatred of the police. Police stations are being burned down and looted. . . . In the snow nearby they are making a bonfire of bursting files out of which fall cascades of papers. . . .

Wednesday 14th March 1917

. . . The revolution appears to have definitely triumphed. The troops are going to the Duma to take the oath, and on returning from the Embassy I stopped at the corner of Liteiny and Sergevskaya Streets to watch a regiment go past, which was making for the Taurid Palace. The men were in marching order, led by their band, which was playing the march from the ballet of "The Little Hunch-backed Horse." Only the red flags, the men's red arm-bands, and the red rags decorating the bayonets remind one of the sad reality. . . .

Sunday 6th May 1917

The state of anarchy is confirmed and extends further and further every day. Petrograd is no longer the only centre: it's the same everywhere, in Moscow, in Kiev, and confusion and disorder reign. . . . It is possible that the High Command might give the order to attack but, in my opinion, it is incapable of carrying out the order and especially of *organizing* the attack, which is the only real condition of success. . . .

Wednesday 7th November 1917

Yesterday's quiet was deceptive. In fact, during the night the Bolsheviks pulled off the surprise attack which they have been planning for a long time. . . . They are now in possession of the telegraph office, the stations, and the departments of state: in short, they are masters of the capital. The government collapsed like a house of cards without the least resistance, and the apparent order has not been disturbed. . . .

Wednesday 21st November 1917

This evening we received the first official communication from the new government, notifying us of its succession, and proposing the conclusion of an armistice between all the belligerents while awaiting the opening of peace negotiations. . . .

Whatever happens, this scrap of paper marks a new era, and I have even preserved the envelope itself: some day it will be interesting to find it in the Embassy archives. . . .

Thursday 22 November 1917

. . . Meanwhile, the government is carrying on with its programme of socialization and has issued a decree purely and simply abolishing the bourgeois newspapers. Its explanation of this attempt against liberty is that paper and printing should be for the use of all, that is to say, of the masses. It would therefore be unfair to let the capitalist bourgeois keep their newspapers, as they are a minority and through their money they occupy a position in the press which is out of all proportion to their numbers. . . .

Friday 23rd November 1917

Trotsky has wasted no time, and as soon as he had proposed the conclusion of an armistice with Germany to the Allies, the council of Commissars ordered General Dukhonin [the commander of the Russian army] to open negotiations with the enemy, and gave the order to all front-line units to cease hostilities. This order received an enthusiastic welcome from all the regiments. . . .

At the same time, the Soviet government this morning started the publication of the "secret agreements" . . . it seems odd to see these documents published in the newspapers, when we used to lock them up in the strong-room with such care and with so many keys. . . .

Thursday 6th December 1917

The territories of the Empire are being frittered away. . . . Finland has proclaimed its independence and has asked the foreign governments to recognize it. . . .

Russia does not exist: a Russian Empire was the only thing which existed, and from the moment when the Imperial backbone became dislocated, there was no more Russia.

At this moment when the different nationalities which composed the Empire are regaining their independence and constituting themselves as countries, in the Western sense of the word, we must make friends for ourselves who will be bound to our cause by bonds of sympathy for our ideas, or by gratitude for the help which we give them. . . .

Wednesday 2nd January 1918

. . . The natural goodness of the Russian still sometimes comes out in these rough characters, who are good at heart. But nevertheless what scenes of savagery there are when these brutes are let loose. At Tashkent, the soldiers struck down a general who was trying to restore order and put him on view in a room where, for thirty kopeks, people could buy the right to watch his dying agonies and spit at him.

. . . Old Goremykin [a former prime minister] and his wife have had their throats cut by a gang of thieves in their villa at Sochi on the Black Sea, and I have been told this evening that several Frenchmen have been massacred at Irkutsk. . . .

Friday 11th January 1918

M. Dumas, a socialist who has been sent on a mission by the Ministry of Foreign Affairs, brings good news from France. The state of mind is excellent, and people are much reassured by the hope of American reinforcements.

But they have got delusions about Russia. The French are imbued with the spirit of the *Marseillaise* and still believe that the Russian revolution was caused by patriotism. Nobody has yet understood that from the very beginning the revolution was just as much against the war as against the régime. . . .

Sunday 13th January 1918

Disturbances continue. In the wake of Finland, the Ukraine, the Don, the Caucasus, Siberia and many others whose names I forget, we now have the Republic of Archangel which has just proclaimed its independence.

It is the end of a world. And on the last day of the old year as I crossed the Troitsky Bridge I gazed at the Imperial city in rays of the setting sun: it is already dead, and its magnificence will soon be only a memory.

Source: Louis de Robien, *The Diary of a Diplomat in Russia, 1917–1918*, trans. Camilla Sykes (New York: Praeger, 1970), pp. 16–17, 51, 130–31, 149–51, 161–62, 184, 189–90.

Annotated Bibliography

PRINT SOURCES

General Histories of the War

The American Heritage History of World War I. New York: American Heritage, 1964. A lavishly illustrated popular account of the war featuring a brilliantly drawn set of maps.

Ferro, Marc. *The Great War, 1914–1918*. London: Routledge and Kegan Paul, 1973. A dramatic and colorful comparative account of the major participating countries' wartime experience; it stresses military operations, the use of propaganda, and the social and economic impact of the war.

Livesay, Anthony. *The Historical Atlas of World War I*. New York: Henry Holt, 1994. A useful set of maps.

Lyons, Michael J. *World War I: A Short History*. Englewood Cliffs, N.J.: Prentice-Hall, 1994. A recent and valuable survey of all the major facets of the war.

Schmitt, Bernadotte, and Harold Vedeler. *The World in the Crucible, 1914–1919*. New York: Harper and Row, 1984. An important scholarly survey of the war stressing military events and the political revolutions at the close of the conflict.

Winter, J. M. *The Experience of World War I*. London: Macmillan, 1988. A rich collection of maps, photographs, timelines, and essays treating all major aspects of the war.

Origins of the War and the Summer 1914 Crisis

Bosworth, Richard. *Italy and the Approach of the First World War*. New York: St. Martin's Press, 1983. A readable and balanced introductory account that contends that Italian leaders sought above all to establish Italy's place as one of the Great Powers.

Cassels, Lavender. *The Archduke and the Assassin: Sarajevo, June 28th, 1914.* London: Frederick Muller, 1984. A detailed and well-written dual biography of Franz Ferdinand and Princip with a splendid account of the assassination plot and its implementation.

Herrmann, David G. *The Arming of Europe and the Making of the First World War.* Princeton: Princeton University Press, 1996. An important, pioneering study of the arms race on land among the Great Powers and how it led to the outbreak of hostilities in 1914.

Joll, James. *The Origins of the First World War.* London: Longman, 1984. A balanced and comprehensive analysis of the domestic and international factors that led the countries of Europe into armed conflict in 1914.

Keiger, John F. V. *France and the Origins of the First World War.* London: Macmillan, 1983. A useful study stressing the role of Raymond Poincaré, France's president, in directing his country's prewar diplomacy; Keiger sees France leaving the initiative to other countries during the July crisis of 1914.

Kennan, George. *The Fateful Alliance: France, Russia, and the Looming of the First World War.* New York: Pantheon, 1984. An important, elegantly written account of how diplomatic developments in the 1890s contributed to the outbreak of war in 1914.

Lafore, Laurence. *The Long Fuse: An Interpretation of the Origins of World War I.* 2nd ed. Philadelphia: Lippincott, 1971. A useful introductory survey.

Langdon, John W. *July 1914: The Long Debate, 1918–1990.* New York: Berg, 1990. An extremely useful summary and analysis of the controversy that has raged over responsibility for the outbreak of the war.

Lee, Dwight E. *Europe's Crucial Years: The Diplomatic Background of World War I, 1902–1914.* Hanover, N.H: University Press of New England, 1974. A balanced introductory survey of prewar diplomacy designed for the general reader.

Lieven, D.C.B. *Russia and the Origins of the First World War.* New York: St. Martin's Press, 1983. A scholarly study of the domestic pressures and events on the international scene that led Russia into war.

May, Ernest, ed. *Knowing One's Enemies: Intelligence Assessment before the Two World Wars.* Princeton: Princeton University Press, 1985. Contains a number of original and informative essays on the successes and failures of pre-1914 European intelligence services.

Mayer, Arno. "Domestic Causes of the First World War." In Leonard Krieger and Fritz Stern, eds., *The Responsibility of Power: Historical Essays in Honor of Hajo Holborn.* Garden City, N.Y.: Doubleday, 1967. A provocative article.

Remak, Joachim. *Sarajevo: The Story of a Political Murder*. New York: Criterion, 1959. A clear and readable account of the act that led to war; it takes a strong position in favor of Austria-Hungary and bitterly criticizes Serbia.

Steiner, Zara. *Britain and the Origins of the First World War* London: Macmillan, 1977. An introduction to the domestic and external factors that shaped Britain's role in European international affairs from 1900 through the July 1914 crisis.

Williamson, Samuel R. *Austria-Hungary and the Origins of the First World War*. New York: St. Martin's Press, 1991. A useful study concentrating on the two years leading up to the war.

—————— . *The Politics of Grand Strategy: Britain and France Prepare for War, 1904–1914*. Cambridge, Mass: Harvard University Press, 1969. A valuable scholarly account of the growing military relationship between the two future World War I allies.

Wartime Leaders

Barnett, Correlli. *The Swordbearers: Supreme Command in the First World War*. London: Eyre and Spottiswoode, 1963. Brilliant studies on four key wartime leaders: Moltke, Jellicoe, Pétain, and Ludendorff.

De Groot, Gerard J. *Douglas Haig, 1861–1928*. London: Unwin Hyman, 1988. A highly critical biography of the British commander stressing how the roots of his wartime leadership can be found in his upbringing in Victorian society.

Epstein, Klaus. *Matthias Erzberger and the Dilemma of German Democracy*. Princeton: Princeton University Press, 1959. A fine biography of a leading German diplomat and political figure during the war, the Armistice negotiations, and the debate over the peace treaty.

Heckscher, August. *Woodrow Wilson*. New York: Scribner, 1991. An admiring biography of the American president stressing his personality, his political views, and his foreign policy during the war and the era of peacemaking.

Herwig, Holger, and Neil Heyman. *Biographical Dictionary of World War I*. Westport, Conn.: Greenwood Press, 1982. Presents the lives and significance of 327 key political and military figures.

Jarausch, Konrad H. *The Enigmatic Chancellor: Bethmann Hollweg and the Hubris of Imperial Germany*. New Haven, Conn.: Yale University Press, 1973. The standard biography of the German prime minister; presents him as an ambitious and active leader but one incapable of effectively directing the course of events in 1914 and thereafter.

Klachko, Mary, and David Trask. *Admiral William Shepherd Benson: First Chief of Naval Operations*. Annapolis, Md.: Naval Institute Press, 1986. An informative study of a leading American naval policy maker during the war.

Marshall-Cornwall, James. *Foch as a Military Commander*. London: Batsford, 1972. A good popular introduction to the career of the Allied supreme commander in 1918.

Morison, Elting E. *Admiral Sims and the Modern American Navy*. Boston: Houghton Mifflin, 1942. A dated but still valuable study of the American naval commander-in-chief in Europe.

Palmer, Alan. *The Kaiser: Warlord of the Second Reich*. London: Weidenfeld and Nicolson, 1978. An informed and readable account of the life of Wilhelm II for the general reader.

Parkinson, Roger. *Tormented Warrior: Ludendorff and the Supreme Command*. London: Hodder and Stoughton, 1978. A readable and informative biography of the most significant German leader.

Patterson, A. Temple. *Jellicoe: A Biography*. London: Macmillan, 1969. The standard biography of the British naval commander; balanced and well informed.

Rowland, Peter. *Lloyd George*. London: Barrie and Jenkins, 1975. A good general account of the British leader's life including three chapters on his role in World War I.

Ryan, Stephen. *Pétain the Soldier*. South Brunswick, N.J.: A. S. Barnes, 1969. The standard work on the French commander's military career, with more than one-half of the text devoted to World War I.

Smythe, Donald. *Pershing, General of the Armies*. Bloomington: Indiana University Press, 1986. The most useful and up-to-date biography of the American commander, with an extensive and balanced assessment of his wartime role.

Terraine, John. *Ordeal of Victory*. Philadelphia: Lippincott, 1963. A vigorous rebuttal to the long-standing criticism of Haig's leadership in the war. Sometimes listed under the title *Douglas Haig: The Educated Soldier*.

Ulam, Adam. *The Bolsheviks: The Intellectual and Political History of the Triumph of Communism in Russia*. New York: Macmillan, 1965. Despite its title, this is a useful and informed biography of V. I. Lenin. Sometimes entitled *Lenin and the Bolsheviks*.

Watson, David Robin. *Georges Clemenceau: A Political Biography*. New York: 1974. The best general biography of the French political leader; one-third of the book is devoted to his role as opposition figure, then prime minister during the war.

Wilson, Jeremy. *Lawrence of Arabia*. New York: Atheneum, 1990. A lucid account of the war's greatest romantic hero and his exploits in the Middle East.

Strategy and Tactics

Bucholz, Arden. *Moltke, Schlieffen, and Prussian War Planning*. New York: Berg, 1991. A scholarly study that analyzes the Prussian tradition of war planning and how it influenced the way in which Germany fought the first campaigns of World War I.

Griffith, Paddy. *Battle Tactics of the Western Front: The British Army's Art of Attack, 1916–1918*. New Haven: Yale University Press, 1989. An important study that contends that British tactics improved drastically after the Battle of the Somme and led to a well-deserved success in the fall of 1918.

Haber, L. F. *The Poisonous Cloud: Chemical Warfare in the First World War*. New York: Oxford University Press, 1986. A study of how scientists and military men developed and used this novel weapon.

Hartcup, Guy. *The War of Invention: Scientific Developments, 1914–1918*. London: Brassey's Defence Publishers, 1988. A good survey of the new weaponry that was developed during the war.

Millet, Allan R., and Murray Williamson, eds. *Military Effectiveness*. Vol. 1, *The First World War*. Boston: Allen and Unwin, 1988. Essays on how the major powers conducted their war efforts in politics, strategy, operations, and tactics.

Richter, Donald. *Chemical Soldier: British Gas Warfare in World War I*. Lawrence: University of Kansas Press, 1992. A well-written study of one of the British units that conducted gas warfare on the western front; it stresses the experiences of the individual fighting men involved in this form of warfare.

Ritter, Gerhard. *The Schlieffen Plan: Critique of a Myth*. Reprint. New York: Praeger [1958]. An informed, engrossing, and sharply critical study of the plan with which Germany entered the war.

Travers, Tim. *How the War Was Won: Command and Technology in the British Army on the Western Front, 1917–1918*. London: Routledge, 1992. Describes how the British army used tanks, infantry, and artillery to turn the tide in the final period of the war.

————. *The Killing Ground: The British Army, the Western Front and the Emergence of Modern Warfare, 1900–1918*. London: Allen and Unwin, 1987. An important critical evaluation of the prewar British officer corps and its basic ideas, the leadership of General Douglas Haig, and the British performance at the Battle of the Somme.

The Social History of the War

Barnett, L. Margaret. *British Food Policy During the First World War*. Boston: Allen and Unwin, 1985. A densely detailed but valuable study of how the British government came to understand and to cope effectively with the nation's wartime food problems.

Becker, Jean-Jacques. *The Great War and the French People*. New York: St. Martin's Press, 1986. An important examination of various segments of

French society showing how and why the French stood up to the strain of the war.

Bessel, Richard. *Germany after the First World War.* Oxford: Clarendon Press, 1993. The first three chapters are invaluable for an understanding of German society during the war and the subsequent return of its defeated fighting men.

Braybon, Gail. *Women Workers in the First World War: The British Experience.* London: Croom Helm, 1981. A well-written study that questions whether the wartime economy brought significant social change to British women.

Fridenson, Patrick, ed. *The French Home Front.* Providence, R.I: Berg, 1992. Fourteen scholarly essays including case studies of industrial firms, women workers, and portions of the French labor movement.

Greenwald, Maurice Weiner. *Women, War, and Work: The Impact of World War I on Women Workers in the United States.* Westport, Conn.: Greenwood Press, 1980. A detailed scholarly investigation of how the war and the economic opportunities it brought affected American women working in the railroad, telegraph, and streetcar industries.

Grieves, Keith. *The Politics of Manpower, 1914–1918.* Manchester, Eng.: Manchester University Press, 1988. A valuable scholarly investigation of the clash between advocates of a large army and those who wanted to reserve a significant pool of manpower for British industry.

Higonnet, Margaret Randolph, et al., eds. *Behind the Lines: Gender and the Two World Wars.* New Haven, Conn.: Yale University Press, 1987. This informative collection of essays on how women have been affected by war contains important pieces on Vera Brittain, the French woman's rights movement in World War I, and Germany's treatment of the widows of its fallen fighting men.

Hoover, A. J. *God, Germany, and Britain in the Great War: A Study in Clerical Nationalism.* New York: Praeger, 1989. A brief but informative study of how clergymen from both sides defended their countries and attacked the enemy.

Horn, Pamela. *Rural Life in England in the First World War.* New York: St. Martin's Press, 1984. Examines the human losses among the rural population, the wartime expansion of agriculture, and the changing relations among the segments of rural society.

Kocka, Jurgen. *Facing Total War: German Society, 1914–1918.* Leamington Spa, Eng.: Berg, 1984. A difficult but important study of wartime society in Germany presented from a Marxist perspective.

Lih, Lars T. *Bread and Authority in Russia, 1914–1921.* Berkeley and Los Angeles: University of California Press, 1990. A scholarly examination of how first Russia's monarchy and then its revolutionary governments tried to cope with the nation's wartime food crisis.

Marwick, Arthur. *The Deluge: British Society and the First World War*. Boston: Little, Brown, 1966. A rich and lively introduction to changes on the British home front.

Waites, Bernard. *A Class Society at War: England, 1914–1918*. Leamington Spa: Berg, 1987. A scholarly study that argues that the war did not lower but rather raised barriers between Britain's social classes.

Wall, Richard, and Jay Winter, eds. *The Upheaval of War: Family, Work and Welfare in Europe, 1914–1918*. Cambridge: Cambridge University Press, 1988. A collection of sixteen informative essays on topics ranging from the living standards in the belligerent countries to the efforts of various governments to encourage women to bear more children.

Williams, John. *The Other Battleground: The Home Fronts, Britain, France and Germany, 1914–1918*. Chicago: Regnery, 1972. A popularly written but valuable introduction to the experience of civilians in three of the main warring nations.

Winter, J. M. *The Great War and the British People*. Cambridge, Mass.: Harvard University Press, 1986. An important study employing statistics to evaluate the impact of the war on the home front; it contends that the war affected civilians' health and economic conditions in a positive way.

The Higher Direction of the War

Asprey, Robert. *The German High Command at War: Hindenburg and Ludendorff Conduct World War I*. New York: William Morrow, 1991. A vivid and well-informed account of how Ludendorff and Hindenburg directed the German war effort, first on the eastern front, then throughout Europe.

Hunt, Barry, and Adrian Preston, eds. *War Aims and Strategic Policy in the Great War, 1914–1918*. London: Croom Helm, 1977. Six brief essays on the grand strategy of Britain, France, Canada, the United States, Italy, and Germany.

Snyder, Jack. *The Ideology of the Offensive: Military Decision Making and the Disasters of 1914*. Ithaca, N.Y.: Cornell University Press, 1984. An important scholarly study of prewar strategic thinking in France, Germany, and Russia and the 1914 war plans it produced.

Trask, David F. *The AEF and Coalition Warmaking, 1917–1918*. Lawrence: University Press of Kansas, 1993. A valuable account of Allied operations during the last year of the war stressing the difficulties of cooperation between the American high command under Pershing and its French and British counterparts; sharply critical of Pershing's leadership.

Woodward, David. *Lloyd George and the Generals*. Newark, Del.: University of Delaware Press, 1983. A valuable study showing how British strategy was determined by the difficult interaction between British politicians like Lloyd George and the nation's military leaders.

The Economic History of the War

Burk, Kathleen. *Britain, America, and the Sinews of War, 1914–1918*. London: Allen and Unwin, 1984. A study of how the financial strain of the war led to increasing British dependence on the United States.

Feldman, Gerald D. *Army, Industry, and Labor in Germany, 1914–1918*. Princeton: Princeton University Press, 1966. A pioneering scholarly study showing the wartime cooperation among various segments of German society.

Hardach, Gerd. *The First World War, 1914–1918*. Berkeley and Los Angeles: University of California Press, 1977. The standard economic history of the war.

Offer, Avner. *The First World War: An Agrarian Interpretation*. Oxford: Oxford University Press; Clarendon, 1989. A novel examination of the war's economic side stressing such topics as the evolution of British agriculture before and during the conflict and the influence of agricultural factors on German strategic planning.

Olson, Mancur. *The Economics of the Wartime Shortage: A History of British Food Supplies in the Napoleonic War and in World Wars I and II*. Durham, N.C.: Duke University Press, 1963. Contains a lucid description of how Britain was able to adjust its economy to overcome the strains of the U-boat blockade.

Vincent, C. Paul. *The Politics of Hunger: The Allied Blockade of Germany, 1915–1919*. Athens: Ohio University Press, 1985. A valuable book on the food blockade, its wartime effectiveness, and its impact in the immediate postwar period.

Wartime Diplomacy

Jaffe, Lorna S. *The Decision to Disarm Germany: British Policy Towards Postwar German Disarmament, 1914–1919*. Boston: Allen and Unwin, 1985. A good scholarly study of how the disarmament of Germany became an important British war aim during the course of the conflict.

Mamatey, Victor. *The United States and East Central Europe, 1914–1918: A Study in Wilsonian Diplomacy and Propaganda*. Princeton: Princeton University Press, 1957. Still a valuable source of information on the nationalist movement within the Austro-Hungarian Empire and how it came to get American support.

Neilson, Keith. *Strategy and Supply: The Anglo-Russian Alliance, 1914–1917*. London: Allen and Unwin, 1984. A detailed scholarly account stressing the British role in this important wartime alliance.

Shanafelt, Gary W. *The Secret Enemy: Austria-Hungary and the German Alliance, 1914–1918*. Boulder, Colo.: East European Monographs, 1985. A scholarly account of how Germany came to dominate the wartime alliance with Austria-Hungary.

Stevenson, David. *The First World War and International Politics*. New York: Oxford University Press, 1988. A study of how Europe's government officials and diplomats led the continent into war, developed war aims, and, with the United States, produced a flawed peace settlement.

Wheeler-Bennett, John. *Brest-Litovsk: The Forgotten Peace, March 1918*. New York: W. W. Norton, 1971. Sometimes entitled *The Forgotten Peace*. An important study of the peace treaty the victorious Central Powers imposed on revolutionary Russia.

Woodward, David R. *Trial by Friendship: Anglo-American Relations, 1917–1918*. Lexington: University of Kentucky Press, 1993. Examines this crucial relationship in World War I stressing the growing friction between Woodrow Wilson and David Lloyd George.

The Naval War

Bennett, Geoffrey. *Coronel and the Falklands*. New York: Macmillan, 1962. A good popular account of the first major surface actions of the naval war.

Halpern, Paul. *A Naval History of World War I*. Annapolis, Md.: Naval Institute Press, 1994. A detailed and scholarly account of the entire war at sea.

———. *The Naval War in the Mediterranean, 1914–1918*. A scholarly examination of the surface and U-boat war in an important area of naval operations.

Herwig, Holger. *"Luxury" Fleet: The Imperial German Navy, 1888–1918*. London: Allen and Unwin, 1980. One-third of this useful general work examines World War I naval operations from the German standpoint.

Hezlet, Arthur. *The Submarine and Sea Power*. New York: Stein and Day, 1967. Contains a lucid account of the early development of submarines and their use in World War I.

Hough, Richard. *The Great War at Sea, 1914–1918*. Oxford: Oxford University Press, 1983. A vivid and readable survey of the naval war for the general reader.

Keegan, John. *The Price of Admiralty: War at Sea from Man of War to Submarine*. London: Hutchinson, 1988. This treatment of naval warfare from the age of Nelson through World War II includes a vivid description of surface warfare operations by battleships and battle cruisers, especially in the Battle of Jutland.

Marder, Arthur J. *From the Dreadnought to Scapa Flow: The Royal Navy in the Fisher Era, 1904–1919*. 5 vols. London: Oxford University Press, 1961–1970. The most extensive modern examination of the naval war, told brilliantly from the British perspective; volume 3 is devoted to the Battle of Jutland.

O'Connell, Robert L. *Sacred Vessels: The Cult of the Battleship and the Rise of the U.S. Navy.* Boulder, Colo.: Westview Press, 1991. A wide-ranging account of capital ships in the United States Navy with several useful chapters on the challenge to the battleship in World War I.

Trask, David F. *Captains and Cabinets: Anglo-American Naval Relations, 1917–1918.* Columbia: University of Missouri Press, 1972. An essential work on the war against the U-boat and other aspects of cooperation between the two strong Allied navies.

Winton, John. *Convoy: The Defence of Sea Trade, 1890–1990.* London: Michael Joseph, 1983. Presents an excellent account of how the Allies used convoys to win the war against World War I German submarines.

The Common Soldiers

Ellis, John. *Eye-Deep in Hell: Trench Warfare in World War I.* New York: Pantheon, 1976. A vivid and harrowing description of the experience of British, French, and German soldiers on the western front.

Keegan, John. *The Face of Battle.* London: Jonathan Cape, 1976. An examination of the nature of battlefield combat since the Middle Ages with an extensive treatment of the Battle of the Somme.

Leed, Eric. *No Man's Land: Combat and Identity in World War I.* London: Cambridge University Press, 1979. An important scholarly study of the psychological impact of the war on front-line combatants.

Macdonald, Lyn. *Somme.* Salem, N.H.: Salem House, 1983. An account of the bloody battle told through the words of its British participants.

Rawling, Bill. *Surviving Trench Warfare: Technology and the Canadian Corps, 1914–1918.* Toronto: University of Toronto Press, 1992. A study showing both the horror of trench warfare and how Canadian forces became increasingly skilled and effective in waging it.

Smith, Leonard V. *Between Mutiny and Obedience: The Case of the French Fifth Infantry Division During World War I.* Princeton: Princeton University Press, 1994. A study of how one renowned French combat unit was transformed into a center of mutiny in 1917.

Winter, Denis. *Death's Men: Soldiers of the Great War.* Harmondsworth, Eng.: Penguin Books, 1979. A valuable and gripping account of how the men of Great Britain were trained for military service, how they experienced the trauma of trench warfare, and how they were abruptly transformed again into civilians.

Pictorial Histories

Freidel, Frank. *Over There: The Story of America's First Great Overseas Crusade.* Boston: Little, Brown, 1964. A valuable examination of the American experience of the fighting told through photographs and contemporary letters.

Haythornthwaite, Philip J. *A Photohistory of World War One*. London: Arms and Armour, 1993. Treats all the fighting armies, with particular emphasis on their fighting equipment and uniforms.

Terraine, John. *The Great War, 1914–1918: A Pictorial History*. New York: Macmillan, 1965. A rich collection of pictures showing all the principal fighting fronts.

Opposition to the War

Carsten, F. L. *War against War: British and German Radical Movements in the First World War*. Berkeley and Los Angeles: University of California Press, 1982. A detailed scholarly account of the antiwar movement in two of the major belligerent countries.

Gibbs, Christopher C. *The Great Silent Majority: Missouri's Resistance to World War I*. Columbia: University of Missouri Press, 1988. The author contends with passion that labor unions, individuals, and even the state government provided varying degrees of resistance to the war effort.

Melancon, Michael. *The Socialist Revolutionaries and the Russian Anti-war Movement, 1914–1917*. Columbus: Ohio State University Press, 1990. An important study of how one of Russia's radical parties agitated vigorously against the war effort.

Robbins, Keith. *The Abolition of War: The "Peace Movement" in Britain, 1914–1919*. Cardiff: University of Wales Press, 1976. A study of the wartime organizations and activities of British pacifists and their sympathizers.

The War by Countries and Areas

Austria-Hungary and the Balkans

Adams, John Clinton. *Flight in Winter*. Princeton: Princeton University Press, 1942. A classic account of the defeat of the Serbian army in 1915 and its heroic escape westward to the Adriatic Sea.

Fest, Wilfried. *Peace or Partition: The Habsburg Monarchy and British Policy, 1914–1918*. New York: St. Martin's Press, 1978. A detailed scholarly account of Britain's shifting policies toward one of its principal wartime opponents.

Kann, Robert A., Béla K. Király, and Paula S. Fichtner, eds. *The Habsburg Empire in World War I: Essays on the Intellectual, Military, Political and Economic Aspects of the Habsburg War Effort*. Boulder, Colo.: East European Quarterly, 1977. A set of twelve essays; the most useful are five on military affairs.

Király, Béla K., and Nándor Dreisziger, eds. *East Central European Society in World War I*. Boulder, Colo.: Atlantic Research and Publications, 1985.

More than thirty essays dealing with the armies, military campaigns, and home fronts of the Habsburg Empire, Bulgaria, Poland, Rumania, Serbia and Montenegro, Czechoslovakia, and the Ottoman Empire.

May, Arthur J. *The Passing of the Hapsburg Monarchy, 1914–1918.* 2 vols. Philadelphia: University of Pennsylvania Press, 1966. This valuable study stresses government policy; it is weak on the social history of the war.

Rothenberg, G. E. *The Army of Francis Joseph.* West Lafayette, Ind.: Purdue University Press, 1976. A valuable account of the Austro-Hungarian army before and during World War I.

Zeman, Z.A.B. *The Break-up of the Habsburg Empire, 1914–1918: A Study in National and Social Revolution.* London: Oxford University Press, 1961. An important scholarly study of the internal and external forces that led to the collapse of Austria-Hungary.

Britain

Adams, R.J.Q., and Philip P. Poirer. *The Conscription Controversy in Great Britain, 1914–1918.* Basingstoke, Eng.: Macmillan, 1987. Stresses how conscription was a commanding political issue in the first two years of the war.

Bond, Brian, ed. *The First World War and British Military History.* Oxford: Oxford University Press, Clarendon Press, 1990. Eleven valuable essays showing how historians, memoir writers, and filmmakers have treated the war.

Burk, Kathleen, ed. *War and the State: The Transformation of British Government, 1914–1919.* London: Allen and Unwin, 1982. Seven scholarly essays showing how the British government grew to meet the demands of the war.

French, David. *British Strategy and War Aims, 1914–1916.* London: Allen and Unwin, 1986. A scholarly examination of how the Asquith government formulated and implemented its war aims vis-à-vis both Britain's allies and Britain's opponents.

Pugh, Martin. *Electoral Reform in War and Peace, 1906–1918.* London: Routledge and Kegan Paul, 1978. A scholarly study showing how the war contributed to a vast widening of the British electorate.

Simkins, Peter. *Kitchener's Army: The Raising of the New Armies, 1914–1916.* Manchester, Eng.: Manchester University Press, 1988. A valuable work on War Minister Horatio Kitchener's leadership and the citizen army he created.

Wilson, Trevor. *The Myriad Faces of War: Britain and the Great War, 1914–1918.* Cambridge: Polity Press, 1986. A brilliantly written and provocative treatment of all aspects of the British role in the war.

France

Cruikshank, John. *Variations on Catastrophe: Some French Responses to the Great War*. London: Oxford University Press, 1982. A lucid scholarly study showing the variety of reactions by French writers to the war and the values of a wartime society.

King, Jere. *Foch Versus Clemenceau: France and German Dismemberment, 1918–1919*. Cambridge, Mass.: Harvard University Press, 1960. A sequel to *Generals and Politicians*, it describes how the French prime minister managed to restrain the desire of military men for an even more punitive peace to be placed on defeated Germany.

————. *Generals and Politicians: Conflict Between France's High Command, Parliament and Government, 1914–1918*. Berkeley and Los Angeles: University of California Press, 1950. An old but still valuable account of tensions between France's civilian and political leaders throughout the war.

Porch, Douglas. *The March to the Marne: The French Army, 1871–1914*. London: Cambridge University Press, 1981. A study of the prewar French army that attributes the army's weaknesses and mistakes at the start of the war to the harmful influence politicians had exerted over it.

Stevenson, David. *French War Aims Against Germany, 1914–1919*. Oxford: Oxford University Press, 1982. A pioneering work that shows how France moved from merely trying to avoid defeat to a program of territorial gains and other goals that would assure its postwar security.

Watt, Richard M. *Dare Call It Treason*. New York: Simon and Schuster, 1963. A good popular study of growing tensions in the French army, the Nivelle offensive, and the subsequent mutinies.

Germany

Craig, Gordon A. *Germany, 1866–1945*. New York: Oxford University Press, 1978. The best survey of German history during this period; two chapters present a good introduction to Germany's role leading up to the war and its wartime experiences.

————. *The Politics of the Prussian Army, 1640–1945*. London: Oxford University Press, 1955. A classic account of relations between German military and civilian leaders; it contains treatments of the prewar and wartime years.

Herwig, Holger H. *The First World War: Germany and Austria-Hungary, 1914–1918*. New York: St. Martin's Press, 1997. An important recent work on the cooperation between the two great Germanic powers.

Kitchen, Martin. *The Silent Dictatorship: The Politics of the German High Command under Hindenburg and Ludendorff*. New York: Holmes and Meier, 1976. A study of Germany's military leadership and its domination of the political scene from 1916 to the close of the war; written from a Marxist perspective.

Moyer, Laurence V. *Victory Must Be Ours: Germany in the Great War, 1914–1918*. New York: Hippocrene Books, 1995. The best book in English on the German side of the war; particularly strong on events at home.

Italy

Burgwyn, H. James. *The Legend of the Mutilated Victory: Italy, the Great War, and the Paris Peace Conference, 1915–1919*. Westport, Conn.: Greenwood Press, 1993. Stresses Italian diplomacy and policy-making; gives equal weight to the problems of making war and conducting peace negotiations.

Seton-Watson, Christopher. *Italy from Liberalism to Fascism, 1870–1925*. London: Methuen, 1967. The standard survey of Italian history for this period, with an extensive treatment of the war years.

Thayer, John A. *Italy and the Great War: Politics and Culture, 1870–1915*. Madison: University of Wisconsin Press, 1964. Contains a good account of how Italy came to enter the war.

Whittam, John. *The Politics of the Italian Army*. Hamden, Conn.: Archon Books, 1977. Contains a useful chapter dealing with the war.

Russia

Debo, Richard. *Revolution and Survival: The Foreign Policy of Soviet Russia, 1917–1918*. Toronto: University of Toronto Press, 1979. A lucid study of how V. I. Lenin and Russia's new Communist government led that country out of the war.

Lincoln, W. Bruce. *Passage Through Armageddon: The Russians in War and Revolution, 1914–1918*. New York: Oxford University Press, 1994. An informed and readable account of Russia's experience during and after the war, intended for a general audience.

Pearson, Raymond. *The Russian Moderates and the Crisis of Tsarism*. Basingstoke, Eng.: Macmillan, 1977. An important study of the leading parties in the Russian parliament (Duma) during the war.

Rutherford, Ward. *The Russian Army in World War I*. London: Gordon Cremonesi, 1975. A good popular introduction to the subject.

Smith, C. Jay, Jr. *The Russian Struggle for Power, 1914–1917: A Study of Russian Foreign Policy During the First World War*. New York: Greenwood Press, 1969. Reprint of 1956 edition. Still a valuable survey of Russian diplomacy during the conflict.

Wade, Rex A. *The Russian Search for Peace, February–October 1917*. Stanford: Stanford University Press, 1969. A lucid account of how the failure of moderate governments to remove Russia from the war after the March 1917 Revolution opened the way for the Bolsheviks to take power.

Wildman, Alan K. *The End of the Russian Imperial Army.* 2 vols. Princeton: Princeton University Press, 1980–1987. An important study of how the army disintegrated during the revolutionary year 1917.

Ottoman Turkey

Shaw, Stanford J. *History of the Ottoman Empire and Modern Turkey.* New York: Cambridge University Press, 1976–1977. 2 vols. Volume 2 contains a good discussion of Ottoman Turkey during the war years.

Trumpener, Otto. *Germany and the Ottoman Empire, 1914–1918.* Princeton: Princeton University Press, 1968. A well-informed and lucid study of the Turkish role in the war and its relationship with its powerful ally.

United States

Barbeau, Arthur E., and Florette Henri. *The Unknown Soldiers: Black American Troops in World War I.* Philadelphia: Temple University Press, 1974. A valuable study of how black Americans participated in their country's military effort and how the war changed their expectations for the future.

Braim, Paul F. *The Test of Battle: The American Expeditionary Forces in the Meuse-Argonne Campaign.* Newark, Del.: University of Delaware Press, 1987. A study of the largest battle in which the American forces took part.

Clements, Kendrick A. *The Presidency of Woodrow Wilson.* Lawrence: University of Kansas Press, 1992. The best brief account of Wilson's presidency; half of the book is devoted to America's role in World War I and the peacemaking.

Coffmann, Edward M. *The War to End All Wars: The American Military Experience in World War I.* New York: Oxford University Press, 1968. A good older account of how America's armed forces took shape and fought the war.

Devlin, Patrick. *Too Proud to Fight: Woodrow Wilson's Neutrality.* New York: Oxford University Press, 1975. A study of American foreign policy stressing the personality and motivations of Woodrow Wilson.

DeWeerd, Harvey. *President Wilson Fights His War: World War I and the American Intervention.* New York: Macmillan, 1968. An account of the entire war that moves on to consider the American role in the fighting and the effect of the war on Americans at home.

Ferrell, Robert H. *Woodrow Wilson and World War I, 1917–1921.* New York: Harper and Row, 1985. A brilliantly written treatment of the mobilization of American military power, combat operations, and the parallel developments on the home front.

Harries, Meiron, and Susie Harries. *The Last Days of Innocence: America at War, 1917–1918.* New York: Random House, 1997. Intended for a popular audience, this work deals with both the battlefields and the home front.

Kennedy, David. *Over Here: The First World War and American Society.* New York: Oxford University Press, 1982. A lucid and well-informed study of the American home front during the war; it puts the conflict into the larger context of American history in the early twentieth century.

Knock, Thomas J. *To End All Wars: Woodrow Wilson and the Quest for a New World Order.* New York: Oxford University Press, 1992. An important and provocative study of the background and nature of Wilson's plans for the postwar international community.

May, Ernest R. *The World War and American Isolation, 1914–1917.* Cambridge, Mass.: Harvard University Press, 1959. A balanced account of the events and pressures that brought the United States to enter the war.

Mock, James R., and Cedric Larson. *Words that Won the War: The Story of the Committee on Public Information, 1917–1919.* New York: Russell and Russell, 1968. Reprint from Princeton University Press, 1939. A classic account.

Schaffer, Ronald. *America in the Great War: The Rise of the War Welfare State.* New York: Oxford University Press, 1991. A well-written account of the spread of federal power during the wartime administration of Woodrow Wilson.

Thompson, John A. *Reformers and War: American Progressive Publicists and the First World War.* Cambridge: Cambridge University Press, 1987. A study of the divisive effect the war had on the important group of American political theorists and writers that included Herbert Croly.

Tuchman, Barbara. *The Zimmermann Telegram.* New York: Macmillan, 1958. A good popular account of a key event that helped to bring the United States into the war.

War and Revolution

Carsten, F. L. *Revolution in Central Europe, 1918–1919.* Berkeley and Los Angeles: University of California Press, 1972. An account based largely on local records of how revolution erupted and developed in Germany and Austria at the close of the war.

Hasegawa, Tsukoshi. *The February Revolution: Petrograd, 1917.* Seattle: University of Washington Press, 1981. A detailed and complete scholarly account of the fall of the Russian monarchy.

Kirby, David. *War, Peace, and Revolution: International Socialism at the Crossroads, 1914–1918.* New York: St. Martin's Press, 1988. A study of how most socialist leaders supported their countries' wartime governments while pressing those governments to end the conflict.

Koenker, Diane. *Moscow Workers and the 1917 Revolution.* Princeton: Princeton University Press, 1981. An account of how the Russian workers in this key city promoted the radicalization of the course of the revolution in 1917.

Mawdsley, Evan. *The Russian Revolution and the Baltic Fleet: War and Politics, February 1917–April 1918*. London: Macmillan, 1978. An informative study of how the navy took part in the revolution.

Rabinowitch, Alexander. *The Bolsheviks Come to Power: The 1917 Revolution in Petrograd*. New York: W. W. Norton, 1978. An informed scholarly interpretation of how Lenin's Marxist faction defeated its rivals and took control of Petrograd in November 1917.

Read, Christopher. *From Tsar to Soviets: The Russian People and Their Revolution, 1917–1921*. New York: Oxford University Press, 1996. A good survey embodying the most recent research on the period.

Upton, Anthony. *The Finnish Revolution, 1917–1918*. Minneapolis: University of Minnesota Press, 1980. A scholarly account of a part of the Russian Empire whose revolution became a battleground for competing Russian and German interests.

Watt, Richard M. *The Kings Depart: The Tragedy of Germany, Versailles and the German Revolution*. New York: Simon and Schuster, 1968. A vivid popular account of the fall of the German monarchy and subsequent events in revolutionary Germany.

The Great Battles

Brook-Shepherd, Gordon. *November 1918*. Boston: Little, Brown, 1981. A good popular account of the final phase of the fighting in Europe and the Middle East.

Falls, Cyril. *The Battle of Caporetto*. Philadelphia: Lippincott, 1966. A good popular account of the most important battles on the Italian front.

Horne, Alistair. *The Price of Glory: Verdun 1916*. New York: St. Martin's Press, 1962. A fine account of the war's longest battle.

Isselin, Henri. *The Battle of the Marne*. Garden City, N.Y.: Doubleday, 1966. A French historian's view of the most decisive battle on the western front in 1914.

James, Robert Rhodes. *Gallipoli*. New York: Macmillan, 1965. The best work to date on this controversial campaign.

Middlebrook, Martin. *The First Day on the Somme: 1 July 1916*. New York: W. W. Norton, 1972. A masterful reconstruction of the bloodiest single day in the war based on interviews with hundreds of the survivors.

Palmer, Alan. *The Gardeners of Salonika*. New York: Simon and Schuster, 1965. A vividly written and informative account of the important Balkan operations centered on the Greek port of Salonika from the fall of 1915 to the close of the war.

Pascall, Rod. *The Defeat of Imperial Germany, 1917–1918*. Chapel Hill, N.C.: Algonquin Books of Chapel Hill, 1989. A vivid and informed account of the final two years of fighting on the western front.

Showalter, Dennis. *Tannenberg: Clash of Empires*. Hamden, Conn.: Archon Books, 1991. A rich account of the first great battle on the eastern front, with an extensive discussion of the characteristics of the Russian and German armies.

Stone, Norman. *The Eastern Front, 1914–1917*. New York: Charles Scribner's Sons, 1975. The best account to date of what Winston Churchill called "the unknown war."

Terraine, John. *Mons: The Retreat to Victory*. New York: Macmillan, 1960. A vivid account of the first military clashes between the British and German armies leading up to the start of the Battle of the Marne.

————. *To Win a War: 1918, the Year of Victory*. London: Sidgwick and Jackson, 1978. A fine, well-informed account of the last German offensive and the subsequent Allied offensive on the western front.

Tuchman, Barbara. *The Guns of August*. New York: Macmillan, 1962. A classic popular account of the war's early weeks up to the eve of the Battle of the Marne.

Wolff, Leon. *In Flanders Fields: The 1917 Campaign*. New York: Viking, 1958. An embittered popular account of the Passchendaele offensive stressing the incompetence of the British high command and the suffering of the men in the rank and file.

The Air War and the Tank War

Chamberlain, Peter, and Chris Ellis. *Tanks of World War I: British and German*. New York: Arco Publishing, 1969. An informative and well-illustrated description of the two belligerents' armored forces.

Citino, Robert M. *Armored Forces: History and Sourcebook*. Westport, Conn.: Greenwood Press, 1994. Contains a good brief account on the early development of tank warfare.

Fredette, Raymond H. *The Sky on Fire: The First Battle of Britain, 1917–1918, and the Birth of the Royal Air Force*. New York: Holt, Rinehart and Winston, 1966. A colorful account of the sustained German air assault against Britain.

Kennett, Lee. *The First Air War, 1914–1918*. New York: Free Press, 1991. A good survey of all aspects of the air war.

Liddell Hart, B. H. *The Tanks: The History of the Royal Tank Regiment*. Vol. 1. New York: Praeger, 1959. Contains a detailed account of the development of tanks in the British army and their employment on the western front.

Macksey, Kenneth. *Tank Warfare: A History of Tanks in Battle*. New York: Stein and Day, 1972. A lucid account of the development of armored warfare; includes a good account of the Battle of Cambrai in 1917.

Morrow, John H. *German Air Power in World War I*. Lincoln: University of Nebraska Press, 1982. An important study of how German industry provided the tools of aerial warfare.

——— . *The Great War in the Air: Military Aviation from 1909 to 1921*. Washington, D.C.: Smithsonian Institution, 1993. A fine scholarly study of how the major European powers and the United States developed their air arm before the war, employed it between 1914 and 1918, and took their experiences into the postwar era.

Norman, Aaron. *The Great Air War*. New York: Macmillan, 1968. A good survey that stresses combat operations on the western front and the colorful aerial heroes who fought there.

The Cultural Impact of the War

Adams, Michael C. C. *The Great Adventure: Male Desire and the Coming of World War I*. Bloomington: Indiana University Press, 1990. A provocative study of the British and American upper classes and how the reigning social mores and sexual tensions encouraged young men from these groups to go to war.

Bonadeo, Alfred. *Mark of the Beast: Death and Degradation in the Literature of the Great War*. Lexington: University Press of Kentucky, 1989. A study of the reaction of soldiers to the experience of combat; especially useful for its material on the Italian front.

Buitenhuis, Peter. *The Great War of Words: British, American, and Canadian Propaganda and Fiction, 1914–1933*. Vancouver: University of British Columbia Press, 1987. A study comparing the propaganda and fiction produced in wartime with the more realistic writing about the conflict in the postwar generation.

Dibbets, Karel, and Bert Hogenkamp. *Film and the First World War*. Amsterdam: Amsterdam University Press, 1995. A valuable set of essays on filmmaking during the war and subsequent examinations of the conflict in this important art form.

Eberle, Matthias. *World War I and the Weimar Artists: Dix, Grosz, Beckmann, Schlemmer*. New Haven, Conn.: Yale University Press, 1985. Shows how four German artists served in the military and found their ideas and their work transformed by the horrors they witnessed.

Eksteins, Modris. *Rites of Spring: The Great War and the Birth of the Modern Age*. Boston: Houghton Mifflin, 1989. A sweeping and provocative work that links the war to the overall transformation of European, especially German, cultural values at the turn of the century.

Ferguson, John. *The Arts in Britain in World War I*. London: Stainer and Bell, 1980. A good popular introduction to the changes that took place in writing and the visual arts during the war.

Field, Frank. *British and French Writers of the First World War: Comparative Studies in Cultural History*. Cambridge: Cambridge University Press, 1991. A study of the cultural pessimism the war created or deepened in the writers of two of the principal belligerents.

———. *Three French Writers and the Great War*. Cambridge: Cambridge University Press, 1963. Considers how the experiences of World War I pushed Henri Barbusse toward communism in the postwar era while his countrymen George Bernanos and Pierre Drieu la Rochelle moved toward fascism.

Fussell, Paul. *The Great War and Modern Memory*. New York: Oxford University Press, 1975. An important and influential study that contends that the British literary tradition was reshaped by World War I.

Hibberd, Dominic. *The First World War*. Houndmills, Eng.: Macmillan, 1990. An intriguing selection of contemporary writing about various phases of the war from such authors as H. G. Wells and Rudyard Kipling.

Hynes, Samuel. *A War Imagined: The First World War and English Culture*. London: Bodley Head, 1990. An examination of the ways a bitter view of the war emerged in wartime poetry and the postwar novel.

Jahn, Hubertus F. *Patriotic Culture in Russia During World War I*. Ithaca, N.Y.: Cornell University Press, 1995. A study of how popular culture in Russia expressed support for the war.

Kahn, Elizabeth Louise. *The Neglected Majority: "Les Camoufleurs," Art History, and World War I*. Lanham, Md.: University Press of America, 1984. An interesting account of the work of French artists drafted into military service.

Sillars, Stuart. *Art and Survival in First World War Britain*. Basingstoke, Eng.: Macmillan, 1987. A valuable study of how British artists and popular writers were impelled to sanitize their depictions of the carnage of 1916 for the civilian public.

Silver, Kenneth. *Esprit de Corps: The Art of the Parisian Avant-garde and the First World War, 1914–1925*. Princeton: Princeton University Press, 1989. Stresses how the wartime atmosphere pushed the art of the time in a conservative direction.

Stromberg, Roland. *Redemption by War: The Intellectuals and 1914*. Lawrence: Regents Press of Kansas, 1982. Considers Europe's prewar climate of opinion and how it encouraged the intellectuals of many nations to support their respective nations at the start of the conflict.

Wallace, Stuart. *War and the Image of Germany: British Academics, 1914–1918*. Edinburgh: John Donald Publications, 1988. Shows how British scholars contributed to raising and maintaining popular enthusiasm for the war.

Wohl, Robert. *The Generation of 1914*. Cambridge, Mass.: Harvard University Press, 1979. An ambitious study of how the war contributed to the disaffection of a generation of intellectuals in England, France, Germany, Italy, and Spain.

Propaganda

Knightley, Phillip. *The First Casualty: From Crimea to Vietnam: The War Correspondent as Hero, Propagandist, and Myth Maker*. New York: Harcourt Brace Jovanovich, 1975. Contains three informative chapters on the war and the Russian Revolution.

Messinger, Gary S. *British Propaganda and the State in the First World War*. Manchester, Eng.: Manchester University Press, 1992. A popular account of the propaganda campaign focused on fourteen key individuals.

Sanders, Michael, and Philip M. Taylor. *British Propaganda in the First World War, 1914–1918*. New York: Crane, Russak, 1983. A valuable examination of the organization and methods of the complex British propaganda system.

Vaughan, Stephen. *Holding Fast the Inner Lines: Democracy, Nationalism, and the Committee on Public Information*. Chapel Hill: University of North Carolina Press, 1980. A good scholarly account of the American government's propaganda agency, the CPI, created to mobilize public opinion behind the war effort.

The War's Aftermath and Consequences

Albert, Bill. *South America and the First World War: The Impact of the War on Brazil, Argentina, Peru, and Chile*. Cambridge: Cambridge University Press, 1988. An important survey of the relationship of the warring powers with Latin America and how the war disrupted the economy of these four important countries.

Albrecht-Carrié, René. *The Meaning of the First World War*. Englewood Cliffs, N.J.: Prentice-Hall, 1965. An extended essay that stresses how the war was a dramatic break with the patterns of European life in the nineteenth century.

Dockrill, Michael, and Douglas J. Gould. *Peace Without Promise: Britain and the Peace Conferences, 1919–1923*. Hamden, Conn.: Archon Books, 1981. A study of the peace settlements that stresses the Allies' negotiations with Ottoman Turkey.

Egerton, George W. *Great Britain and the Creation of the League of Nations: Strategy, Politics, and International Organization, 1914–1919*. Chapel Hill: University of North Carolina Press, 1978. Shows how a combination of political idealists and pragmatists among British political leaders successfully promoted the creation of the international body.

Goldstein, Erik. *Winning the Peace: British Diplomatic Strategy, Peace Planning, and the Paris Peace Conference, 1916–1920*. Oxford: Clarendon Press,

1991. A scholarly study of how British government leaders skillfully prepared and then achieved Britain's program of war aims.

Kent, Bruce. *The Spoils of War: The Politics, Economics, and Diplomacy of Reparations, 1918–1932*. Oxford: Oxford University Press (Clarendon Press), 1989. A scholarly study that contends that domestic political pressures pushed Allied leaders to impose and maintain the reparations burden on Germany.

Lederer, Ivo J. *Yugoslavia at the Peace Conference: A Study in Frontiermaking*. New Haven, Conn.: Yale University Press, 1963. A good scholarly treatment of the role of one of Europe's newest nations at the great international gathering of 1919.

Lentin, A. *Lloyd George, Woodrow Wilson, and the Guilt of Germany*. Baton Rouge: Louisiana State University Press, 1985. A provocative extended essay on how the British blocked Wilson's desire for a mild peace with Germany and then, tormented by guilt, turned toward appeasing Germany in the postwar period.

Maier, Charles S. *Recasting Bourgeois Europe: Stabilization in France, Germany, and Italy in the Decade after World War I*. Princeton: Princeton University Press, 1975. An important study showing how three major countries overcame the unrest generated by the war.

Marks, Sally. *Innocent Abroad: Belgium at the Paris Peace Conference of 1919*. Chapel Hill: University of North Carolina Press, 1981. A useful scholarly analysis of how this small nation's expectations were frustrated at the peace conference.

Marwick, Arthur. *War and Social Change in the Twentieth Century: A Comparative Study of Britain, France, Germany, Russia and the United States*. New York: St. Martin's Press, 1974. Contains valuable essays on the disruptive effects of World War I on each of these four countries.

Mayer, Arno. *Politics and Diplomacy of Peacemaking: Containment and Counterrevolution at Versailles, 1918–1919*. New York: Knopf, 1967. An important study of the peace conference stressing the influence of the Bolshevik Revolution on the peacemakers and the settlement they produced.

Mosse, George L. *Fallen Soldiers: Reshaping the Memory of the World Wars*. Oxford: Oxford University Press, 1990. An important examination of how the grim losses Germany and other countries suffered in the war were transformed into the basis for a glorious myth of national unity.

Roth, Jack, ed. *World War I: A Turning Point in Modern History*. New York: Knopf, 1967. Four useful essays on the significance of the war as seen by experts in international relations, European culture and political systems, and American history.

Schwabe, Klause. *Woodrow Wilson, Revolutionary Germany, and Peacemaking, 1918–1919: Missionary Diplomacy and the Realities of Power*. Chapel

Hill: University of North Carolina Press, 1985. A scholarly study of how Germany's expectations for a mild peace settlement were disappointed by Wilson's shifting positions and by the stand taken by the British and French governments.

Silverman, Dan P. *Reconstructing Europe after the Great War*. Cambridge, Mass.: Harvard University Press, 1982. A scholarly study of how the United States and Great Britain tried to restore the continent's financial order.

Sontag, Raymond J. *A Broken World, 1919–1939*. New York: Harper and Row, 1971. The best overall treatment of Europe in the postwar era.

Spector, Sherman David. *Rumania at the Paris Peace Conference: A Study of the Diplomacy of Ion Bratianu*. New York: Bookman Associates, 1962. A useful discussion of how one small power succeeded in achieving its goals at Versailles.

Walworth, Arthur. *America's Moment: American Diplomacy at the End of World War I*. New York: Norton, 1977. A readable account of Woodrow Wilson's diplomacy as the war ended and the U.S. government prepared for the peace conference.

———. *Wilson and His Peacemakers: American Diplomacy at the Paris Peace Conference, 1919*. New York: Norton, 1986. A detailed account of the American role in the diplomatic meeting that produced the peace settlement.

Whalen, Robert Weldon. *Bitter Wounds: German Victims of the Great War, 1914–1939*. Ithaca, N.Y.: Cornell University Press, 1984. An examination of what the war was like for the German fighting man, and how the Weimar Republic and the Nazi regime treated wounded veterans and the families of the slain.

FILMS AND CD-ROM

Documentary Films

Are We Making a Good Peace? The Results of the War (color, 52 minutes). *Europe: The Mighty Continent* series. BBC, 1976. A good account of how the victorious Allies made peace at Versailles in 1919.

Arming of the Earth (color, 55 minutes). *A Walk Through the Twentieth Century with Bill Moyers* series. PBS, 1983. A vivid examination of the impact of the submarine, the machine gun, and the airplane on warfare in our century; the first half of the film deals brilliantly with World War I.

The Battle of the Somme: 1916 (color, 94 minutes). Films for the Humanities and Sciences, 1994. An extensive and enlightening account of one of the bloodiest battles of the war using personal accounts and contemporary scenes of the combat zone.

Cavalry of the Clouds (color, 38 minutes). Films for the Humanities and Sciences, 1988. A colorful account of Britain's Royal Flying Corps emphasizing lives and exploits of individual pilots on the western front.

The Drums Begin to Roll (color, 52 minutes). *Europe: The Mighty Continent* series. BBC, 1974. A notably successful effort to describe in clear fashion the growing tensions in early twentieth-century Europe that led to war.

Good-bye Billy: America Goes to War (black and white, 25 minutes). Cadre Films, 1972. A poignant, brilliantly filmed set of impressions of America at war, dealing with both the home front and the fighting in France.

The Great War and the Shaping of the Twentieth Century (color, 8 hours). PBS, 1996. A brilliantly composed examination of the war and its aftermath featuring rare film footage and commentary by leading experts on various aspects of the conflict.

Lenin and the Great Ungluing (color, 57 minutes). *Age of Uncertainty* series. BBC, 1977. An account of both the Russian leader's wartime preparation for revolution and the slaughter of the conflict that helped him reach his goal; it features a witty narrative by economist John K. Galbraith.

This Generation Has No Future: The Great War (color, 52 minutes). *Europe: The Mighty Continent* series. BBC, 1974. A vivid, clear chronological account of the war and its consequences in revolutionary Russia.

Verdun (black and white, 30 minutes). *Legacy* series. WNET, 1965. A strikingly effective depiction of both the strategy of the war's longest battle and its effects on the soldiers who fought there.

World War I (color, 70 minutes). *American Heritage Historical Collection* series. Clearvue/eav, 1985. A vivid depiction of the war with an emphasis on the American role in the conflict; it successfully captures the wartime atmosphere with extensive samples of the music and popular art of the time.

Feature Films

All Quiet on the Western Front (black and white, 140 minutes). USA, 1930. Directed by Lewis Milestone. One of the most famous antiwar movies of all time, it features Lew Ayres as a young German soldier who fights, and eventually dies, in the hideous conflict. Remade in an impressive 1979 television version with Richard Thomas and Ernest Borgnine.

Big Parade (black and white, 125 minutes). USA, 1925. Directed by King Vidor. An account of three American soldiers in France, it gives a good sense of the dirt and boredom of service behind the lines as well as the carnage, fear, and comradeship of battle.

A Farewell to Arms (black and white, 78 minutes). USA, 1932. Directed by Frank Borzage. Set on the Italian front and derived from a novel by Ernest Hemingway, who served there, this is a tragic story of an ambulance driver and a nurse caught up in the great retreat after Caporetto. Remade in an inferior version with Rock Hudson and Jennifer Jones in 1957.

The Fighting 69th (black and white, 89 minutes). USA, 1940. Directed by William Keighley. Made as America prepared to fight once again in Europe, this film with James Cagney and Pat O'Brien shows the battlefield cost of the war but also fondly commemorates the heroism of the American fighting men.

Gallipoli (color, 111 minutes). Australia, 1981. Directed by Peter Weir. The film takes two young Australian ranchers from their home to the bloody and futile fighting on the Turkish peninsula in 1915.

Grand Illusion (black and white, 117 minutes). France, 1937. Directed by Jean Renoir. Set mainly in a German prisoner-of-war camp, it makes a powerful antiwar statement by showing the essential similarities of the people on both the French and the German side and the transnational comradeship, and even love, that develops between them.

J'accuse (black and white, approximately 2 hours). France, 1919. Directed by Abel Gance. A bitter indictment of the war's waste and brutality made during the last months of the fighting and told through the experiences of a French family. Remade in a sound version by the same director in 1937.

Lawrence of Arabia (color, 221 minutes). Great Britain, 1962. Directed by David Lean. A brilliant film depiction of the great hero of the 1917–1918 desert war in the Middle East; it presents the exhilaration of successful battle on this secondary front, the psychological complexity that makes Lawrence into a hero, and the petty diplomatic maneuvering that robs his Arab allies of what they had earned on the battlefield.

The Light Horsemen (color, 110 minutes). Australia, 1988. Directed by Simon Wincer. Set in the Palestine campaign of 1917, it shows the human cost of the war, but it stresses the heroism and successful battlefield performance of an Australian cavalry unit.

Oh! What a Lovely War (color, 144 minutes). Great Britain, 1969. Directed by Richard Attenborough. A bitter film that uses devices like the music of World War I to highlight the war's horror and ultimate lack of meaning.

Paths of Glory (black and white, 87 minutes). USA, 1957. Directed by Stanley Kubrick. A film about the Nivelle offensive, it presents the fighting on the western front as a futile effort to come to grips with an invisible and deadly enemy while Allied soldiers suffer under commanders indifferent to their fate.

Sergeant York (black and white, 134 minutes). USA, 1941. Directed by Howard Hawks. Like *The Fighting 69th*, this is a film made as the United States prepared to enter World War I. It revolves around the heroic battlefield performance of a onetime pacifist from rural Tennessee.

Westfront (black and white, 90 minutes). Germany, 1930. Directed by G. W. Pabst. A somber film about the horror and futility of the war at the front and the degradation fighting men find when they go home on leave.

Wings (black and white, 136 minutes). USA, 1927. Directed by William Wellman. Presenting the aerial war on the western front, it features brilliant flying sequences as well as valuable views of the fighting on the ground; the German enemy is presented in a complex, sometimes sympathetic and admiring, fashion.

Zeppelin (color, 97 minutes). Great Britain, 1971. Directed by Etienne Périer. The film shows how the new aerial weapon was employed, and, as the leading members of the cast escape to be interned in a neutral country, it concludes with an antiwar message.

CD-ROM

The Causes of World War I CD-ROM (32 minutes). Clearvue/eav, 1994. Directed primarily at a high school audience, this material gives a lucid presentation of the war's immediate and remote origins, including the nationalism and imperialism of the nineteenth century, the arms race, and the events of the summer of 1914.

Index

About the Author

NEIL M. HEYMAN is Professor of History at San Diego State University. He is a specialist in Russian and modern European history and has written extensively on military affairs. He is the author of *Western Civilization: A Critical Guide to Documentary Film* (Greenwood, 1996) and *Russian History* (1993), and coauthor (with Holger H. Herwig) of *Biographical Dictionary of World War I* (Greenwood, 1982). He is currently preparing a study of the final year of World War I from a global perspective.

Glossary of Selected Terms

AEF (American Expeditionary Forces). The American army and marine troops that arrived in Europe starting in June 1917 under the command of General John Pershing. Most of these troops fought on a separate American sector in the Meuse Valley. By the close of the war, Pershing led 2 million troops in Europe.

The Allies. Sometimes called the Entente, one of the two opposing coalitions that took part in the war. It first consisted of Great Britain, France, and Russia. Italy became a member when it entered the war in May 1915, as did Rumania when it became a belligerent in August 1916.

BEF (British Expeditionary Force). The British land forces that fought on the western front from August 1914 to the close of the war. Beginning as a contingent of six infantry divisions and one cavalry division, 160,000 professional soldiers under the command of General Sir John French, it grew to a force of fifty-seven divisions of volunteers and conscripts (including troops from the Dominions) under General Sir Douglas Haig, who took command in December 1915.

Black Hand. A radical nationalist organization directed by officers in the intelligence section of the Serbian army, it probably helped to plan the assassination of Archduke Franz Ferdinand of Austria. In any case, it provided the assassins with weapons and assistance in entering Bosnia to carry out their plot.

Blank check. Germany's declaration of full support, on July 6, for Austria-Hungary's move to humiliate Serbia following the assassination of Archduke Franz Ferdinand of Austria. This encouraged the Austrians to provoke a war with Serbia that would probably draw Russia, and perhaps other major powers, into confrontations with Austria-Hungary and Germany.

Central Powers. One of the two opposing coalitions that took part in the war, it first consisted of Germany and Austria-Hungary, whose formal alliance had been formed before the war. Ottoman Turkey became a member when it joined the war in late October 1914; Bulgaria followed in October 1915.

Eastern front. The battle front established at the start of the war running from the Baltic Sea through the Polish provinces of the Russian Empire to the borders of Rumania. It moved a considerable distance northward and eastward as a result of successful German offensives against the Russians in 1915 and against Rumania in 1916.

Fourteen Points. A set of principles for a future peace settlement presented to the United States Congress by President Woodrow Wilson on January 8, 1918. Motivated by the need to block the call of Russia's new Bolshevik government for an immediate peace settlement and to bolster Allied morale, these principles included general aims such as freedom of the seas and specific territorial goals such as restoring Alsace-Lorraine to France. In October 1918, the German government asked for an armistice leading to a peace settlement based on the Fourteen Points.

March Revolution. A spontaneous revolution that broke out in Russia in the second week of March 1917. Sparked by food riots in the capital, Petrograd, it tapped deep reserves of popular discontent due to the ineptitude of the tsarist government, the colossal military and territorial losses of the war, and the hardships imposed by the conflict on the country's urban population. Within less than a week, the monarchy fell and was replaced by a Provisional Government.

November Revolution. The deliberate and successful effort of Russia's Bolshevik party, led by V. I. Lenin and Leon Trotsky, to seize power from Alexander Kerensky's Provisional Government in November 1917. Aided by a militia force (Red Guards) of armed factory workers, the Bolsheviks took over key locations in the capital city, Petrograd, without encountering serious resistance. This event placed a radical Marxist government in power for the first time and constitutes one of the most important consequences of World War I.

No man's land. The area between the opposing trench lines on the western front. Stripped bare of trees and other vegetation by repeated bombardments, it often contained unburied corpses and undetonated shells as well as barbed wire entanglements and other hindrances to movement. Opposing forces aimed their artillery and machine guns at likely attack routes here, and advancing troops often suffered immense casualties passing through this dangerous and desolate zone.

Supreme War Council. An organization containing military and political leaders from the Allied countries and the United States. Initially set up to coordinate Allied strategy in dealing with the crisis in Italy in late 1917, it provided a mechanism for directing Allied strategy during the final year of the war.

Treaty of Brest-Litovsk. A peace settlement signed on March 3, 1918, by Russia and the Central Powers. It removed Russia from the war and gave Germany effective political control over Russia's former Polish, Baltic, and Ukrainian territories. The treaty permitted Germany to shift troops from the former eastern front to France for the 1918 offensive, but its harsh terms gave the Allies a clear signal of what to expect if Germany won the war. It thereby stiffened their will to continue fighting until Germany had been defeated.

Treaty of Versailles. The peace treaty between Germany and the victorious Allies, signed on June 28, 1919. The treaty compelled Germany to pay reparations to the countries it had injured during the war, to surrender its colonies and 15 percent of its territory in Europe, and to limit severely its future military power. It also set up a League of Nations. The treaty was presented to the German government without permitting its representatives to negotiate regarding its provisions, and it was seen by most Germans as an unjust, dictated settlement.

Unrestricted submarine warfare. A policy of naval warfare that the Germans adopted in early 1917 despite long-standing American objections. It called for attacks without warning on all shipping, Allied and neutral, in an extensive zone around the British Isles. Following the loss of American ships and lives, this German policy was a significant cause of U.S. entry into the war.

War guilt clause. One of the most controversial elements in the Treaty of Versailles, Article 231 assigned to Germany and its allies full responsibility for waging a war of aggression and thereby causing losses and damage to Germany's opponents. This clause, which most Germans saw as a particularly offensive part of the treaty, was used as the basis for imposing on Germany the obligation to pay reparations.

Western front. The principal battle front of the war. It was established at the start of the war and ran from the North Sea southward through western Belgium and northeastern France. It turned eastward along the Aisne River and extended all the way to Switzerland. Heavily fortified, especially on the German side, it barely moved for most of the war even in the face of fierce Allied offensives.